To Patrick Eby
Slàinte mhath!

John J. Tiffey

A Woman Nobly Planned

A Woman Nobly Planned

*Fact and Myth
in the Legacy of
Flora MacDonald*

John J. Toffey

CAROLINA ACADEMIC PRESS
Durham, North Carolina

Library of Congress Cataloging-in-Publication Data

Toffey, John J., 1931–
    A woman nobly planned: fact and myth in the legacy of Flora
MacDonald/John J. Toffey
        p.   cm.
    Includes bibliographical references.
    ISBN 0-89089-957-6
    1. MacDonald, Flora, 1722–1790. 2. Charles Edward, Prince,
grandson of James II, King of England, 1728–1788. 3. North
Carolina — History — Revolution, 1775–1788 — Historiography.
4. Jacobite Rebellion, 1745–1746 — Historiography. 5. Scotland —
History — 18th century — Historiography. 6. American loyalists —
North Carolina — Biography. 7. Scots — North Carolina — History —
18th century. 8. Jacobite Rebellion, 1745–1746 — Biography. 9. Women
heroes — Scotland — Biography. 10. Jacobites — Biography. I. Title.
DA814.M14T64   1997
941.107'092 — dc21
[B]   97-12376
                                                                          CIP

CAROLINA ACADEMIC PRESS
700 Kent Street
Durham, NC 27701
Telephone (919) 489-7486
Fax (919) 493-5668
www.cap-press.com

Printed in the United States of America

To Punky,
of whom my father used to say,
"Your mother is a remarkable woman."

Contents

Maps on pages 9 and 10.
Illustrations on pages 95–106.

Acknowledgments

AT THE HEAD OF THIS LIST of those who have helped me in this endeavor stands my wife, Irene. To her I am deeply grateful for accompanying and encouraging me along the way and for critically reading this book in its several manuscript drafts.

Early in my inquiry into the history and heritage of Flora MacDonald, a new-found friend called me "a stranger within the gates" of Scottish history. The land within these gates, I quickly and happily learned, was a rich and fascinating terrain, most of which had been carefully explored by distinguished men and women. In this new and only slightly foreign land, I needed help. Everyone to whom I turned for directions gave them generously. Indeed, one of the greatest pleasures accruing from this study has been the people I have met along the way.

To Mrs. James Kellogg and to James R. Moore I am grateful for the opportunity to set foot in Scotland for the first time. I am grateful for the early orientation to Scottish history provided by T. C. Smout and by Norman MacDougall at the University of St. Andrews. Bruce Lenman led me into the eighteenth century in general and to the Jacobites in particular. Michael Fry, too, has helped greatly in my introduction to 18th-century Scottish history. John Gibson and Alasdair Maclean offered their expertise on Jacobite and Hebridean matters. Sheila Craik at the Glasgow University Library, Rosalind Marshall and members of the staff of the Scottish National Portrait Gallery, Maggie MacDonald at the archives of the Clan Donald Centre on Skye, and Christine Gascoigne of the St. Andrews Library have been especially helpful. In addition, for their replies to my questions or requests for material, I am grateful to members of the staffs of the Aberdeen University Library, the Ashmolean Museum, the British Newspaper Library, the Burrell Collection in Glasgow, the Inverness Branch Library, the National Library of Scotland, the National Portrait Gallery in London, and *The Oban Times*. Robert Lambert at St. Andrews and Tom Millard at Aberdeen also provided valuable assistance.

In this country, Elizabeth Holmes and Margaret Gefford at the De-Tamble Library of St. Andrews Presbyterian College introduced me to

Flora MacDonald in North Carolina. Eloise Knight generously allowed me to look at material in her possession. Anne-Marie Logan at the reference library of the Yale Center for British Art introduced me to the Jennings Collection there and helped me with my many questions on 18th-century British art. Also at Yale, help was generously provided by the staffs of the Sterling Memorial Library and the Beinecke Rare Book and Manuscript Library. In addition, I am grateful to the staffs at the Boston Public Library, Library of Congress, the Frick Art Reference Library, the New York Historical Society, the New York Public Library, and the Williams College Library. I thank Ellen Miles at the National Portrait Gallery in Washington, David Steel at the North Carolina Museum of Art, and Martha Tonissen Mayberry at the Mint Museum of Art for their help with questions about portraits, and I thank Susan Maclean Kybett for some helpful background information.

To any whose service I have failed to acknowledge either here or in the book's footnotes and bibliography, my apologies. I hope I have followed well the guidance of all who have so generously given it. If I have not, the responsibility is mine.

A Woman Nobly Planned

Introduction: Realms of Gold

> "I am now in the land of military and romantic adventures, and it only remains to be seen what will be my own share in them."
>
> —CAPT. EDWARD WAVERLEY

"WHY SCOTLAND? Did your family come from there?" asked a friend just back from Morocco. I did not ask if his people had come from there. I do not ask if ancestral origin prompts one to visit France or Portugal or London, Hawaii or Alaska or Cancun. But like Ireland, that other legendary nursery of countless American family trees, Scotland seems to connote roots. Unless, of course, it connotes golf.

The historian Bruce Lenman has noted "the Great American Public's propensity to envisage Britain as a romantic theme park with Mary Poppins Land to the south and Brigadoon to the north."[1] In such a setting, I suppose, golf and history could merge. After all, it is said that the theme park's favorite Scottish queen, Mary, enjoyed golf; and more than one biographer asserts that Bonnie Prince Charlie, another big tourist attraction, was a golfer.

As I began my research in this land of family ties and tees, perhaps I should not have been surprised to find that many who had preceded me in my chosen subject presented family identification at the entrance. One was Flora MacDonald's granddaughter; another had a grandmother from the Hebrides; this one's great-great-grand uncle was Flora's husband; that one's maternal grandfather spoke Gaelic; another's forebear had been with the Prince throughout the rising of 1745. The ancestral connection is often displayed early and prominently among the author's credentials. With no tartan to call my own, no clan with which to gather, I was, as one new-found Scots friend called me, a "stranger within the gates."

Why Flora MacDonald? In the rain on the northern tip of Skye I had stood before the Celtic cross that marks her grave and read Samuel Johnson's tribute to the "Preserver of Prince Charles Edward Stuart [whose] name will be mentioned in history and, if courage and fidelity be virtues, mentioned with honour." Other Scots hearsed in history might be more important or worthy of study, but there remains something compelling about this woman whose moment in the spotlight has generated so much heroine-worship and myth-making.

More than most, the Scots infuse their monuments with romance: Bannockburn, Flodden Field, Glencoe, Linlithgow and Loch Leven, Glenfinnan and Culloden, Murrayfield. And where the stuff of romance isn't immediately at hand, a Scot is ready to invent it. Look at Ossian, perhaps the mistiest and most romantic figure of all, born in the midst of the eighteenth century out of the medieval bardic tradition. In fact Prince Charles Edward Stuart, through whom Flora MacDonald came to fame, is as much a real product of the eighteenth century's love of the lost as Ossian, who some will say influenced Flora, is an invention.

Perhaps more than anyone other than Flora herself, it was the twentieth-century traveler H. V. Morton who drew me to the narrative and let me put down my own requisite roots. In 1932, on his second visit to Scotland, Morton paused at Glenfinnan to meditate upon the events suggested and commemorated by the monument. To Morton "it was as sad as Charlie's grave in the crypt of St. Peter's in Rome."

> A haze of almost impenetrable romance has been cast round the Rebellion of '45, so that everything that happened in those not so distant times seems to shine with an epic splendour. I have seen grim Presbyterians, who would refuse to bend the knee to an altar, thrown into a state of romantic emotionalism by thoughts of Bonnie Prince Charlie. The more one knows about the rebellion and the deeper one delves into the plotting, the lying, the jealousy, the self-seeking and the indifferent leadership, the more one doubts the romance; and yet—and yet.... And I, while I sat on the wall that runs round an ugly decaying tower in Glenfinnan,

fell into that reverie to which every man must surrender in this place.[2]

The reverie arrests, rivets. Before dawn on January 9, 1744, a coach passes out of Rome and heads down the Appian Way. In the coach are Prince Charles Edward Stuart and his tutor seemingly on their way to shoot some ducks in the Pontine marshes near Cisterna. But the shooting party is a ruse. In fact, the Prince will leave the coach on some pretense and continue on horseback. As the coach goes on to Cisterna, the Prince will turn and ride for five nights north to Genoa, there to find a ship that will take him to France and thence on to Scotland and his place in history and romance.

Cisterna. Two hundred years later to the month, an army of American and British troops waded back into Italy at Anzio and Nettuno, just west of Cisterna. Because of an initial command failure to seize the moment and press their advantage inland, these troops lay pinned down on their beachhead for four months. At last they broke out and began their advance on Highway 6. The war in southern Italy would end in another week, and young Americans and British, most of them, anyway, would ride in triumph into Rome like Caesars before them. Troop commanders studied their field maps, fixing on Cisterna as a reference point. Did any of them, noting Cisterna, think of the Prince and the sequence of events he was about to initiate? Did my father, on his way to that command post in the farmhouse near Palestrina in which he would pass into legend and history of his own, know of Cisterna as a landmark in the life of Bonnie Prince Charlie?

Morton's reverie is no insubstantial dream; he knows what he is writing about. He concludes the reverie thus:

> In this melodramatic way—a night escape, a disguise, a secret journey—began the slow train of events which, piling melodrama upon drama, and adding a touch of the operatic now and then, were to culminate in Culloden and the wanderings of Bonnie Prince Charlie.[3]

I share Morton's romantic musings as countless other readers must have. But to me the image of Cisterna, amid "tombs and cypresses," as Morton reconstructs it, or amid sunlight and olive groves, as I recall my own ride from Rome to Nettuno in 1982, has a special meaning. Later we shall follow Flora MacDonald and part of her divided family to Fayetteville, North Carolina, where in October of 1942, my family parted—my father east to the events above by way of North Africa and Sicily, the rest of us north to wait out the war.

As I began to learn my way around in eighteenth-century Scottish history, it became clear that Flora MacDonald had not been a subject of serious scholarly inquiry. To be sure, she has been the subject of several biographies over the years, and she has played parts of more or less importance in the many books written on Bonnie Prince Charlie, the Jacobites, the Isle of Skye, and other tangential topics. But scholars devote little attention to Flora and her moment in the spotlight.

Why? Is the record, once presented, so clear and definitive that there remains nothing more to be examined? In 1988, the bicentennial of Prince Charlie's death and thus of the end of the Jacobite century, several new scholarly studies of both topics appeared; but 1990, the bicentennial of Flora MacDonald's death, seems to have produced no new work on her. Where was the customary spate of retrospections? A stranger within the gates indeed, where was I to look for Flora, in the library or the theme park?

Though part of the Great American Public, I did not invent the images in the theme park, nor in all cases did the British Tourist Board. The Reverend G. V. R. Grant writes,

> One of the great peculiarities of Scottish history is the extremely strange way that Scots have treated it. Understanding what really happened hardly ever gets beyond the old traditional myths that have been trotted out for many years.[4]

R. C. Jarvis puts it another way. The historian, he says, "has been seduced from history to romance: he has, perhaps all unwillingly or possibly quite unwittingly, been converted—corrupted—from historian to romancer."[5] And historian Frank McLynn says that myth in moderation can actually be good for us.

> But every historian of the Jacobites who believes that the truth about the past cannot be totally retrieved from documents and archives must be open to the dimension of the

imagination. The honest historian of Jacobitism, recognizing how powerful is the sway of the irrational over human beings, will always have the door ajar to myth.[6]

If Flora is merely a costumed character greeting tourists as they queue up for the theme park's "Speed Bonnie Boat Ride," then perhaps she yields little to academics seeking credit for their contributions to the scholarly minutiae that fill the learned journals and foster departmental preferment. But even if she is not fit food for academic thought, Flora is a significant part of the Scottish cultural diet. Bruce Lenman speaks of the shortbread-tin and Drambuie-bottle reading of Scottish history designed to appeal to visitors to the theme park.[7] And there was that magnificent, hand-painted, one-of-a-kind Culloden chess set in the antique shop down in England. Beautifully done, meticulously researched to make the tartans of the Highlander pawns authentic; Bonnie Prince Charlie as the king of the board and Flora as his queen ranged against their counterparts, the Duke of Cumberland and Britannia. Elsewhere, too, the Scottish past is important in the Scottish present. Even a stranger within the gates watching on television had to be moved as, in the tense lull before the World Cup rugby match against England in Murrayfield, players and spectators sang with considerable emotion of sending home "proud Edward's army" "tae think again".[8] Surely, the taking up an historical event into the popular national mythology need not diminish the original event despite the danger of its contemporary corruption.

On the 1700 ScotRail express from Edinburgh one evening I fell into conversation with two Aberdonian school teachers returning from a conference. From Inverkeithing to Burntisland we compared notes on aspects of secondary education in our respective countries, and, as Kinghorn slipped by, the topic of learning disabilities inevitably came up. As we left Kirkcaldy, I mentioned that Bonnie Prince Charlie had been dyslexic, at which one of the teachers said, "I knew he died of syphilis, but I didn't know he was dyslexic." I asked where the teacher thought Charlie might have contracted syphilis. "Why, from Flora MacDonald, of course," came the reply. "Where in the world did you get that idea?" I asked with amiable superiority arising from years of listening to adolescent answers to my questions in the classroom. "Why, from a teacher in school, I suppose," she said.

In the few moments left to me I tried to set the record straight while pointing out the dangers inherent in taking seriously everything one is told by a teacher. But the impact of the disquieting encounter lingered long after I had alighted in Leuchars. So much for a clear and definitive historical record of one whose name "will be mentioned in history and, if courage and fidelity be virtues, mentioned with honour." Here was a glimpse of how one educated Scot regarded Flora MacDonald. I'll have the shortbread and Drambuie, please.

Flora's story has been told in biography, novel, play, poem, song, opera, and film. Portraits alleged to be of her abound. Artifacts and relics said to have been hers are cherished on both sides of the Atlantic. For two centuries fact and fancy have blended in the images we have of her. Her name has been invoked in support of countless worthy causes. Dr. Johnson's prediction about her name enduring has proven true, and on her statue in Inverness immortality is implicit in the lines "While the flowers bloom in the meadow/The name of the fair maiden will endure." She was, as William Jolly said, borrowing from William Wordsworth, "a woman nobly planned."[9] Remembering to guard against seduction and corruption, and leaving the door slightly ajar for myth, let us consider both the woman and the plans.

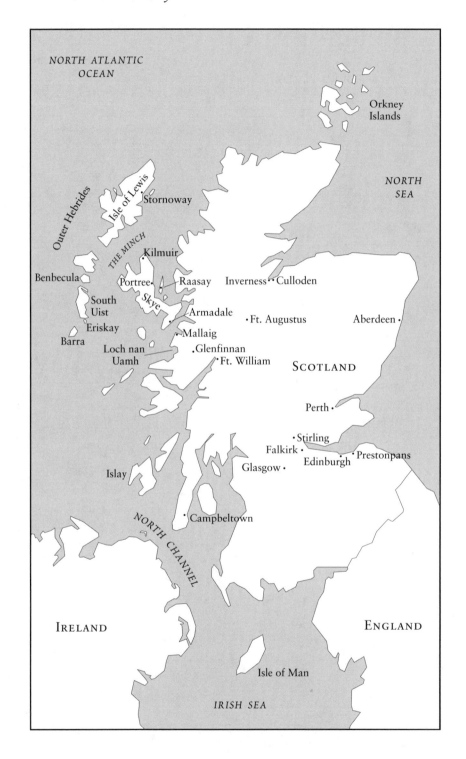

Chapter 1

The 'Forty-Five

Wha widna' fecht for Charlie,
Wha widna' draw the sword,
Wha widna' up and rally,
At the royal Prince's word?

—ANONYMOUS

WITHOUT THE JACOBITE RISING OF 1745, it is unlikely that Flora MacDonald's name would have been mentioned in history at all. To begin to understand her, it is helpful to know something of the events that placed her upon the stage of history. "Bliadhna Thearlach" —Charlie's Year—began with his first appearance on Scottish soil in July 1745, and ended with his departure therefrom in September, 1746. Though a stranger in Scotland when he got off the boat, Charles Edward Louis John Casimir Silvester Severino Maria carried credentials steeped in tradition. He was a Stuart; descendants of Banquo, Stuarts had sat upon the throne of Scotland, and more recently, of Scotland and England, since the accession of Robert II in 1371. Robert's mother Marjory, daughter of the heroic King Robert the Bruce, had married Walter, 6th High Steward of Scotland (hence the dynasty's name); and Queen Mary, Charlie's French-educated great-great-great-grandmother had not been good with "w's" (hence its spelling).[1]

The Protestant reformations in Scotland and England took their toll on the traditionally Catholic House of Stuart. In Scotland, Queen Mary's Catholicism contributed significantly to the loss of her crown, her country, and her life. Mary's son by her second marriage, James VI of Scotland, was, by virtue of his Protestant persuasion, able to succeed the childless Elizabeth I of England when she died in 1603. In James VI of Scotland & I of England, the crowns of the two countries were thus united.

11

Charles I, born in Dunfermline, Scotland, succeeded his father in 1625, only to lose his crown and head to Oliver Cromwell and the Puritans in 1648. Upon the death of Cromwell, James's elder surviving son returned to the throne in 1660. He died in 1685 and was succeeded by his younger brother, James VII & II.

Catholic James married twice. Of the many children born to James and his first wife, Anne Hyde, only two Protestant daughters, Mary and Anne, survived. Both women would reign over England and Scotland. Upon the death of his first wife James married again, this time to Mary of Modena, and they had a son, James Francis Edward, who would be raised a Catholic. The zeal with which King James imposed Catholicism upon his subjects caused considerable unrest in the kingdom. In June 1688, English Protestants invited to the throne Prince William of Orange, husband of James's half-sister Mary. In December, James chose to leave office alive and, having sent his wife and infant son before him, fled to France and later settled in Rome. The Stuart line remained alive and, upon the death of James VII & II in 1701, young James Francis Edward became "The King over the Water," and often was so toasted by Jacobites in Britain. To the other side he would come to be "The Old Pretender." Either way, he would be the father of Bonnie Prince Charlie.

Back in Britain, William and Mary died without issue, and the succession passed to Mary's sister Anne. Having improbably outlived all of her seventeen children, Queen Anne, despite death-bed thoughts of her Catholic half-brother in exile,[2] became "the lass" with whom the Stuart dynasty would end* — at least for the time being. Succession was established upon the Protestant Hanovers. Through his mother Sophia and grandmother Elizabeth, King George I and first of the House of Hanover was the great-grandson of James VI & I. Though the Jacobite Rising of 1745 was not exclusively a Catholic revolt, the Catholicism of the Stuarts had cost them the throne.

---

* Legend has it that upon hearing of the birth of his daughter Mary, James V said of the Stuart dynasty, "It cam wi' a lass, and it will go wi' a lass." Though he was referring to Margaret as the former lass and Mary as the latter, the end came with the death of Queen Anne.

A Royal Genealogy

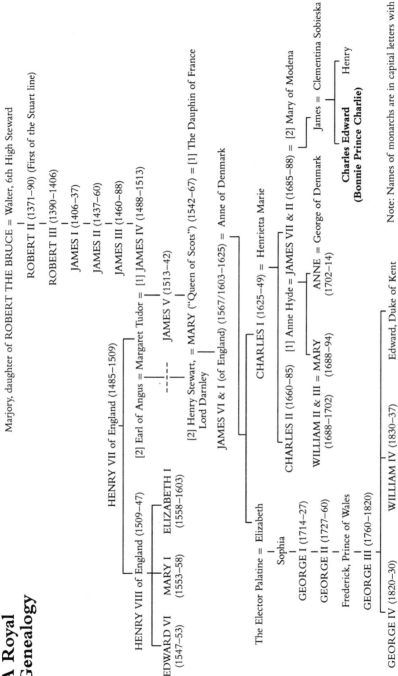

Marjory, daughter of ROBERT THE BRUCE = Walter, 6th High Steward

ROBERT II (1371–90) (First of the Stuart line)

ROBERT III (1390–1406)

JAMES I (1406–37)

JAMES II (1437–60)

JAMES III (1460–88)

HENRY VII of England (1485–1509)

[2] Earl of Angus = Margaret Tudor = [1] JAMES IV (1488–1513)

JAMES V (1513–42)

[2] Henry Stewart, = MARY ("Queen of Scots") (1542–67) = [1] The Dauphin of France
Lord Darnley

HENRY VIII of England (1509–47) ELIZABETH I
(1558–1603)

JAMES VI & I (of England) (1567/1603–1625) = Anne of Denmark

CHARLES I (1625–49) = Henrietta Marie

[1] Anne Hyde = JAMES VII & II (1685–88) = [2] Mary of Modena

ANNE = George of Denmark
(1702–14)

James = Clementina Sobieska

EDWARD VI MARY I
(1547–53) (1553–58)

CHARLES II (1660–85)

WILLIAM II & III = MARY
(1688–1702) (1688–94)

Charles Edward Henry
(Bonnie Prince Charlie)

The Elector Palatine = Elizabeth

Sophia

GEORGE I (1714–27)

GEORGE II (1727–60)

Frederick, Prince of Wales

GEORGE III (1760–1820)

Edward, Duke of Kent

VICTORIA (1837–1901)

GEORGE IV (1820–30) WILLIAM IV (1830–37)

Note: Names of monarchs are in capital letters with
the dates of their reigns are in parentheses. Some
marriages, spouses, and offspring have been omitted.

Many on both sides of the English Channel would have preferred to see the Stuart line continue to occupy the British throne. Many in Scotland would have found the maintenance of a royal Scottish tradition a palliative at least to the recent and somewhat unpopular Act of Union, which in 1707 united the English and Scottish parliaments and thus removed Scotland's legislative representation to London. English and Scottish traditionalists, looking to a potential monarch with good Stuart bloodlines alive and well in Rome, called themselves "Jacobites" after the Latin "Jacobus" for "James." Almost immediately upon the departure of James VII & II and on several occasions thereafter,[3] Jacobites had risen up to various but always unsuccessful heights.

Born in Rome in 1720 to James and his Polish wife Clementina Sobieska and raised as one who might be king, young Charles had undertaken a regimen of physical training to compensate for a rather frail physique and had tasted military action at the siege of Gaeta before he was fourteen.[4] Both the physical training and the limited knowledge of military matters would play vital parts in his Scottish adventures.

On the eve of the Prince's departure in search of his royal fortune in the January dawn in 1744, agents and intriguers were all over Europe. France would certainly have been interested in restoring a Catholic to the throne of Britain or at the very least in worrying England with that prospect and had readied an invasion fleet, which because of some bad weather and bad planning never got going. Its hands full of war on the continent, France put on hold the invasion scheme. Meanwhile shadowy figures were blowing in Charlie's ear and telling him that if he would come to Britain at the head of an army, Jacobites all over the kingdom were ready to rise again and follow him.

So Charlie started for Scotland at the head of a force that could be carried in two ships. Antoine Walsh, an ardent Irish Jacobite, privateer, and slaver, provided and commanded the light frigate *Du Teillay*,[5] which carried the Prince and "the seven men of Moidart," his inner circle of four Irish and three Scots advisers. They were joined by the well-stocked sixty-four-gun warship, *L'Elisabeth*. Four days into their voyage they encountered the British warship *HMS Lion*, which engaged the larger of the Frenchmen, while the smaller, faster frigate stood off out of range. After a fierce but inconclusive gun fight in which both ships took heavy damage, they broke off and repaired to their respective ports. With *L'Elisabeth* went 1,500 muskets, 1,800 broadswords, 700 men, as well as other arms, ammunition, and money.[6]

Against a lot of good advice, Charlie insisted that his ship press on alone to Scotland. On July 23 he stepped onto Scottish soil on Eriskay, a tiny island just south of the Uists perhaps more celebrated in this century as the "Whisky Galore" island than as the Young Pretender's first Scottish landing place. Here, too, the first of the legion of legends about the young adventurer would have its start. On the very spot of beach where he first stood grows the sea-bindweed or convolvulus. It grows nowhere else in that remote and barren part of the world. When the Prince stepped ashore, so the story goes, seeds which had attached themselves to his cloak in France fell from it and sprouted.[7] On Eriskay, Charles expected to receive support from the powerful MacDonald and MacLeod clans. Instead he received only an emissary, Alexander MacDonald of Boisdale, who told Charlie to go back home ("tae think again"?), to which Charlie may have replied, "I am come home."[8]

On the 25th, again against good advice, Charlie pressed on, crossed the Minch, sailed into Loch nan Uamh, and stepped ashore on the Scottish mainland at Borrodale, in Morar. He spent the next several days sending for and interviewing local leaders, among whom may have been the stepfather of the woman who would be his conductress a year later in his hour of greatest need.[9] Support for the Prince was less than he had hoped for or been led to believe he would receive. Neither Sir Alexander MacDonald nor MacLeod of MacLeod, the two most powerful men on Skye, would meet or support the Prince. Some men did step forward, though. When the Prince asked Ranald Mac-Donald, "Will you not assist me?", the young man is said to have replied, "I will though no other man in the Highlands should draw his sword."[10]

Heartened by this heroic response, the Prince scheduled a formal standard-raising for August 19 at Glenfinnan. Here again, the turnout was not great. Prominently absent was Cameron of Locheil with his clansmen. Without Locheil's strength, even Charlie may very well have seen the light and abandoned his plan. Then, after about two hours of waiting and frustration, there occurred a scene right out of the Hollywood of old.[11] Historians recorded it and subsequent generations of romantics have embroidered it. When Queen Victoria visited Glenfinnan in September 1873, she imagined in her journal Charlie with his head in his hands. "Suddenly the sound of the pipes aroused him, and he saw the clans coming down Glenfinnan."[12] It was Locheil with seven hundred men. "I'll share the fate of my prince," he may have said, "and so shall every man over whom nature or fortune hath given me any power."[13] This force and this expression of fidelity were enough in Charlie's mind to set him on the road to the throne.

Isn't it a great scene? Remember one like it in *Gunga Din* when the three swash-buckling sergeants and Sam Jaffe are near the end of their ropes atop the Thugs' mountain stronghold in India? And as they lie there wounded, thirsty, they hear—faintly at first—the sound of the pipes at the head of the relief column away off down the valley. And do you remember what those "beautiful Scotties" are playing and singing as they come to the rescue? "Will Ye No Come Back Again," the Jacobite tear-jerker written by Lady Nairne long after the fact. On which tune the pipers were playing as they led the clan down the glen in 1745 history is silent, but remember Alec Guinness citing "The Gathering of Locheil" among the Tunes of Glory in the movie of the same name.

Romantic musings aside, who would in fact fight for Charlie? What motivated those who sought out the Prince in his mainland headquarters at Borrodale? There is some evidence that food had a more profound effect than did political principle. Though Charlie arrived relatively empty-handed, he did come into some supplies of oatmeal and barley, captured by Antoine Walsh before quitting Scottish waters. These were delivered to the Prince for distribution to starving Highlanders. Wrote Colonel John William O'Sullivan,

> the poor people had not a Scrap of meal for above six months before. The prince bought the meal & got it distributed proportionably to the numbre yt was in each family; people came from all parts to get their proportion.[14]

The Earl of Kilmarnock said much the same thing just before he was executed in London:

> In the two kings and their rights I cared not a farthing which prevailed, but I was starving, and, by God, if Mo-

hammed had set up his standard in the Highlands, I had
been a good Muslim for bread and stuck close to the party,
for I must eat.[15]

Even Cameron of Locheil's noble expression of loyalty to the Prince,
some say, came only after Charlie had told Locheil to join up or "stay
at home, and learn from the newspapers the fate of [your] prince."[16]

More probably, Locheil would have readily rallied to the Jacobite
cause had the prospect of French support been clearer. As it was, the
Prince needed Lochiel and applied a different kind of coercion. He had
sent away the *Du Teillay*, thereby stranding himself on Scottish soil.
Locheil, "alive above all else to the danger to which the Prince's person
was exposed,"[17] had no choice but to declare his support, bringing with
him "the majority of his people whom he made to take up arms."[18]

There were other such men around the Prince; men who had been
loyal to and active in the Jacobite cause for a generation or longer.
Lord George Murray comes to mind: he, like Locheil, "whose heart
got the better of his head;" he who ever after the Jacobite defeat
would carry his copy of *The Office and Authority of a Justice of the Peace*
open to the page on which were summarized the pains and penalties
for high treason.[19] But in the ranks were many who would lay down
their lives for a ration of oatmeal.

The standard was raised and to it came men enough for the opti-
mistic Charlie to push forward into Scotland. On August 22, as a
brash reply to the government's offer of £30,000 for his capture, the
Prince offered the same sum for the Elector of Hanover.[20] After
spending the rest of August marching in the Highlands seeking to engage the army of General Cope, Charlie's unopposed army moved
southeast to Edinburgh, where early on the morning of September 17,
Locheil's men slipped through the Netherbow Gate and without
bloodshed gained control of the town, though not of the castle. The
first real battle of the war occurred on September 21 at Prestonpans
(or Gladsmuir), just east of Edinburgh, and lasted about four minutes.
Led by a local who knew a secret path, Charlie's Highlanders sneaked
around the government army, made up largely of raw troops, and
charged the exposed flank, which folded and fled. General Cope repaired to Berwick and was maligned as the first general in history to
bring back the report of his own defeat.

Charlie had his father proclaimed king and set up court at the Palace of Holyrood House while his army trained and grew. The ladies of Edinburgh society flocked to the palace to see the handsome Prince. "The figure and presence of Charles Stuart were not ill-suited to his lofty pretensions. He was in the prime of youth, tall and handsome," observed one contemporary.[21] At 5' 11" he was tall for the age, with sensual lips, a ruddy complexion, red hair, and "large, melancholy rolling brown eyes," the Prince cut quite a figure. Besides, wrote his secretary, John Murray of Broughton, there was that "unspeakable majesty diffused through his whole mien" that made it impossible for beholders to look long upon him unless encouraged to do so by "his excessive affability."

Miss Christian Threipland was forty-four years old and her brother had just been killed at Prestonpans.[22] Still, after meeting the Prince and receiving his expression of sympathy, she wrote:

> Oh had you beheld my beloved Hero you must confess he is a Gift from Heaven; but then, beside his outward appearance, which is absolutely the best figure *I ever saw*, such Vivacity, such piercing Wit, woven with a clear Judgement and an active Genius, and allowed by all to have a Capacity apt to receive such impressions as are not usually stampt on every brain: in short, Madam, he is *The Top of Perfection* and *Heaven's Darling*.[23]

Another young lady was moved to wonder in verse if one so fair could command in battle.

> O Glorious Youth! 'tis evidently plain,
> By thy majestick Eyes, thou'rt born to reign:
> But when thy warlike and extended Hand,
> Directs the foremost ranks to charge or stand;
> Retract thy Face, lest that so fair and young,
> Should call in doubt the Orders of thy Tongue:
> May ev'ry Action, ev'ry Grace of thine,
> O latest Son of Fame, Son of Bruce's Line,
> Affect thy Troops with all that can inspire,
> A blooming Sweetness and a martial Fire;
> Fatal to none but thy audacious Foe:

So Lightenings which to all their Brightness show
Strikes but the Man alone who has provok'd the Show.
I on no other Terms a Man would be,
But to defend thy glorious Cause and Thee;
For both, my Life I'd bravely chuse to lose:
I now can only serve Thee with my Muse;
But were my Pen a Sword, thy Foes I'd meet,
And lay the conquer'd World beneath thy Feet.[24]

Such protestations of admiration and willingness to give their all, as well as the roles of Flora and other women in the drama of the Prince, doubtless prompted Lord President Forbes to declare later that men's swords did less for Charlie than did women's tongues.[25] The ladies, however, did not turn Charlie's head. A man with a purpose, the Prince apparently did not take part in the dancing at Holyrood. Said he,

It is very true I like danceing and am very glad to see the Ladys and yu divert yr selfs but I have now another Air to dance [and] until that be finished I'll dance no other.[26]

Thus, even had she been in Edinburgh at the time, it is unlikely that Flora MacDonald would have danced with Charlie at Holyrood, as at least one writer would have us believe.[27]

In late September, the government side began to pick up reinforcements as troops were recalled from Flanders to help out at home. Around the first of November the Prince's army began to move south and on November 8 crossed the River Esk into England. Carlisle put up minimal resistance before yielding to the rebels, at whose head were a hundred pipers and Charlie on a white horse. Farther south, Manchester supplied a regiment to the cause, about the only show of support Charlie found south of the border. The army continued its march to Derby, 130 miles from London. Significantly, the invaders were not gaining the numbers of supporters they had been led to believe awaited them in England. They were, however, apparently causing quite a stir. Some historians say that London was on the verge of panic and the King on the verge of flight.

At 130 miles from London, the Highlanders of Charlie's army were about 250 miles from home. Though they had not been engaged in significant combat since crossing into England, they knew that there were now two—rumors said three—government armies in the field against them. Perhaps their enthusiasm for young, foreign "Tearlach" did not extend to placing him upon the English throne. Perhaps they were tired and wanted to go home.

It has to be noted, too, that leadership of the Jacobite army was far from ideal. Egos, personalities, politics, and preferment frequently interfered with military management. Under the influence of followers like Thomas Sheridan and Quartermaster-General O'Sullivan, the Prince never really trusted the Scots commanders. Nor was there always unity of opinion or purpose among men like Lord George Murray, Cameron of Locheil, Lord Elcho, James, Duke of Perth, and John Murray of Broughton.

Though the vote was not unanimous, the Jacobite council for whatever reasons decided on Black Friday, December 6, 1745, to turn around. On the way back, the Prince's army won a minor victory in a skirmish at Clifton Moor. To prove he was not retreating, Charlie left a garrison at Carlisle. What befell these men at the hands of the Hanoverian government gave promise of what awaited Jacobite prisoners.

On his birthday, December 20,* Charlie recrossed the Esk. After a week in hostile, largely loyalist Glasgow, he moved on to Bannockburn House, where he stayed while his army, under the direction of a French consultant, wasted time and energy in an ineffectual siege of Stirling Castle. At Bannockburn House the Prince seems to have met Clementina Walkinshaw, the namesake of the Prince's mother and the daughter of a man who had served the Prince's father in France. Whatever the nature of their relationship at Bannockburn that winter, later on the Continent Miss Walkinshaw would become the Prince's mistress and the mother of his only child.

At Falkirk on January 17, the Prince's army engaged and routed their government pursuers. Instead of pressing their advantage, the rebels broke off and withdrew, wandering north to the area around Inverness.

A month later there occurred a minor, almost comic-opera event in the annals of the '45. On the night of February 16 the Prince was

---

* In Rome, where the Prince was born, the date was December 31. The eleven-day difference in "Old Style" Continental and "New Style" British dates lasted until 1752.

the guest of Lady Anne Mackintosh, at Moy Hall, near Inverness. Though things were quiet in the area, Lady Anne had sent four men under her blacksmith to watch the approaches to Moy. In Inverness, Lord Loudon received a tip that the Prince was at Moy and set out to take him by surprise and collect the £30,000 bounty. A young lass and lad relayed a warning to Moy Hall, upon receipt of which the royal guest was removed from the house. As Loudon's force of some fifteen hundred militia marched along the road from Inverness, the vigilant blacksmith and his associates made such a racket including some gun-shots and military commands to phantom troops that the militiamen fled in panic. There were two significant casualties of this "engage-ment": Donald Mackrimmon, piper to the MacLeods was shot and killed, thus fulfilling his own prophecy, and the Prince, from running through the winter landscape in his sleeping attire, caught pneumonia. Thus ended the "Rout of Moy."[28]

In late March a French attempt to succor Charlie's ragged army failed when four government ships chased and ran aground on the north coast of Scotland a Jacobite ship carrying money and supplies. Prophetically perhaps, the ship was named the *Prince Charles.*

The government army was closing on the Jacobites. Its commander now was William, Duke of Cumberland and third son of the King. Less than a year younger than Charlie, Cumberland had already made a name for himself as a military figure, having led his troops in an heroic but futile assault at Fontenoy. Despite that defeat, Cumberland seems to have been popular with his men and managed to keep his military reputation unsullied. He was just the man to take the field against Charlie's largely Highland army. The military issue would be settled at Culloden. The government army, which included a large contingent of Scots, was rested and fed. The Jacobite army wasn't. Lord George Murray and other leaders advised withdrawing north across the Great Glen to fight guerrilla action on friendlier Highland ground. But Charlie would have none of it. Here he would fight. After all, his Highlanders[29] were two for two against the government army; he be-lieved them to be invincible.

Remembering perhaps the success at Gladsmuir, Charlie tried to sneak his army up to the enemy's camp near Nairn. There, under the cover of the darkness just before dawn, they would fall upon the Hanoverians, who would have dropped their guard after a night of celebrating their commander's birthday. But there had been no birthday party, and the Highlanders, too slow and strung out, were caught short of their objective at sunrise. They pulled back, hungry and exhausted, to unfavorable open ground on the moor. In his first exercise in military command, Charlie saw his army savaged in less than an hour in the sleet on Drummossie Moor.

The reasons for the Jacobite rout were many: the condition of the Jacobite army; the poor choice of terrain; orders delayed or given and not received; disputes about which clan would take which position in the Jacobite line of attack; vastly superior government numbers of men and artillery; a new government tactic for withstanding the awesome Highland charge.

Perhaps to get even for earlier military embarrassments, perhaps because they believed the rebels were under orders to give no quarter, the government troops gave none. In what must rank high on the all-time list of military atrocities, they—English and Scots—hacked to pieces not only the wounded Highlanders but any innocent but unfortunate bystanders as well. To one Scot, "...the contest between Charles and Cumberland was that of a civilized and chivalrous commander against a foe as treacherous and cruel as a Huron or an Iroquois."[30]

What was left of the Prince's army was scattered. Some of it made for Ruthven to regroup. Lord George Murray wrote to the Prince a bitterly accusatory letter. Though he made some valid points, his timing was bad. But Lord George had put much on the line in the service of the Jacobite cause and had been badly used at every turn. In such a climate, the remnants of the Jacobite army were not likely to reform as an effective fighting force. Charlie gave out the word to his followers that they were on their own. He would return to France for help.

But before the Prince would see France again, he would undergo five months of extreme hardship in the Highlands and Islands of western Scotland. His conduct and the adventures that befell him during the period of his life that many regard as his finest hour have been written and sung about for two hundred fifty years.

Chapter 2

Flora Meets Prince Charlie

There are twa bonny maidens,
And three bonny maidens,
Come over the Minch,
And come over the main,
Wi' the wind for their way,
And the corrie for their hame:
Let us welcome them bravely
Unto Skye again.

—HOGG's *Jacobite Minstrelsy*

WHERE FLORA MACDONALD WAS while the Jacobites rose and fell in 1745–46 we do not know. Indeed, despite all that has been written about her, we have few verifiable facts of her life before she met the Prince. We do know that she was born sometime in the year 1722 at Milton, one of her father's tacks on the South Uist in the Outer Hebrides. We know also that Flora was well born. On one side of her family she could trace her ancestry back to the first Lord of the Isles and on the other to Margaret, daughter of King Robert II and the start of the Stuart line. Thus, notes A. R. MacDonald, "the Prince and she were eleventh and twelfth in descent from King Robert II, in their respective branches."[1]

Flora's father, Ranald, had died when Flora was a year or so old, and in 1728 her mother was aggressively wooed and won by Hugh MacDonald, a Skye man who had been in the French service and was noted for his strength, swordsmanship, and loss of an eye.[2] By the time our story opens, Hugh and Flora's mother had moved to Skye, living on ground that is now part of the Clan Donald Centre, at Armadale.

Flora may have left South Uist in 1744 to visit relatives at Largie, in Kintyre, but was home in the spring of 1745. We have no information about her activities for the next year, but in June 1746 she was on South Uist, perhaps having come over from Skye to visit her brother, Angus. She was thus conveniently placed, whether by fate or by man, to assist the Prince.

Meanwhile, Prince Charles and a few close followers moved southwest from Culloden heading for the coast. On April 26, on the shore of Loch nan Uamh, where he had first set foot on the Scottish mainland nine months earlier, the Prince and four followers[3] stepped into a boat piloted by Donald MacLeod of Gualtergill. All night they sailed through a severe storm and arrived at Rossinish, on Benbecula, part of the Outer Hebrides locally called the Long Island and including North and South Uist and Harris and Lewis. The plan was to seek a French ship in these waters. Ironically, the Prince missed by a week two French ships looking for him in Loch nan Uamh and subsequently saw but did not recognize these ships as they sailed past the Long Island on their way back to France.[4] The Prince's party went north hoping to have Donald MacLeod obtain a vessel in Stornoway suitable for carrying them to Europe. Negotiations fell through when rumors spread that the ship was for the fugitive Prince, of whom the townsfolk wanted no part.

Throughout May, the Prince moved from place to place to avoid search parties by land and by sea. For about three weeks he enjoyed relative comfort and stability in a cottage at Coradale, in South Uist, where he shot birds and ate better than he had in some time. But government troops and local militia were closing in. By mid-June, there were some twenty-three hundred troops and militia searching an island area of about two hundred fifty square miles.[5] The Prince, with a reward of £30,000 on his head, could not expect to remain safely where he was much longer, and the likelihood of a French vessel eluding the British fleet in the surrounding waters seemed ever slighter.

The job of combing the rough Highland and Island terrain in search of the fugitive Prince fell to a regiment of militia under the command of Lord Loudon and to the Argyll militia commanded by Lt. Col. Campbell. In overall command was Major General John Campbell, father of the colonel and later 4th Duke of Argyll. Commanding one company of Lord Loudon's militia was Captain Hugh MacDonald of Armadale, Flora's stepfather. The captain's loyalty to the crown does not seem to have prevented him from helping the Prince. It was probably his idea to get the Prince off of the Long Island and over to Skye disguised as an Irish maid traveling in the company of Flora, who would be returning to her mother. Whoever raised the idea to Flora, she at first wanted no part of it. She feared that the project would bring danger and dishonor to her and her family. On the night of June 20, either under a full moon, as some tell it,[6] or in the "perpetual twilight sometimes called the summer dim,"[7] as others tell it, or both, Captain Felix O'Neill, who had accompanied the Prince in his flight, and Neil MacEachain, a cousin of Flora's, brought the Prince to her at a shieling* where she was allegedly tending her brother's cattle. Was this high-born young woman really just helping her brother by herding his cattle, or was she at the shieling for some other and potentially more historic purpose? Inconsistent as reports—even firsthand reports—of the meeting are, it seems that Flora was moved by the charm that shone through the pitiful condition of the Prince, and she finally agreed to help out. One modern writer puts the meeting in a reasonable perspective this way:

> If he had been specifically made up and cued for the part Charles could not have done better. Flora was appalled as he stood before her, filthy, ragged, covered with sores, and yet dignified. She was not a romantic girl...but she was exactly the type to whom Charles appealed. If there was one thing calculated to appeal to a woman who prided herself on her own honesty, decency, and virtue, it was the sight of someone else struggling to maintain those standards in spite of their circumstances.[8]

Thus moved, Flora said she would make arrangements and get back to them.

When she did not return by the appointed time, Charlie, by now quite depressed and on the verge of giving himself up to General

---

*A shieling can be either a pasture or a crude upland shelter for herdsmen or shepherds. The latter meaning is more common and the one usually intended in descriptions of Flora'a meeting with the Prince.

Campbell, sent MacEachain to look for Flora. She had been detained by her stepfather's militiamen, as was MacEachain when he found her, but Captain MacDonald appeared and cleared up everything.

It was time to remove the Prince. The press of searching militia was imminent and ominous in its own right, but a sense of even greater urgency may have been stimulated by a message from no less a figure than General Campbell to Ranald MacDonald of Clanranald, warning him that "tomorrow we are going to carry out some thorough searches. If there is any contraband I think you would do well to get it under cover tonight."[9] Whether the general was referring specifically to the illustrious fugitive or to caches of arms or other forms of contraband is not certain. Of further interest in the note is the implication that persons in high Government ranks may not have wanted to capture the Prince—not necessarily because of latent Stuart sympathies, but because of the problems of potential martyrdom implicit in a captive Prince.[10]

Flora returned with the proposal that they take the Prince to Baleshair, on North Uist, but Hugh MacDonald of Baleshair declined to receive the fugitive.[11] It was up to Flora, Neil MacEachain, and Lady Clanranald* to effect the Prince's escape from South Uist. Lady Clanranald, wife of the elder Clanranald is credited by some with masterminding the Prince's escape to Skye. If she did not engineer it, she certainly contributed materially to its success, preparing the Prince's disguise. After a makeshift dinner party from which Lady Clanranald was summoned by General Campbell, Flora seems to have taken charge of the operation. She put Charlie into his disguise as Betty Burke, Irish spinning maid. The get-up, we are told, included "a white linen dress sprigged with lilac, a cap and apron, a quilted petticoat, and a hooded cape."[12] The Prince wanted to keep a pistol hidden in his costume, but Flora wouldn't let him. She said that if it were discovered it would give him away. Charlie is said to have replied that if he were to be searched that closely, he would be found out anyhow. Flora allowed him to retain a cudgel under his skirts but said that Captain O'Neill would have to remain behind, noting wisely

---

*The MacDonalds of Clanranald had vast holdings in the Hebrides. Though Ranald MacDonald the elder had declined to join the Prince eleven months earlier, his son had rallied to the cause.

that O'Neill was not mentioned in the passport her stepfather had issued, that he was unknown to the locals, and that he did not speak Gaelic. Unable to sway Flora, O'Neill remained in hiding on Uist until, a rendezvous with Col. O'Sullivan and a French ship having failed, he was seized by government troops. In his captivity, O'Neill became the principal narrator of and authority on the events surrounding the prince's skulk.

Another act of Flora's on Uist bears mention as well. In *The White Cockade* (1949), Baron Porcelli quotes a letter allegedly written by Flora at Ormaclade to Ewen MacDonald on June 27, asking for a boat with which to return to Skye with her luggage and "what I have with me."[13] Flora's absence from Ormaclade on that date prompts Alasdair Maclean to conclude that the letter was a decoy intended to fool a family of MacDonalds suspected of treachery.[14]

With preparations at last completed and the Government troops closing in, at sunset on June 28 the little party set out to cross the Minch—Flora, Neil MacEachain, the disguised Prince, and a boat crew which seems to have included a John MacDonald and his brother Rory, another Rory MacDonald, John MacMhuirich, and Duncan Campbell.[15] To pass the time, Charlie sang Jacobite songs and protected Flora's head as she slept in the bottom of the boat.[16] They crossed the Minch undetected and at daylight found themselves to be below Waternish Point on the northwest side of Skye. Here they put in to shore for rest and refreshment before undertaking the last leg of the journey. Soon after returning to sea, they were spotted by a detachment of militia who fired a few perfunctory shots but made little or no attempt to pursue. Once across Loch Snizort, they beached the boat at Kilbride, near Monkstadt House, the seat of Sir Alexander MacDonald of Sleat and Lady Margaret. Sir Alexander, who would have wanted no part of this operation, was conveniently away at Ft. Augustus with the Duke of Cumberland. Lady Margaret, on the other hand, had sent care packages of shirts and newspapers to Charlie on Uist. It is altogether possible that Mrs. MacDonald of Kirkibost, sent from Uist the day before to test the vigilance of the militia and perhaps to advise them not to overdo their duty, had informed Lady Margaret of the prince's imminent arrival on Skye. Still, Lady Margaret was outwardly upset at what Flora had brought to her house. Furthermore, Lt. Alexander MacLeod of the local militia was at Lady Margaret's house as they spoke. Alexander MacDonald of Kingsburgh, factor to Sir Alexander, agreed to take the Prince to his house while Flora and Lady Margaret engaged Lt. MacLeod in "close chit-chat."

Although still cool and in command as she had been thus far, Flora made one tactical error after her party had landed safely on Skye. She sent the boat crew back to Uist where, as General Campbell had warned, Lady Clanranald had already been forcefully interrogated. The boatmen were immediately picked up and needed little prodding to tell all they knew.

The argument has recently been convincingly made that the absence of the Royal Navy from the Minch during Charlie and Flora's voyage to Skye and the apparent lack of effort of the militia on the shore and later at Monkstadt were in fact the results of well-orchestrated actions by supporting players.[17]

On Skye the Prince was unconvincing both as a female and as a servant. Movements and gestures repeatedly threatened to give him away. At one point in their travels Neil MacEachain became so exasperated that he admonished the Prince, "For God's sake, sir, take care what you are doing, for you will certainly discover yourself."[18] However, upon learning that this "very odd, muckle, ill-shapen-up wife" was Irish, puzzled locals dropped their suspicions. "Irish" apparently explained any sort of outrageous behavior. The Prince did fool some of the people. One John MacDonald remembered until the day he died in 1827 at the age of 107 having shown two young ladies the way to the Virgin Well while he was tending his black cattle on Skye.[19]

At Kingsburgh a meal fit for a hungry fugitive was hastily put together. Mrs. MacDonald was quite beside herself to have the royal celebrity under her roof, and she and her daughter apparently dressed up for the impromptu dinner party. Her son-in-law, however, decided to remove himself from the Prince's presence and, according to at least one source, did so quickly via a window. Kingsburgh and the Prince stayed up late over bowls of punch until Charlie broke the bowl. The next day he slept until around noon, causing Mrs. MacDonald more anxiety. She finally sent Flora in to ask the Prince for a lock of his hair, with which he magnanimously parted. When at last he "quitted the sheets," the first, incidentally, he had slept in since mid-April, Mrs. MacDonald had them taken up and put away unwashed to be used as her winding sheets. Though one school of thought gives the sheets to

Flora and another holds that the two women divided them, Flora herself says Mrs. MacDonald kept them.

Rosalind Marshall cites a bit of silliness that took place between Flora and Charlie as he was getting back into his frock with the lilac-sprig design. "'Oh, Miss,' he called out in an absurd voice, 'You have forgot my apron! Where is my apron! Pray get my apron here, for that is a principal part of my dress.'" Dr. Marshall adds that Flora's repressive replies made him tease her all the more, and he behaved "not like one that was in danger, but as cheerfully as if he had been putting on women's clothes merely for a piece of diversion."[20]

Charlie left the house in disguise to avoid further suspicion among the servants, but he changed into Highland garb as soon as he was out of sight. He and MacEachain, guided by a boy named MacQueen, made their way cross country to Portree, on the east side of Skye. Flora on horseback followed the road. At Portree, they met Donald Roy MacDonald, who had made arrangements for the Prince to be conveyed across the Sound of Raasay and into the hands of the MacLeods.

Flora and the Prince parted at an inn[21] in Portree on the night of June 30, 1746. One can find as poignant and romantic an account of their parting as one might wish. In reality, it seems to have been rather restrained, though. The Prince tried to repay Flora a crown he had borrowed, but she said it was only half a crown. He is said to have replied, "For all that has happened, I hope, Madame, we shall meet at St. James's yet and I will reward you there for what you have done," or words to that effect. Most commentators agree that Flora and the Prince never saw or communicated with each other again. Robert Chambers does carry their communication a bit further, though. He says that after the Prince and Flora parted, Charlie took a lump of sugar out of his pocket, gave it to Donald Roy MacDonald and said, "Pray, MacDonald, take this piece of sugar to *our lady*; for I am afraid she will get none where she is going."[22] She was arrested a few days later.

It took only a day to discover that Raasay was too small and too open to hide the Prince. After futilely scouring the island, government troops had only recently withdrawn, but not before they had slaughtered the island's cattle and torched its houses. The Prince and his MacLeod guides returned to Skye and crossed the island to Elgol.

There he came under the protection of John MacKinnon, with whom he set out for the mainland. They landed at Mallaig, back in MacDonald country. The Prince was led on to Borrodale, into the Braes of Morar, and into the hands of the Glenmoriston men on or about July 24.

The defeated Prince thus remained in Scotland longer than his conqueror. On July 18, Cumberland quit Ft. Augustus for England, leaving Lord Albemarle in command of the government forces in the north. In August the search for the fugitive Prince was losing intensity as troops were withdrawn from the field and some began to move back to England. In late August the Prince was at Loch Arkaig, in MacPherson country, and in early September joined Cluny MacPherson and moved into the latter's hideout, called the "cage," for the remainder of his stay. On September 13, having learned that the two French ships had arrived at Loch nan Uamh a week earlier, the Prince and his protectors set out for Borrodale and France. On the 19th, the Prince boarded *L'Heureux*, and shortly after midnight on September 20, left Scotland forever. The encouraging words with which the Prince may have bade farewell to the Highlanders whom he left behind sound appropriately noble:

> My lads, be in good spirits. It shall not be long before I shall be with you, and shall endeavour to make up for all the loss you have suffered. I have left money for your subsistence that are officers and have also left money to provide for all the private men.[23]

Did the Prince's departure resemble the one depicted in John Blake MacDonald's oft-reproduced painting of "Lochaber No More"? Some who remained behind no doubt continued to believe Charlie would come back again; others hoped he wouldn't. Assessing the aftermath of the '45, one angry anonymous writer said,

> But whatever hardships [Charles] had endured, he might have had terrible qualms of conscience, for having been the wicked cause of so much bloodshed, rapine, and desolation. Many innocent people were, by means of his cursed ambition, involved in the most horrid calamities, many useful lives were sacrificed in his quarrel, trade and manufactures

suffered a total stagnation, and his infatuated followers were ruined, and banished their country.[24]

John MacDonald of Borrodale put it a bit more succinctly when he grimly observed, "He left us all in a worse state than he found us."[25]

Chapter 3

Flora's First Biographies

"I suppose you have heard of Flora MacDonald."

—GENERAL JOHN CAMPBELL

THE STATE IN WHICH CHARLES EDWARD STUART, the Young Chevalier, left the people of Scotland has been thoroughly explored by Scottish historians and political economists. Instead, let us look at the state in which he left Flora MacDonald. First, of course, he left her in serious trouble. She was in the custody of a government which was dealing most harshly with those who had recently opposed it in thought, word, or deed. He also left her instant, widespread fame.

Flora MacDonald lived for sixty-eight years in a century that saw the world turned upside down. She bore seven children. In the service of two great ruling houses of Britain, she was caught up in the events of two rebellions on opposite sides of the world. At the age of fifty-two she set out with her family to hack a fresh start out of a strange new world. By any standard, Flora MacDonald was a woman of character, courage, and common sense who lived a full and fascinating life well worthy of note even without her encounter with the Prince. Yet it is because of those ten days in June 1746 that Flora MacDonald's story has been told and has grown in the telling. Indeed, the telling of the story becomes as interesting as the story itself.

Reading different accounts of the life of Flora MacDonald is like listening to "Ah, Yes, I remember it well," the duet from *Gigi* in which virtually every assertion that one person makes is contradicted by the other—but both remember it well.

In the telling of Flora's story we can find some consensus. There is general agreement that she was born in 1722 at her father's farm on South Uist, that she was the third child and only daughter of Ranald and Marion MacDonald, that her father died when Flora was one or two, that her mother married Captain Hugh MacDonald of Skye, and that Flora was well educated. Biographers agree that Flora was on South Uist in 1746 when the Prince arrived in flight, and that she assisted in carrying him to Skye, where they parted at an inn in Portree. There is agreement that Flora was arrested a short time later and held on several ships before being transported to London, where she became something of a celebrity and was taken into the circle of the ardent Jacobite Lady Primrose. It is widely understood that upon her release from custody Flora received from Lady Primrose a purse of £1500 and a post-chaise in which to return home in the company of Malcolm MacLeod. There is agreement that Flora married Allan MacDonald in 1750, had at least seven children, met and delighted Boswell and Johnson in 1773, and went with her husband and some of their children to North Carolina in 1774. Biographers concur in telling that Flora's husband took up arms for the crown and that he and one son were captured in their first military engagement. The biographers agree that Flora suffered during her long separation from her husband, that she returned to Scotland, that she died there in March 1790, and that she had a huge funeral.

Beyond this summary of the mainstream biographical consensus, however, few details or even other events enjoy consensus. As we examine the telling of Flora's story over two and a half centuries, we will note in detail two causes for biographical discrepancies: the lack of factual information about the Highland lass before she met the Prince and long undiscovered and unpublished information after the fact.

In examining factual inconsistency, one must begin with her name. One can find at least three different spellings of "MacDonald." Flora and her husband usually wrote "McDonald." Elizabeth Gray Vining, in her 1966 biography points out that modern usage has tended to "Macdonald." She then cites Dr. Donald MacKinnon, himself an authority on Flora's life, who states that the correct Scots spelling is "MacDonald," adding that only names derived from churchly callings should have a small letter after the "Mac."[1] So be it: "MacDonald" will prevail here unless another spelling is being quoted.

Even with her Christian name we are not on completely solid ground. "Flora," of course, is traditional and predominates. But let us at least observe that Flora often referred to herself as "Flory," most notably perhaps in her marriage contract, which found its way into the hands of Sir Walter Scott and is on display at Abbotsford. In a quaint but undocumented quotation, the Reverend Alexander MacGregor has Hebridean parents chide their children, "C'uin a bhios sibh cosmhuil ri Fionnghal Nighean Roanuill an Airidh-Mhuilinn?" [When will you resemble Flora of Milton?][2] Fionnghal—"the fair one"—has prevailed, but in the light of what Flora called herself, at least one writer would prefer "Floraidh" as a truer rendering of "Flory" in Gaelic.[3]

By whatever name, Flora was instantaneously famous. As early as July 15, 1746, Colonel O'Sullivan, himself recently rescued from Benbecula by a French ship, wrote cryptically to Jacobite friends at Versailles of "a lady who transformed my associate and conveyed him to Heaven."[4] References in a letter from General John Campbell to the commander of Dunstaffnage Castle dated August 1 and in a letter from Henry Seymour Conway to Horace Walpole dated August 12 shall be looked at in a later chapter. On August 11, while the Prince was still at large in the Highlands and Flora, though a prisoner, had not yet been brought to Edinburgh, *Gentleman's Magazine* reported "the exactest account of the pretender's motions we have yet met with," saying that on June 28,

> under the disguise of a lady's maid, he sailed with her in a small boat from South Uist to the isle of Sky, and next day, in the same habit, landed at a gentleman's house....[5]

By October, with Flora now on board the *Bridgewater* in Leith Roads, *Gentleman's Magazine* had identified Flora by name and had elaborated on her involvement in the Prince's "motions."[6] We are told that while a shipboard prisoner in Leith Roads and during her confinement in London, Flora captured the imaginations and earned the admiration of Jacobites and Hanoverians alike. And, as we shall see later, she was celebrity enough to attract the attention of the principal portraitists of the day.

Certainly Flora was famous in 1773, when Johnson and Boswell included Skye in their famous tour of the Hebrides specifically to see her. Indeed, Dr. Johnson's preoccupation with Flora seems to have dislocated the nose of Sir Alexander MacDonald of Skye, who addressed the doctor thus: "At your behaviour every one felt some degree of resentment when you told me your only errand into Skye was to visit the Pretender's conductress, and that you deemed every moment as lost which was not spent in her company."[7] Boswell's account of Johnson's behavior in Flora's presence suggests that Sir Alexander might have had a point. "To see Mr. Samuel Johnson salute Miss Flora MacDonald was a wonderful romantic scene to me," recalled Boswell.

For her part, Flora bantered with Johnson, calling him "a young English buck" and contrived with him that he would sleep in the Prince's bed because, as she says, "You know that young bucks are always the favourites of the ladies." Tickled as he must have been at Flora's attention, Johnson does manage to say of his night in the famous bed that he had "no ambitious thoughts in it."[8]

Flora had become a tourist attraction. The year before Johnson and Boswell's visit, another Englishman had made his way to Skye and had "stopped at Kingsburgh, immortalized by its mistress, the celebrated Flora Mac-Donald, the fair protectress of the fugitive adventurer."[9] Thomas Pennant, whom Dr. Johnson called "the best traveller I ever read,"[10] had not published his account of his 1772 trip to Scotland when Johnson and Boswell visited, so perhaps they did not know that Pennant, though he missed seeing "the fair protectress," had "lodged [the] night in the same bed that formerly received the unfortunate Charles Stuart."[11]

But Johnson and Boswell wanted to hear Flora's account of her adventures with the Prince. "Who was with him?" they asked. "We were told in England that there was one Miss Flora Macdonald with him." "They were very right," she replied. Then, according to Boswell, Flora "very obligingly" told of traveling to Skye with the Prince disguised as Betty Burke, of dining with Lady Margaret MacDonald at Monkstadt, and of deceiving the officer of militia who was dining with them. Johnson told Flora that all this should be written down. She said that Bishop Forbes at Leith had it all.[12]

Regrettably, neither Johnson nor Boswell gives us a source for what they were told in England. But, while we don't know precisely what their sources were, we know generally what was available in print at the time. Thanks to the avid collecting of Walter Biggar Blaikie, W. M. MacBean, and McGillivray of McGillivray, among others, we can examine dozens of pamphlets produced in the aftermath of the '45.

Among these is a piece entitled *The Female Rebels, Being some remarkable incidents in the lives, characters, and families of the titular Duke and Duchess of Perth, The Lord and Lady Ogilvie, and of Miss Florence McDonald* published in London and in Dublin in 1747. Like many pamphlets of this sort, it is unsigned, but the British Museum catalog attributes it to John Drummond.[13] As biography, this is pretty sketchy stuff. Of the nine pages devoted to Flora, six are about her genealogy and three are about her life and character. What facts this pamphlet does present are largely incorrect. The author calls Flora an only child and says that her father "bestowed on her a very genteel and early education, in which she had made a very considerable progress when he died, though she was only about twelve years of age." The author of this pamphlet initiates the on-going idea that Flora completed her education at a finishing school in Edinburgh. He goes on to describe Flora as

> a young person of about 20, a graceful person of good complexion and regular features. She has a peculiar sweetness mixed with sagacity in her countenance; her deportment is rather graver than is becoming her years. Even under confinement she betrays nothing of sullenness or discontent, in all her actions bespeaks a mind full of conscious innocence, and uncapable of being ruffled by the common accidents of life.[14]

The Female Rebels is the only contemporary pamphlet that presents any biographical information about Flora. Most of the other pieces focus on the Prince's coming to Scotland, his heroic adventures at the head of his Highland army, and his lamentable defeat and departure. The typical early pamphlet is embellished with various colorings of the artistic imagination. *Manlius or, The Brave Adventurer, A Poetical Novel*, for example, is poem of some 437 lines of blank verse containing the usual epic conventions and echoing the opening line of Vergil's *Aeneid*. Only the last fifteen lines or so treat post-Culloden events, and Flora MacDonald is not mentioned. *Young Juba* is another such piece. It is subtitled *The History of the Young Chevalier from his Birth to his Escape from Scotland after the Battle of Culloden*. Published in Rome, probably 1747 by Michaele Vezzosi,[15] the Prince's valet, it was translated from the original Italian by one M. Mitchell and first appeared in London in

1748. It is a conventional retelling of the Prince's story in which all of the participants except the Prince retain their real names. He is called "Juba," presumably after the first-century B.C. Numidian king who, having been defeated by the Romans, wandered in the wilderness a fugitive. In *Young Juba*, Flora is briefly mentioned.

Ascanius; or the Young Adventurer, A True History appeared in London in the late forties. It, too, is presented as a translation "from a manuscript...at the Court of Versailles containing a particular account of all that happened to a certain person during his wanderings in the north, from his memorable defeat in April, 1746, to his final escape on the 19th of September of the same year." This sort of semi-transparent cryptic allusion is common in the writings of the time, and barring an incredible coincidence, the identity of this certain person, called Ascanius in the text, can hardly be in doubt. In the introduction, having mused upon the "many and various turns and vicissitudes of Fortune," the author has this to say:

> Enough already has the world heard of his story to excite compassion in the generous breast, but still the greater part remains untold. Such melancholy truths are yet behind as when exhibited to public view, will raise a fresh supply of pity, a tribute justly due to such distinguished sufferings."[16]

In *Ascanius,* the meeting between Flora and the Prince gets some embellished attention. Indeed, the embellishments given to the meeting are sufficiently distinctive to link *Ascanius* with Padre Giulio Cesare Cordara's *Commentary on the Expedition to Scotland Made by Charles Edward Stuart, Prince of Wales.*[17] One or both of these probably served as a source for Voltaire's account of the incident.[18] Both describe the lady as traveling on horseback. Both say that the Prince and the lady had previously met at Inverness. Both have her recognize the voice but not the figure now so wasted and besmirched. Both have the lady dismounting, throwing herself at the Prince's feet, and trying to kiss his hand, which he graciously withdraws because, covered with scabby sores, it is unfit for gentle lips. To help raise that fresh supply of pity, the *Ascanius* author tells us that "The lady's tenderness was quite moved, and she could not avoid shedding tears on seeing the P—— in so forlorn a condition." The lady immediately pledges her aid to the Prince thus: "I, from my heart, pity your condition; my family hath ever been strictly attach'd to the R—l House of St—t. As far as lies in my power you may command my services."[19] Noble as this offer is, it does not square with the initial reluctance to get involved that Flora herself and other contemporaries tell us she expressed. It should be noted as well that here the lady is depicted as executing a "continental thrust." This maneuver, described in both these works, appears again in Voltaire's account of the Prince's adventures. As Voltaire tells it, the lady, upon recognizing the Prince, "se jeta a ses pieds."[20]

It is to this sort of romanticized, pity-raising account that J. C. Hadden refers many years later. The Prince is moved to tears by Flora's expression of devotion. He raises Flora to her feet, kisses her on the forehead, and says:

> Do not kneel to me, my dear. I'm but a poor hunted man, with neither name or home, and never more will Charles Stuart come near the throne of his fathers! Help me to escape from my enemies, and you will help not only your Prince, but a poor, unfortunate mortal who stands sore in need of sympathy.[21]

In *The Aeneid*, it is Ascanius, the son of Aeneas, who shoots a stag and breaks the peace in Latium.[22] *Ascanius* is further noteworthy because it gives a rare view of the Prince expressing concern for the grief he has brought upon Scotland. On the crossing to Skye, Flora tells him of the depredation and arrests that have occurred since Culloden, to which he replies:

> Tis a cutting Reflection to me...that so many brave Men should be ruined by their Attachment to my Interest: that I have involved them in mine and my Families Misfortunes! ...Oh! I cannot bear the Thought![23]

Alexis; or, The Young Adventurer, A Novel was published in London in 1746. Its authorship is uncertain and in dispute. MacDonald of Kingsburgh tells us that Neil MacEachain is the only person other than himself with the firsthand knowledge to tell the story so accurately, and Flora concurs. MacEachain is the favorite of a number of scholars, and his literary prowess is elsewhere shown to be sufficiently strong to sustain the account with all its pastoral machinery and allegorical trappings. In his 1839 edition of the work, however, the Scottish antiquarian Peter Buchan attributes authorship to the soldier-poet and cousin of Flora, Alexander MacDonald, known somewhat more widely by the Gaelic Alasdair MacMhaighstir Alasdair. Perhaps following Buchan's lead, the cataloguer of the MacBean Collection in Aberdeen also credits MacDonald. By whatever mind devised or whatever hand penned, some of the names assigned in the narrative are amusing and worth noting. Our hero (the Prince) is "Alexis, a shepherd of the first rank." Scotland is "Robustia"; England, "Felicia." Culloden is "Lachrymania;" Cumberland, "Sanguinius." Another villain, Captain Fergusson, is "Crudelius," and the principled General Campbell is merely "Militarius." If Neil MacEachain is indeed the author, he gives his character a ring of truth as "Veracius." And Flora? She is "Heroica."[23]

Perhaps the best known and for a while the most often cited authority was the account of Captain Felix O'Neill. Despite his Irish name, O'Neill was of Spanish descent and had served in the Spanish army before joining Lally's Irish regiment in the service of France. He had arrived in Scotland with dispatches for the Prince just before Culloden and remained with the Prince until Flora barred him from the boat to Skye. Captured soon thereafter, O'Neill readily told his story, which was published in *Caledonian Mercury* in October 1746 and in *Gentleman's Magazine* and *London Magazine* in November. Fond of Flora and endowed with a sense of self-worth, O'Neill did nothing in his telling of the story to diminish the importance of his role in it. Despite O'Neill's early eminence as a resource, later historians question his accuracy and his veracity. In the nineteenth century Robert Chambers describes him as being "of a confused intellect"; in the twentieth, Alasdair Maclean calls him a "paranoid liar."[24]

In the first few months after the rising, the pamphlets came thick and fast. The April 1747 issue of *Gentleman's Magazine* reports the publication in that month alone of *The Female Rebels, Alexis, Ascanius,* and *The Wanderer: A Narrative founded upon True Facts.* The author of this last piece acknowledges having read *Ascanius,* from which he borrowed the classical nomenclature. After his army's defeat, the Wanderer, followed by the faithful Sulluvius and Tyronius, is received with open arms by Sempronia, who disguises him as a servant of Porcia.

In addition to the accounts cited above, others by participants on both sides continued to reach the reading public with considerable regularity over the next two decades. Thus, though little was known about Flora's background, her part in preserving the Prince would have been well known.

Actually by the time Dr. Johnson met Flora, she had told her story and had it taken down on at least three occasions. She had, of course, told it to her English captors in the summer of 1746; she had told it during her confinement and shortly after her release to Dr. John Burton of York, a fellow inmate during Flora's detention in London; and she had told it to The Reverend (later Bishop) Robert Forbes in Leith as he began to compile what would become *The Lyon in Mourning*. Of these, only the one she had given to Dr. Burton had been published when Johnson and Boswell went to Skye to see her, and if they knew of it, they do not seem to have paid it much attention. Clearly, the English visitors knew who Flora was and wanted to meet her. They seem to have believed that despite her fame, her story was there to be recorded and passed along to the world at large.

Even so, like those before him, Boswell focused on the adventures of the Prince, in which Flora was, at best, a prominent supporting player, a charming eyewitness. He was not researching the first definitive biography of Flora. From her and others whom he met in the Hebrides, Boswell put together a narrative of the Prince's adventures. Celebrity though she clearly was, Flora drops out of Boswell's account as soon as she passes the Prince along to the MacLeods at Portree.

Every edition of Boswell's Hebridean journal from its first appearance in 1776 until 1936 omitted Flora's statement to Johnson that Bishop Forbes had her story. Not until Professors Pottle and Bennett found, edited, and published the original manuscript did this reference come to light.

A year after Johnson and Boswell's visit, Flora and her family left Scotland to begin their American adventure and for the time being, at least, the interviewing stopped. Upon her return to Skye and less than a year before her death, Flora did provide another account of her adventures both with the Prince and in America, which she dictated at the request of Sir John McPherson, "late Governor General of India." Of these papers Flora says, "I hope they are to the purpose, being exact truth; They are longer than I would wish, but shorter I could not make them...."[25]

Like *The Lyon in Mourning*, however, this memorial seems to have remained unnoticed until well into the twentieth century, when it came into the possession of the National Library of Scotland and was first published in *The Scotsman*, November 29, 1938.[26] Ten years later the eminent Jacobite scholar Henrietta Tayler published it as part of "A Jacobite Miscellany" in the *Roxburghe Club Papers*.

By the end of her century Flora's story was known and her fame established. Though some of the original material would not come to light for many years, enough of Flora's story was available to establish a base on which writers would build for the next two hundred years.

Chapter 4

The Later Biographies

"The life of no female in the history of any country was ever more deserving the attention of the historian."

—JOSEPH SEAWELL JONES

"THE SPIRIT AND PRESENCE OF MIND of Miss Flora MacDonald were again displayed in behalf of the object so strangely thrown under the protection of one of her sex and age."[1] So wrote Sir Walter Scott in Tales of a Grandfather in the winter of 1827–28, and in so doing brought to the historiography of Flora the romanticism of the nineteenth century. In his treatment of her, Scott makes Flora something more than a supporting character in the adventures of the Prince. For the first time we see symbolic value being assigned to the Highland heroine. To Lady Primrose's house in London, where Scott says Flora was staying after her release from custody, came

> persons of rank, who entertained any bias to that unhappy cause.... Many who, perhaps, secretly regretted they had not given more effectual instances of their faith to the exiled [Stuart] family, were desirous to make some amends, by loading with attentions and valuable presents, the heroine who had played such a dauntless part in the drama.[2]

Also in 1827, Robert Chambers brought out the first edition of his *History of the Rebellion in Scotland, 1745–1746*, in which he gave a bit of a biographical sketch of Flora, noting that she was "the daughter of MacDonald of Milton, in the island of South Uist, and therefore a gentlewoman by birth,...."[3] Five years later, in the same year that Chambers and his brother William founded *Chambers' Edinburgh Jour-*

43

nal, Robert Chambers obtained the ten black-bound volumes containing the "collection of speeches, letters, journals, etc." relative to the '45 which The Reverend Robert Forbes[4] had scrupulously (and "as exactly ...as the iniquity of the time would permit")[5] amassed in the months and years just after the events had taken place. Forbes's widow had kept these volumes for some thirty years. They were then bought by Sir Henry Stewart of Allanton in 1806. Chambers tracked down the work and subsequently purchased it from Sir Henry. Thus armed with the Forbes material, Chambers published in 1834 his *Jacobite Memoirs of the Rebellion of 1745*, and then rewrote his *History of the Rebellion* and reissued it in 1840. He held onto the Forbes material until his death in 1871 and bequeathed it to the Advocates Library in Edinburgh. Not until 1895 did Henry Paton edit *The Lyon in Mourning* for publication by the Scottish Historical Society.[6] Throughout the nineteenth century, then, without Boswell's clue to the existence of Bishop Forbes's work and unaware perhaps of Robert Chambers's possession of it, historians of the '45 and biographers of its principal players labored without material that we now take for granted.[7]

In 1834, between the two editions of his *History of the Rebellion*, Chambers published in his *Journal* a biographical sketch of Flora. The piece runs to two and a half large folio columns of fine print and covers all of Flora's life, though about half of the article is devoted to those ten days in June 1746 and their immediate consequences.[8]

To maintain chronological order, we must cross the Atlantic to find the next serious study of Flora. Joseph Seawell Jones published in New York in 1838, *Memorials of North Carolina*, a series of essays that had previously appeared "some years ago in the literary gazettes of the day." In one of the few trail markers left by nineteenth-century writers, Jones cites Chambers as a source. As he finishes the chapter devoted to her tale, Jones gives us a glimpse of how Flora was perceived at the time he was telling it:

> The life of no female in the history of any country was ever more deserving the attention of the historian. Her adventurous deeds in the service of the unfortunate Prince have been celebrated by almost every poet of the age, and have, more than any single subject, infused a spirit of love and war into the minstrelsy of her own poetical country.[9]

Back in Britain in 1845, John Heneage Jesse produced his *Memoirs of the Pretenders and their Adherents*. Jesse devotes a good deal of attention to Flora in his biography of the Young Pretender and an equal amount to her as one of the Adherents. Jesse cites Chambers's *History of the Rebellion* as one of his sources, and Jesse's account of Flora's shipboard life at Leith echoes Forbes through Chambers.[10] The first American edition of Jesse's work was published in Philadelphia in 1846.

In that same year in America, the Reverend William Henry Foote wrote *Sketches of North Carolina*. As the title further tells us, the sketches were "Historical and Biographical, illustrative of the Principles of a portion of her early settlers. Here, again, Flora is presented as the embodiment of ideals:

> Will not posterity admire her more than Prince Charles who led his followers to slaughter? or George II, who envied the popularity of his own son? and draw more instruction from her romance, and affection, and boldness, and devotion, and womanly graces, and feminine loveliness, than from all the court of England that fill the histories of that by-gone period?
>
> Massachusetts had her Lady Arabella; Virginia her Pocahontas; and North Carolina her Flora MacDonald.[11]

From his vantage point, Foote saw the Prince's escape from Uist as a women's effort. He credits Lady Clanranald with the idea of dressing up the Prince as a spinning maid and says that her ladyship approached Flora with the proposition thus: "Will you expose yourself to this danger to aid the escape of the Prince from his enemies that have him here enclosed?" The maiden answered, "Since I am to die, and can die but once, I am perfectly willing to put my life in jeopardy to save his Royal Highness from the danger which now besets him."[12] It is interesting to note that the dialogue that Foote and others attribute to Flora has never been authenticated, and is not likely to be.

Time and distance, too, perhaps cause Foote to mis-identify "an officer named O'Neill, who expressed the same romantic idea to aid the escape of the very man for the apprehension of whom he was then in arms."[13] While we do not know Foote's source for the idea that O'Neill was one of the local militiamen, we can be sure that it was not from O'Neill. Foote also has Flora find "a youth, Neill McDonald

... as noble, generous, and romantic as herself, who entered with devotion into the plan for the escape of the Prince." The part Neil MacEachain, to whom Foote is referring, played in the Prince's escape will be looked at later. For now suffice it to say that Foote underestimates it.

On the celebrated voyage to Skye, "the courage of the maiden never forsakes her." Instead of allowing Flora to rest in the bottom of the boat while the Prince sang Jacobite airs to her, Foote has her exhort the oarsmen to exert their utmost strength. Foote says that at Monkstadt Flora received a "cordial reception" from Lady Margaret. "The lady's heart answers to the maiden's confidence, and she espouses her cause." He reports that local citizens returning from church were curious at the sight of this "coarse, negligent, clumsy-looking, long-legged female figure." However, "without any indignity or suspicion [the Prince and his guides] reached the place of their destination." Foote has Flora take the Prince to Portree and part with him the next morning. He kissed her and said, "Gentle, faithful maiden, I entertain the hope that we shall yet meet in the Palace Royal." Summing it up, Foote notes, "His escape was the work not of his chivalry or courage, but of woman's tenderness, and the loyal feelings of Scottish hearts."[14]

The Reverend Mr. Foote had an audience. In her 1848 compilation of *The Women of the American Revolution*, Elizabeth F. Ellet quotes Foote's comparison at the beginning of her chapter on Flora. Mrs. Ellet draws her material from Foote and Jones, both of whom she cites in her text, and she concludes with the observation that while Flora's memory remains among the lofty pines of her North Carolina home, "the story of her romantic enthusiasm, intrepidity, and disinterested self-devotion, has extended into lands where in life she was unknown."[15]

Next came James Banks, who in 1854 in Fayetteville, North Carolina, delivered a lecture entitled *The Life and Character of Flora Mac-Donald*. The lecture was subsequently published in *University Magazine* and, in 1857, between its own covers. Banks, too, recognizes Flora as ideals personified:

> The incidents in the life of Flora MacDonald are so numerous, that I have refrained from attempting a formal delineation of her character, believing that a simple narrative, a

plain unvarnished tale would best portray those qualities, for which she is distinguished and celebrated throughout the world.[16]

Banks maintains the romantic element in the narrative as can be seen in his description of the Prince rallying support:

> By his talent, eloquence and address, he so operated on the feelings of the various clans, that soon the "fiery cross" traversed the mountain and the vale, calling the clansmen to that last gathering of the "Highland Host," in which a halo of glory was reflected on the prowess and arms, far beyond what they had hitherto attained.[17]

Banks follows eighteenth-century convention in having Flora complete her studies in Edinburgh "to acquire the grace and polish suited to her station in life." He then offers Dr. Johnson's praise of Flora as proof that she had attained these necessary qualities. He also calls as a witness one Malcolm MacKay, a former coronet in the British army, "who had seen the Queen of England and many of her attendants," but said that

> for grace and dignity Flora McDonald excelled all the women he had ever beheld: that it was worth a day's ride to see her graceful manner of sitting, or rising from a chair— that there was a perfection of ease and grace in that simple act, that could be felt but not described.[18]

It is thus easy to understand how Flora rose to the occasion and came to the Prince's rescue "when in the solitude of her mountain home, in the beautiful language of the poet, she exclaimed—

> 'Thy spirit, Independence, let me share,
> Lord of the lion heart, and eagle eye,
> Thy steps I follow, with my bosom bare,
> Nor heed the storm that howls along the sky.'

so that I am enabled to save my sovereign Prince or perish in the attempt." [19] Later, Alexander MacGregor would only "imagine" Flora's recalling of these lines from Smollett.[20]

Despite these sentiments, Banks has Flora take a more cautious position when asked to escort the Prince from Uist. Lady Clanranald again appears as an initiator along with "Captain Neal." On the crossing, Charlie is telling stories, singing, and protecting the slumbering Flora. Banks provides a conventional synopsis of Flora's marriage to Allan, knows that the marriage contract is at Abbotsford, relates Johnson's visit, and brings Flora and family to North Carolina.

In Britain, the next biographer of our lady and first to fill a full-length book was her granddaughter, Flora Frances MacDonald, the eighth of nine children and first of two daughters born to Flora's son, the distinguished Lt. Col. John MacDonald, FRS. Flora Frances, who married Edward Wylde, RN, published in 1870 and again in 1875 *The Life of Flora MacDonald*, "edited by her grand-daughter." Mrs. Wylde maintains the autobiographical spirit by having Flora tell her story to "Maggie" at the latter's request. This device and the considerable use of dialogue properly render the work a biographical novel. As such, it is rather summarily dismissed by subsequent biographers as being of little use. Yet Mrs. Wylde may have been under-appreciated. It is clear that she has researched her subject. The authenticity of incidents which she includes can be independently confirmed by historical documents. She quotes, for example, General Campbell's letter of August 1, 1746, to the commander at Dunstaffnage Castle, referring to the "pretty rebel" and including the postscript alluding to Flora's instantaneous celebrity.[21] Furthermore, given the findings of John Gibson and Alasdair Maclean on the covert role of Neil MacEachain and the possibility of Flora's knowledge of it,[22] it is noteworthy that Mrs. Wylde introduces MacEachain as Flora's cousin and childhood playmate. Is this merely a case of the novelist's introducing early a character who will return in a significant role later in the story, or did Mrs. Wylde know more about her grandmother's doings than we might think?

In addition, Mrs. Wylde suggests that at least some of Flora's fame during her enforced stay in London stemmed from the fact that she was often mistaken for the notorious Jenny Cameron, widely reputed to be mistress to the Prince. Mrs. Wylde has Flora regret the mistake because Miss J—X—, as she is identified in the book, is one "whose reputation brings her no credit." Whether Mrs. Wylde knew of it or not, *Caledonian Mercury* (Monday, January 5, 1747), quotes a dispatch from London that refers to "The famous Miss Flora MacDonald, who has so often been mistaken by the Town for Jenny Cameron...."[23]

To be sure, Mrs. Wylde can be pretty fanciful with some of her invented dialogue, but certainly no more so than the next two "biographers" of Flora MacDonald. First published in 1882 and frequently thereafter, Alexander MacGregor's *Life of Flora MacDonald* stood for almost fifty years as the standard (and presumably definitive) work. The Reverend Mr. MacGregor makes assertions without attribution. He tells us, for example, that Flora "was naturally a precocious little girl, who showed an early taste for the beautiful, great, and grand in nature. She had been known to stand for hours admiring the battling of the elements, when the bold Atlantic rose in mountains of foam."[24] Perhaps she did; if you agree with Melville (Herman, not Andrew), all of us are similarly inclined: "Water and meditation are wedded forever." Flora "was known" to do so? By whom? Who told Mr. MacGregor? In his years at the church at Kilmuir, on Skye, MacGregor did know Flora's daughter Anne and obtained information from her, but how accurate could she be about her mother's childhood activities? MacGregor writes legend and embellishes his work with poetic selections, both English and Gaelic, that contribute effectively to the romantic atmosphere in which he wraps his legend. Fancy asserts with the authority of fact. Even without footnotes, however, it seems clear that MacGregor was indebted to James Banks for much of the material on Flora in North Carolina.

In a sense, Alexander MacGregor is joined in 1886 by William Jolly, who brought forth *Flora MacDonald in Uist*. Jolly promotes MacGregor's work as, in his later editions, MacGregor plugs Jolly's. Calling his biography "A study of the heroine in her native surroundings," Jolly writes meditative and evocative appreciations of the Hebridean land- and seascapes similar to those found in MacGregor's treatment of Flora's childhood. In his preface he states his purpose:

> This outline sketch is an attempt to present [Flora] as she lived, with requisite local colouring, and to indicate the special conditions under which so marked a personality was produced....[25]

Before leaving the nineteenth century, we should at least note that under Flora's name in the British Biographical Archive we find references to seven different biographical compendia published between 1836 and 1881. These entries tend to be short paragraphs that summarize generally agreed-upon details. Among the more provocative titles of these compendia are *A Cyclopaedia of Female Biography* (1857) and *The Impartial Dictionary of Universal Biography* in 16 volumes (1857–63).[26]

The first notable biographical account of Flora to appear in the twentieth century was written by A. R. MacDonald, of Waternish, Skye. It was he who noted that in the Highlands, where "we can claim cousinship to the fortysecond [sic] degree," Flora could have, had she wanted to, claimed kinship to the Prince.[27] MacDonald's biography appeared in seven installments in the Oban *Times* between July 8 and August 19, 1905, as "A True Account of the Life of Flora MacDonald." The appearance of the word "True" in the title is significant. It is the first time since the eighteenth-century pamphlets that the adjective has been used to describe accounts of the adventures in which Flora played a part. Furthermore, it heralds work that was to engage Mr. MacDonald for the next thirty years and culminate in his *The Truth about Flora MacDonald*, published posthumously in 1938. The word of course implies that truth was to some degree absent from earlier accounts of Flora's life.

Like others before and since, MacDonald devotes a large part of the account (almost half) to those ten days in June 1745. MacDonald corrects assertions by earlier writers. He notes, for example, that Ormaclett [sic] had burned down in 1715 and the Clanranalds were living at Nunton. He rejects the idea of an Edinburgh education, saying that Flora first left the islands when she went to stay for eleven months with maternal relatives at "Largie in Argyllshire." He says that Sir Alexander MacDonald's gala ball held in 1747 in Flora's honor could not have happened because Flora was still in Edinburgh and Sir Alexander was dead. MacDonald's "True Account..." was the beginning of a major undertaking, as shall be shortly seen.

The 1906 edition of the venerable *Dictionary of National Biography,* contains a sketch of Flora MacDonald written by T. F. Henderson. He draws upon such sources as *The Female Rebels* and MacGregor's *Life* and joins MacGregor in dismissing Mrs. Wylde's work as "of little value." Taken as a starting point in one's biographical research, which it often is, the *DNB* seems to state with absolute authority. It is the first word, if not the last, on the subject. Consulted at the outset, it can define the researcher's attitude and direction. However, taken in its chronological place in the evolution of someone's biography, the *DNB* entry becomes merely an imperfect and not always impartial summary of what was available to the compiler at the time the article was solicited.

In the United States, J. P. Maclean's *Flora MacDonald in America*, was published in book form in Lumberton, North Carolina, in 1909. Like A. R. MacDonald's "Truth...," Maclean's book grows out of an earlier periodical piece — in this case an article that had appeared in *The Celtic Monthly* in 1899. Though he provides more detail about Flora's American sojourn than had his predecessors, in his telling of the story of her early life, time with Prince Charlie, later years, and death, Maclean follows the path laid out by MacGregor and the *DNB*. And two years after the publication of his book J. P. Maclean returned to *The Celtic Monthly* with an assessment of Flora's place in history entitled "Eulogium on the Character of Flora MacDonald."

Seven years later, in 1916, The Scottish Society of America presented *Flora MacDonald: A History and A Message*. Published in Washington for free distribution to "anyone who may be interested in the perpetuation of the memory of the great Scottish heroine,"[28] the book is a recounting of Flora's story and the print version of a speech made by Dr. James MacDonald, Editor-in-Chief of the Toronto *Globe*, calling for the establishment of college bearing Flora's name in the heart of Scottish North Carolina. Since 1896 such a college "for the intellectual, moral and religious development and training of young ladies" had existed in Red Springs (Robeson County), North Carolina, under the name of "Red Springs Seminary," and later as "Southern Presbyterian College and Conservatory of Music." It was Dr. MacDonald's hope that a name change would provide the impetus for new and ambitious fundraising for the college.

The history portion of the book shows a strong indebtedness to Jolly's work, especially in descriptions of Flora's early years in Uist. One glimpse of Flora's activities in North Carolina illustrates both the scope and tone of this history. We learn that before the Highlanders marched off to the battle of Moore's Creek Bridge, Flora,

> mounted on a white pony, addressed the troops in Gaelic.... She appealed to their love of the old land whence they came. She rallied them by memories of Highland heroism

and Highland devotion. The clansmen, wild in their enthusiasm, answered her in fierce Gaelic oaths of loyalty.... As
the Highlanders passed...she called out to each clan its
Gaelic battle-cry.[29]

Dr. MacDonald had been successful in delivering his message in
1914. With a motto of "Flora MacDonald and Half a Million" and a
method of "Sons of the Gael, Shoulders Together,"[30] the name had
been changed and the new college born before the book was ready for
distribution.

Back in Britain, 1934 saw the publication of two significant bits of
Floriana. One was Compton Mackenzie's *Prince Charlie and his Ladies*,
which, as one might expect, devotes considerable space to Flora. The
other was an article by Baroness Orczy entitled "Flora and the Bonnie
Prince." The latter was part of a series under the heading of "Royal
Romances" that appeared in the *North China Herald* that year. The article prompted Allan R. MacDonald to take pen in hand one last time
"to clear [Flora's] memory from the foul slanders of a writer in a London magazine." Indeed, as Donald MacKinnon noted, "everything that
Mr. MacDonald wrote about Flora MacDonald had one great aim, and
that was to vindicate her character."[31] Allan MacDonald's book-length
setting forth of the truth about Flora MacDonald was published
posthumously at Inverness in 1938.

Let us hope that in 1934 Flora's character could have withstood the
Baroness's best shot. Bent though he was on repudiating the titillating
article, Allan MacDonald probably did the world and Flora's memory a
greater service by correcting many of the erroneous and unsubstantiated statements of Flora's earlier biographers. And unlike many of those
earlier writers, MacDonald documented his sources.

In 1941, Dorothy MacKay Quynn published "Flora MacDonald in
History" in the *North Carolina Historical Review*. This well-researched
and carefully documented study packs a great deal of information into
twenty-three pages.

The Baron (Ernest) Porcelli, a Clanranald descendant, brought out
in 1949 *The White Cockade*. Despite its somewhat sweeping subtitle,
*The Lives and Adventures of James Francis Edward Stuart and his Sons
'Bonnie Prince Charlie' and Cardinal York,* the book focuses on Charlie
and the '45 and pays considerable attention to Flora's part in the

Prince's skulk. Baron Porcelli also draws upon Flora's 1789 memorials and publishes, apparently for the first time, the aforementioned letter purported to be from Flora to her kinsman Ewan Macdonald, asking for "the boat for my luggage, and what I have with me."[32]

At this point in the chronology of Flora's biographies it is appropriate to mention one that remains unpublished. The Reverend Donald MacKinnon, who in 1938 saw through to posthumous publication A. R. MacDonald's *The Truth about Flora MacDonald,* wrote in 1953 his own account of her story. He gave one copy of his manuscript to the North Carolina historian Rassie Wicker of Pinehurst, in gratitude for Mr. Wicker's assistance on the American portion of Flora's life.[33]

In 1966 Elizabeth Gray Vining published her thorough and professional *Flora: A Biography.* A year later the British edition carried the somewhat longer title *Flora MacDonald, Her Life in the Highlands and America.* Mrs. Vining's interest in Flora is long-standing. "No child with a Scottish father," she writes, "could fail to have heard the story of Flora MacDonald." In 1930, while living in North Carolina and writing a children's book called *Meggy MacIntosh: A Highland Girl in the Carolina Colony,* in which Flora would appear as a character, Mrs. Vining discovered "how little had been written about [Flora] and how larded with legend that little was...."[34] It is interesting to see how the earlier book picks up and passes along much of the legendary "lard" which the author then corrects in the 1966 biography. Though she clearly benefits from both Bishop Forbes and A. R. MacDonald, as well as others who have gone before, Mrs. Vining has scrupulously done her own work. More than any writer on the subject before her, she has been able to separate fact from fiction. Her research is eminently thorough, and she makes the extra effort to follow up on those small, tangential points that less meticulous biographers might leave unexamined. In so doing, she has produced a biography that has stood for a quarter of a century and continues to deserve the designation "definitive."

The Reverend J. A. Carruth followed in 1973 with *Flora MacDonald, The Highland Heroine.* This pamphlet provides a good introduction to Flora and her world. The biographical material is fairly orthodox and the many illustrations are an interesting cross section of relevant art.

In 1976, James and Ida Huneycutt included in their *History of Richmond County* (North Carolina) a thirteen-page chapter in which they too examine "Flora MacDonald—Facts and Fiction." Implicit in the chapter's title is the focus on the North Carolina sojourn, and the chapter draws upon the most recent local research, especially that of Rassie Wicker, to try to determine which is which.

Jonathan MacDonald, of Duntulm, Skye, presented in 1989 an illustrated twenty-seven-page pamphlet entitled *Flora MacDonald, The Famous Highland Heroine.* Though limited in scope and slightly off the mark in its treatment of Flora in America, the piece offers to curious tourists on Skye an inexpensive and perhaps provocative introduction to the life of the island's most celebrated inhabitant.

Nineteen ninty-three brought Hugh Douglas's study of *Flora MacDonald, The Most Loyal Rebel.* Douglas, who had previously written one book about Prince Charles and has subsequently written another, contributes significantly to the body of knowledge of Flora's life by giving us the most detailed and therefore the most credible evidence thus far that the relationship between Flora and Allan and Sir Alexander and Lady Margaret MacDonald was not so close as the nineteenth-century commentators would have us believe.

While Hugh Douglas was finishing his study, Ruairidh MacLeod was at work on his, which he published as *Flora MacDonald: The Jacobite Heroine in Scotland and North* America early in 1995. The use of the partisan label "Jacobite" in the title meshes nicely with the book's publication early in the year that marked the 250th anniversary of the start of the last Jacobite rising. MacLeod's book is another strong piece of historical research. The author uses a log entry here, a letter there, and a bit of background precisely placed to expand, clarify, and elaborate on the story.

These, then, are most of the accounts of the life of Flora MacDonald that have accumulated over the two centuries since her death. This compilation does not include treatments of Flora in fiction, drama, poetry, music, and art, which shall be considered later. There are, of course, a great many other sources of information about Flora MacDonald. For example, virtually all the biographies of Bonnie Prince Charlie, of which there is a plethora, recount the events which precipitated Flora's fame, and in so doing many include a digressionary chapter on Flora herself. Likewise the many histories of the '45, of Skye, and of the MacDonalds mention Flora. A stop at any checkpoint along the biographical path will give the newcomer a sense of who

Flora was, what she did, and how the world has received her. A study of the path as a whole points up different and often conflicting views of who she was, what she did, and how the world has received her.

Chapter 5

Educating Flora

More gentleness of manners, or a more pleasing appearance of domestick society is not to be found in the most polished countries.

—SAMUEL JOHNSON

WAS FLORA EDUCATED IN EDINBURGH or wasn't she? Like so many others, Flora caught her biographers by surprise. Because her eventual fame was not heralded at her birth, the documentation of Flora's pre-celebrity years has not been preserved for examination by researchers. Furthermore, of course, Flora lived in a time and place where educational record keeping had not reached the frenzied state in which we see it today.

Thus forced to work without such modern conveniences as report cards, transcripts, and standardized test scores, biographers must speculate on the kind of education available to a young girl in the Outer Hebrides in the middle of the eighteenth century. One commentator, fairly typically of the consensus, tells us that "Flora learned at home to speak well, like other Scots of her class, without Scottish accent, to sing, to sew, to read, to write after a fashion. She was brought in touch with the best society of the islands."[1] Another describes Flora as "intelligent and sensible, a creditable product of the classical learning found so surprisingly in Skye at that time, where Latin was taught for half-a-crown a quarter, and English and writing for a shilling."[2] Yet another notes that she "plied her book" and won local fame as a player of the spinet and reciter of long Gaelic poems.[3] Still another writer joins in noting her proficiency at the spinet and assures us that "She could feelingly recite ancient Ossianic lays, and fervently sing the old Celtic songs to the sweet old tunes. She thus became in many ways precocious, and grew up a wise little maiden, informed beyond her years."[4] In other words, "She was naturally smart, clever, and active, cautious in her movements, and was invariably the principal or leader in every game, or juvenile frolic in which she engaged."[5]

Continuing his account of Flora's education, MacGregor points out that this interesting girl "became a particular favourite with all the respectable families in the Island, especially with Clanranald and his lady."[6] Then, he adds, when Flora was about thirteen, Lady Clanranald had Flora stay in the family house at Ormiclade and receive tuition with the Clanranald children. That Flora stayed at Ormiclade is questionable, in light of a strong contradictory claim by several scholars that it had burned down in 1715 and the Clanranalds were living at Nunton.[7] At any rate, so MacGregor's story goes, despite mild friction and "every appearance of" adolescent jealousy on the part of the young Clanranalds because Flora "by far excelled in her lessons the daughters of the family," Flora is said to have lived with the Clanranalds for about three years. That Flora studied with the family is unlikely, however, because the only daughter among Clanranald's nine children was seventeen years younger than Flora and was educated in Ireland.[8]

Here, perhaps, we are in need of a context. Robert Chambers says that as the daughter of MacDonald of Milton, Flora was a gentlewoman by birth.[9] In assessing the intellectual climate of the Highlands and Islands in the middle of the eighteenth century, social historians note that among the clans, and especially among the ranking members and their families, education and those societal attributes that we would gather under the heading of "culture" were held in high regard. W. B. Blaikie says that when the Jacobite army occupied Edinburgh, the local citizens were surprised at the "wonderful behaviour of the dreaded Highlanders, whose appearance was so wild and tatterdemalion." He notes that the clan chiefs were most courteous gentlemen, well-educated, many of them fond of letters.[10] Blaikie's prime example of the educated Highlander is Donald Roy MacDonald, who while hiding in a cave on Skye wrote two Horatian odes, one a lament on Culloden and the other on his own wounded foot. And, says Blaikie, Donald Roy MacDonald was "but the younger brother of a subordinate chieftain in Baleshare, a small island in the westernmost Hebrides, who had never gone further for his schooling than the Isle of Skye." Blaikie adds that an Oxford don pronounced the two odes "quite respectable Latin."[11] This counters the sneering snipe of Henry Fielding, noted Whig propagandist, who said that "Jacobites are no scholars and understand no Latin."[12]

During his 1773 visit Dr. Johnson found in Hebridean homes books in more than one language, and adds this observation on an island education:

> The family of Raasay consists of the laird, the lady, three sons and ten daughters. For the sons there is a tutor in the house, and the lady is said to be very skillful and diligent in the education of her girls. More gentleness of manners, or a more pleasing appearance of domestick society, is not found in the most polished countries.[13]

W. G. B. Murdoch studied at some length Jacobite men and women of letters, citing the literary achievements of Mrs. Lumisden, William Hamilton of Bangour, Neil MacEachain, and Alexander Mac-Donald (Alasdair MacMhaigster Alasdair) as praise-worthy and indicative of the presence of education.[14]

It is, thus, reasonable to believe that Flora MacDonald could have had an excellent education in and around her island home. With the wind and the rain, the sea and the hills, and all the gifts that nature can bestow on the one hand, and as a woman of some standing in a society that had an abiding respect for formal education on the other, Flora might well be thought to have had at her disposal all the ingredients of an ideal education.

But a number of biographers have taken her education further. As the story goes, at about sixteen Flora went from Uist to Skye to be with her mother. There she became close to Sir Alexander and Lady Margaret MacDonald of Sleat. Sir Alexander was the clan chief of Hugh MacDonald, Flora's stepfather. Through the arranging of Lady Margaret, most biographers assert, Flora spent three years ("continuously," say at least two) in Edinburgh at a ladies' seminary run by a Miss Henderson in Old Stamp-House Close, just off High Street and near the town residence of the Countess of Eglinton, who was Lady Margaret's mother and, by many accounts, one of the most beautiful pillars of Edinburgh society.[15] Without actually placing Flora in an Edinburgh prep school, Winifred Duke agrees that Flora "had been much in the company of Sir Alexander and Lady Margaret MacDonald in

Edinburgh."[16] Alexander Nicholson, in his *History of Skye* (1930), not only puts Flora in school there, but even goes so far as to say that one of Flora's fellow pupils was her future husband, who, like Flora, was there under the patronage of Sir Alexander MacDonald of Sleat.[17] Actually, the evidence to support Allan's Edinburgh tuition is stronger than that for Flora's. According to at least one writer, in a charter chest at Sleat are receipts dated 1739 for money paid by Sir Alexander in connection with education of Allan in Edinburgh, but no evidence of money paid for the Edinburgh education of Flora, Allan's future wife.[18]

And how did the young lady from the Highlands do at Miss Henderson's school? On the BBC one night in 1927, W. Forbes Gray told his listeners that Flora was said to have proved a diligent and clever scholar and to have been foremost as a player on the spinet. He adds that she sang Gaelic songs so well that her services were in frequent demand in the drawing rooms of Edinburgh.[19] In these assertions Gray is in large part repeating what MacGregor had written almost half a century earlier. Because of all that she acquired in Edinburgh, says W. D. Norie, Flora "was possessed, in addition to her many personal charms, of all the accomplishments and graces of the well-educated and cultured gentlewoman of her time."[20]

Though none of the writers who place Flora in an Edinburgh prep school provides any substantiating source or evidence, the idea was generally accepted among the primary and secondary commentators into this century. Wrong about Flora's age and the time of her father's death, the author of *The Female Rebels*, in 1747, had been the first to mention an Edinburgh education. In this account, upon the death of Flora's father, "her mother left the country, and came up to Edinburgh for the benefit of her daughter's education."[21] But that work does not seem to have been a major source for future biographers, none of whom mentioned it until Henderson wrote his *DNB* article of 1906. Whatever its source, the idea of finishing school seems firmly fixed in nineteenth-century tradition. Two American biographers, Foote and Banks, mention an Edinburgh education, and Mrs. Wylde said her grandmother "was sent for a short time to school in Edinbro'." MacGregor and the rest of the writers at the end of the century concur. Remember, however, that no biographer except Robert Chambers had had access to *The Lyon in Mourning*, in which the scrupulous and meticulous Bishop Forbes, describing Flora during her shipboard captivity in Leith Roads, says:

> Her behaviour in company was so easy, modest, and well-adjusted that every visitant was much surprised; for she had never been out of the islands of South Uist and Sky [sic] till about a year before the Prince's arrival that she had been in the family of MacDonald of Largie in Argyllshire for the space of ten or eleven months;[22]

A bit further on he adds:

> One could not discern by her conversation that she had spent all her former days in the Highlands; for she talks English (or rather Scots) easily, and not at all through the Earse tone. She has a sweet voice and sings well; and no lady, Edinburgh bred, can acquit herself better at the tea-table than what she did at Leith Road. Her wise conduct in one of the most perplexing scenes that can happen in life, her fortitude and good sense, are memorable instances of the strength of a female mind, even in those years that are tender and unexperienced. She is the delight of her friends and the envy of her enemies.[23]

"Never been out of the islands...spent all her former days in the Highlands;...." Here, then, is highly respected contemporary testimony against Flora's having gone to school in Edinburgh. Had biographers mistaken an extended visit to Largie with schooling in Edinburgh?

Whether Chambers got *The Lyon in Mourning* after he had written the biographical sketch of Flora for his *Edinburgh Journal*, or whether he had not read the passages quoted above, or whether he simply ignored them, he does in the sketch refer to Flora's Edinburgh schooling. And most of the nineteenth-century writers agree with one another.

With the advantage of Bishop Forbes's testimony to guide them, most twentieth-century writers have agreed that, tradition to the contrary not withstanding, there is little or no evidence to support the claim of Flora's having attending Miss Henderson's school for young ladies (or ladies and gentlemen).

The Lyon in Mourning provides another clue. We learn that when Flora left London in 1747 and returned northward, she made a couple of stops. The first was at York, to see and be further deposed by Dr. John Burton; the second was at Edinburgh, where she had engaged one David Beatt to help her with her writing. Beatt saw this as a sufficiently challenging undertaking to require him to stay pretty close to the city for a while. It seems unlikely that someone who had excelled at her lessons during her three years in a fashionable Edinburgh finishing school would deem it necessary to engage a writing tutor after being released from a year's confinement. Who was Mr. Beatt? Who referred Flora to him? Before his appearance in history as Flora MacDonald's writing coach, Mr. Beatt had stood for a moment in the spotlight on one other occasion. It was he who was selected to proclaim Prince Charlie's father King James VIII outside Holyrood in September 1745.[24]

As puzzling as the question of "Did she or didn't she?" is the one of why the nineteenth-century writers persisted in their assertion that she did. Is it merely a matter of one writer's taking another's unquestioned word for it? the Reverend A. MacDonald, DD, offers what is perhaps as good an explanation as any when he writes: "That a well-bred, cultured and educated lady should have issued from the outlandish Hebrides may have, in the opinion of the southerner, needed special explanation."[25] If the cultural climate in the Hebrides of the mid-eighteenth century was such that this Highland lass could have acquired the attributes of breeding and education in her native isles, had the climate so changed by the time the Reverend Alexander MacGregor took up his post as minister at Kilmuir on Skye in the next century that he could not recognize the possibility of Flora's homegrown learning?

Did Flora need gentrification as her eighteenth-century life evolved into nineteenth-century legend? Colonel David Stewart, quoting Mrs. Grant's *Superstitions of the Highlands*, sees the Lowlander and Highlander in these terms:

> The Lowlander considered the Highlander as a fierce and savage depredator, speaking a barbarous language, inhabiting a gloomy and barren region, which fear and prudence forbade all strangers to explore....

Cultural relativists will appreciate the flip side:

The Highlander regarded the Lowlanders as a very inferior
race of mongrel intruders, sons of little men, without heroism, without ancestry, or genius;...who could neither sleep
upon the snow, compose extempore songs, recite long tales
of wonder or of woe, or live without bread or without shelter for weeks together....[26]

The eighteenth-century Whig view of the Highlander is, of
course, less romantic. One broadside ballad, undecorously describes
Prince Charlie's followers thus:

Thieves and Rogues come at his Back,
These Amorites from the North,
A bare-ars'd Lousy Pack
Come o'er the Water of Forth.

Another, decrying the alleged behavior of Charlie's army in England,
curses them as

You scurvy Lowns with Buttocks bare,
That robs and plunders every where.[27]

Certainly it would not do for Flora to be seen as a female counter-
part of these people. Despite the favorable impression made by Highlanders in Edinburgh as cited by Blaikie, it seems that a still greater
claim to civility was needed. Bishop Forbes gave Flora the gift of cul-
tivated speech even though she had never been out of the Highlands.

Even into this century, many young Scotswomen are taught to
drop their local accent in favor of the more generic and refined accent
of a BBC newscaster. And even into this century how Flora spoke has
been a matter of some concern. As Sir Compton Mackenzie tells it:

When [I] allowed a young actress representing Flora Macdonald in a broadcast play to speak with the faintest of
brogues, [I] was reproached by one or two socially sensitive
Macdonalds who thought her gentility would have been
better demonstrated by addressing the scene in the nice ac-
cents of contemporary Murrayfield.[28]

Some of Flora's fans, fearful that Flora's universally recognized
virtues would be insufficient for respectability, have presented Flora in

a mantle of gentrification. And all those nineteenth-century biogra-phers who in reconstructing Flora's Hebridean youth found all sorts of admirable qualities already in the young lady before she ever left her is-land home, still, as if "to make assurance doubly sure," sent her packing off to Edinburgh for confirmation.

Chapter 6

Captive

Why, madam, what you call your misfortune is truly
your greatest honour.

—CAPTAIN FELIX O'NEILL

ON AUGUST 12, 1746, Henry Seymour Conway[1] took quill in hand
to write his distinguished cousin and man of many letters, Horace Walpole. In years to come, August 12—"the glorious 12th"—would mark
the opening of grouse season in Scotland, but in 1746, August 12 was
for Conway just another day of dreary duty at Ft. Augustus, a government outpost about halfway along the Great Glen. We may assume that
Conway was tired. He had recently returned from leading a detachment of government troops in search of the fugitive Prince in the
wilds of Morar and Knoydart in western Scotland, country that Conway describes as "one continued scene of rocks, bogs, and mountains."
After nearly two weeks of swatting at the legendary midges and clam-
bering around in this inhospitable terrain "with little more variety than
one would see in the Western Ocean,"[2] Conway was probably ready for
a change.

Besides, they weren't having any luck finding the Prince. As Conway tells cousin "Horry," "I can at present give no further intelligence
of him than he's thought to be still in the country."[3] He was very
right. Even as Conway wrote, the Prince, in the hands of some good-
hearted outlaws known as the Glenmoriston men, was probably less
than ten miles from Conway's writing table, and he would remain at
large in Scotland for another five weeks before being delivered to the
French rescue mission in Loch nan Uamh. Conway does pass along to
his cousin that when "he [the Prince] parted with O'Neil he put on
woman's clothes and put himself under the care of a Miss Flora Mac-
Donald, a young girl who is since taken."[4]

And Conway was right about Flora. She had been taken about a month before the letter and about ten days after she had parted from the Prince at Portree. She was taken aboard *HMS Furnace*, commanded by the notorious Jacobite-hunter Captain John Fergusson.[5] Fortunately, though, General John Campbell was also on board directing search operations, and his presence may have caused Flora to receive better treatment than Fergusson was inclined to give. Flora herself writes that General Campbell ordered her "used with the utmost respect."[6] After one feeble attempt to lie her way out of her situation, Flora told her story pretty truthfully.[7] She apparently impressed Campbell with her forthright manner, for he wrote to a friend, "I have a great deal of compassion for the young lady, she told me she would have in like manner assisted me or any one in distress."[8] This is the first recorded use of a line that Flora seems to have used often and with considerable success during her captivity.

At one point, when the *Furnace* was in the Sound of Sleat, Flora was granted leave to go ashore under guard to visit her mother, provided she speak no Gaelic. She also was allowed to bring back with her a serving girl, Katie MacDonal, who accompanied her throughout her captivity. For the general's compassion Flora seems to have been genuinely appreciative. Later, Captain Knowler of the *Bridgewater*, aboard which Flora spent some time, wrote to the general that "She esteems you her best friend she has in the world."[9]

From July 12 until August 7, Flora was detained aboard the *Furnace*. As the search for the Prince continued, so did the round-up of those who had given him succor. Sir Alexander MacDonald of Sleat, who had been with the Duke of Cumberland at Ft. Augustus when Flora brought the Prince to Monkstadt, sought further to distance himself from the event in a letter to Lord President Duncan Forbes on July 29:

> When the young Pretender made his unhappy visit to Skye, from South Uist, in a small boat, he landed near my house, in woman's clothes, by way of being maid-servant to one Florence Macdonald, a girl of Clanranald's family, now a prisoner with General Campbell. Miss Macdonald went and made a visit to Lady Margaret, dined with her, and put her in the utmost distress by telling her of the Cargo what she had brought from Uist.[10]

Lady Margaret sent to Lord President Forbes her own disclaimer under the same cover:

> Your Lordship can't yet be a Stranger to the trouble which has been lately brought upon this Island by the indiscretion of a foolish Girl, with whom the unhappy disturber of this Kingdom landed at this place; tho' I cannot but look on myself and family as peculiarly favoured by Heaven, in drawing that unlucky Visitant so quickly away from the place of his landing, that there was no room for considering Him as a Person in Disguise; far less my knowing any thing of it.[11]

Though they didn't bother to check the congruence of their stories, both Sir Alexander and Lady Margaret lay blame for the unfortunate event upon Flora, or "Florence," as Sir Alexander calls her. Sir Alexander seems far more interested in interceding for his factor, MacDonald of "Kingsborrow," already confined at Edinburgh Castle, than in the plight of Flora. Perhaps Sir Alexander and Lady Margaret knew that Flora would be in no real danger and sought to mitigate her culpability by calling the incident "the indiscretion of a foolish girl." A less charitable and more probable interpretation is that these letters suggest that the affection felt by Sir Alexander and Lady Margaret for Flora was not so great as some of the early biographers would have us believe.

Meanwhile, the *Furnace* was actively engaged in searching for the Prince or for French ships sent to bring him out, and Flora would have to be held elsewhere. In ordering her transfer to Dunstaffnage Castle near Oban, General Campbell wrote to the commanding officer telling him and his wife to prepare

> to receive a very pritty young rebell; her zeal and the perswasion of those who ought to have given her better advice, has drawn her into a most unhappie scrape by assisting the younge Pretender to make his escape.[12]

The general adds as a kind of postscript, "I suppose you have heard of Flora MacDonald." In a month, then, Flora's fame had spread through western Scotland and, as noted earlier, even reached France. General Campbell doesn't seem to see Flora's crime or her situation as particularly serious. Perhaps Sir Alexander and Lady Margaret were reading the situation correctly.

A dissenting voice is that of Angus W. McLean, author in 1919 of the long-unpublished manuscript *Highland Scots in North Carolina*. McLean was a direct descendant of Flora's half-sister along a branch of the family tree that includes MacQueens and MacEachens. During an active life in public service he was, variously, director of the War Finance Corporation under Woodrow Wilson, governor of North Carolina, and president of the board of trustees of Flora MacDonald College.[13] Because McLean's work was not published until late in this century, it was omitted from the chronological survey of biographies above; nevertheless, it is significant as yet another telling of Flora's story. In his long chapter on Flora, Governor McLean reports that General Campbell was quite worried about what might happen to Flora. "He knew that in all probability the fair maiden would be publicly executed. Would it not be better that she should be lost at sea?"[14] On this thinking, then, the general sent Flora from Dunstaffnage to her next ship "in a wherry, with but one boatman, and before a stiff breeze the frail craft started on its long and perilous journey, with every prospect of being swallowed up by the ocean waves." However, good seamanship on the part of the boatman brought Flora safely to the *Bridgewater*, "and on that vessel she was taken to Leith Roads, near Edinburgh."[15]

Of Flora's stay at Dunstaffnage we have little record. In fact, some doubt that she was ever there. However, a letter from General Campbell to the commander of the castle ordering Flora's transfer would seem to make her stay there highly likely.[16] That General Campbell wanted to drown Flora to save her from public execution is hard to accept. Furthermore, she went from Dunstaffnage to Leith on board the *Eltham*, not the *Bridgewater*.

On Monday, September 8, *Caledonian Mercury* reports the arrival of four ships from the northwest: the *Scarborough, Bridgewater, Greyhound,* and *Furnace*. The article goes on to report that Captain Clanranald is a prisoner on board the *Loo*, a forty-gun man of war, and "Miss Florence MacDonald on board the *Eltham*, both at Stromness." On Thursday, September 18, the paper reported that on Tuesday, "the *Eltham* Man of War came into this Road, having Commodore Smith aboard, who landed here this forenoon." And the same paper reports the departure of the *Eltham* for London on Sunday, the 21st. According to the Public Records Office, Flora was transferred to the *Bridgewater*, Captain Knowler commanding, on September 21, and stayed on the *Bridgewater* in Leith Roads until it sailed for London in early November.

What her captors had in mind for Flora is not clear. At some point during her stay on the *Bridgewater*, Flora persuaded Captain Knowler to write General Campbell asking "if you'll be pleased to let her know what is to become of her."[17] Whether or not the Crown intended to charge Flora, there is one letter written in early August that suggests that, at the very least, the government was considering using her as a witness against others who abetted the Prince.[18]

Meanwhile Flora remained on board the *Bridgewater* in Leith Roads. It was not total hardship, however. Upon her arrival at Leith, all biographers agree, Flora found herself famous, "no doubt," says one of them, "to her own surprise."[19] We are told that she had numerous visitors of all classes and professions. As they had been drawn to the handsome Prince at Holyrood a year before, so now the young ladies of Edinburgh society were drawn his protectress. Bishop Forbes reports that

> some of them with raptures cried out: 'O Miss, what a happy creature are you who had that dear Prince to lull you asleep, and to take such care of you with his hands spread about your head, when you were sleeping! You are surely the happiest woman in the world![20]

A Miss Mary Clerk concurred:

> I could wipe your shoes with pleasure, and think it my honour so to do, when I reflect that you had the honour to have the Prince for your handmaid. We all envy you greatly.[21]

Bishop Forbes then tells of a person "of rank and dignity," one Lady Mary Cochran, who was visiting Flora on the *Bridgewater* when a storm came up, making it dangerous to row back to shore in a small boat.

> The lady whispered to Miss MacDonald that she would with pleasure stay on board all night that she might have it to say that she had the honour of lying in the same bed with

that person who had been so happy as to be guardian to her Prince.[22]

Several ladies lavished gifts upon Flora. The Bishop mentions "gowns, skirts, headsutes, shoes, stockings, etc., etc." He identifies among the donors Lady Bruce, at whose house in Leith Forbes did much of his interviewing for the *Lyon*, and Miss Rachie Houston, who subsequently became the second Mrs. Forbes. One recounter told his listeners that a Miss Rachael Houston presented Flora with copies of the scriptures in "two pretty pocket volumes, handsomely bound."[23] Bishop Forbes tells us that Commodore Smith gave Flora "A handsome sute of riding-cloaths, with plain mounting, and some fine linen for riding shirts, and also a gown to her woman (Kate MacDonal)...."[24] Useless though the Commodore's gift was in Flora's situation, it perhaps gave some cause to believe that Flora might eventually emerge from her situation in a condition to use the riding habit.

Famous though she clearly was, it appears that Flora's fame, at least among the ladies of Edinburgh, arose more from her proximity to the Prince during their adventure than from any symbols that the public saw embodied in the modest young woman. And while fashionable Edinburgh flocked to see the Prince's conductress, near Leith a Mr. Stewart Carmichael sold in "great numbers" reproductions of the Prince's Betty Burke get-up, "so exactly done as not to be distinguished from the original even by Miss MacDonald herself."[25]

In the midst of all this celebrity, Flora remained somehow detached. Like the Prince at Holyrood, Flora did not join the other young ladies and ship's officers in the dancing that was swirling around her on the ship. Romantic biographers say that her concern for the fate of her Prince kept a pall over her. It is perhaps more likely that she was anxious about her own fate. The government had rounded up large numbers of rebels and was dealing harshly with them. Seemingly innocuous acts drew rigorous consequences. MacDonald of Kingsburgh would spend a year in Edinburgh Castle for providing the Prince with a night's lodging, and one Jacobite sympathizer had been incarcerated for seeking to shake the Prince's hand. For more flagrant acts against the government one could expect to be hanged, beheaded, disemboweled, transported to the colonies, or left to rot in chains on a prison hulk.

During Flora's confinement in the port of Edinburgh, Commodore Smith "behaved like a father to her, and tendered her many good advices as to her behaviour in her ticklish situation."[26] Felix O'Neill would have us believe that he, too, served as a consultant to Flora during her captivity. A frequently repeated story has Flora encountering O'Neill when they are both prisoners on a ship, presumably the *Furnace*. Those who have studied carefully the chronology of Flora's captivity question whether the alleged meeting and close chit-chat ever took place given a window of opportunity of one day on which Flora was probably on shore and O'Neill had his hands full with Captain Fergusson and General Campbell.[27] Still, O'Neill's account persists. In it, Flora gently slaps O'Neill's face and says to him, "To that black face do I owe all my misfortune." To which O'Neill is said to have replied,

> Why, Madam, what you call your misfortune is truly your greatest honour. And if you be careful to demean yourself agreeably to the character you have already acquired, you will in the event find it to be your happiness.[28]

Flora tells him that she is afraid of what will befall her if she is taken to London. Bishop Forbes quotes O'Neill as telling Flora that he did not think "that the Government can be so very barbarous and cruel as to bring you to trial for your life. . . ." Indeed, O'Neill predicts that in London Flora "will meet with much respect and great and good friends" for what she has done. He provides her with this formula for behavior:

> Only be careful to make all your conduct of a piece. Be not frighten'd by the thoughts of your present circumstances either to say or do anything that may in the least tend to contradict or sully the character you are now mistress of, and which you can never be robbed of but by yourself. Never once pretend (through an ill-judg'd excess of caution and prudence) to repent or be ashamed of what you have done, and I dare to take upon me to answer for the rest.[29]

Later, during his confinement in Edinburgh Castle, O'Neill continued to tell those who visited him that he had been at the same pains as a parent would be with a child to lay down rules to Miss MacDonald for her future behaviour under the misfortune of being a prisoner, and it gave him infinite pleasure to find that things had happened to her hitherto according to his words.[30]

Either Captain O'Neill or Commodore Smith or both could have advised Flora "as to her behaviour in her ticklish situation." As shall be seen later, there is evidence of Flora's gratitude to Commodore Smith, and the O'Neill account is repeated enough to have a place in tradition. The advice is, presumably, consistent and hardly innovative: Flora is advised to be true to herself. In the brief glimpses of Flora's statements while in captivity, we see her keeping her conduct "of a piece" in acknowledging her actions without repentance or shame. She had told General Campbell that she would have done the same for him had he required assistance, and later, in London she would give the same reply to at least one person of considerable rank when presented to him.

In addition to Smith and O'Neill, another man comes upon the scene during Flora's time in Leith Roads. He is Nigel Gresley. When Flora was taken aboard the *Eltham*, Gresley was a midshipman in the ship's company. When the *Eltham* reached Leith and Flora was transferred to the *Bridgewater*, Gresley was transferred to it as well, and he served on that ship until it sailed for London in November.[31] Coincidentally, it turns out that Gresley had previously served on Flora's last vessel, the *Royal Sovereign*, that carried her up the Thames to London and the next chapter in her story. Gresley will rejoin the narrative later.

Chapter 7

London

Mid the pomp of huge London her heart was still
  yearning
For her home in the corrie, the crag, and the glen;
Though fair be the daughters of England, the fairest
And stateliest walks in the land of the ben.

—JOHN CAMPBELL OF LEDAIG

IN LATE OCTOBER, 1746, Flora's fear was about to come to pass. She would need Smith's "advices" and O'Neill's prophecy because she had been ordered to London. On the 27th, William Anne, Second Earl of Albemarle, commander of government forces in Scotland, wrote to the Duke of Newcastle, Secretary of State of the Northern Department (hence Scotland), that

> Miss Flora McDonald sailed this morning on board the Bridgewater under the care of Captain Knowler; her behaviour has been such during her confinement, that Commodore Smith and General Campbell begs [sic] of your Grace, that when she arrives she may rather be put in the hands of a messenger than into any common prison, this favour the poor girl deserves, her modest behaviour having gained many friends.[1]

So here again Miss Flora receives special handling from a person of rank and dignity. Campbell and Albemarle were not, it should be noted, just a couple of softies in their dealings with female prisoners. In August, Campbell had written Albemarle about Lady Clanranald. He said that the lady had not only been zealous herself in serving and assisting the young P.....but has also brought her husband and several others into the same scrape, for which reason I think she ought to be sent to London.[2]

The general, then, sees Lady Clanranald as an instigator and Flora as merely the recipient of some bad advice, presumably from Lady Clanranald. Nor is the general alone in his assessment; a number of commentators have made the Prince's escape from South Uist a bold and clever piece of women's work, masterminded by Lady Clanranald and carried out by Flora and a number of other women of the island.

Another anecdote about General Campbell is worth relating. When the Prince's boatman Donald MacLeod was picked up, the general asked him if he knew of the thirty thousand-pound price on the Prince's head "which would have made you and all your children after you happy forever."

> MacLeod: "What then? Thirty thousand pounds! Though I had gotten 't, I could not have enjoyed it eight and forty hours. Conscience would have gotten up upon me. That money could not have kept it down. And though I could have gotten all England and all Scotland for my pains, I would not allow a hair of his body to be touched, if I could help it."

> General Campbell: "I will not say that you are wrong."[3]

Albemarle's report of Flora's departure was not, strictly speaking, true. It was probably true as far as Headquarters Scotland knew, but *Caledonian Mercury*, that noted observer of marine goings and comings, reported on August 27 that several vessels were to proceed under convoy of the *Bridgewater* to London and Holland "this Day or Tomorrow Morning." On the 28th, "The Wind being Southerly, the Fleet continues still in the Road." Though the paper does not report the eventual sailing of the fleet, in writing *The Truth about Flora MacDonald*, Allan R. MacDonald says that she "sailed for London on 7th November 1746, amid the cheers of thousands of the people of Edinburgh and Leith who came to see her depart."[4] W. D. Norie, too, has her leave on the 7th "amid the cheers of thousands of her countrymen and countrywomen who had assembled on the pier and other places of vantage to see the heroine depart."[5] From Leith the *Bridgewater* carried her to the Nore, where she was transferred to the *Royal Sovereign* for transport up the Thames. She seems to have reached London on December 7.

All of London that mattered was celebrating the triumph of Cumberland and the enlightened establishment over the Pretender and his "bare-ars'd" Highland rebels. One ethnic joke making the rounds had it that if you put a louse upon a table, it would invariably turn north, the direction from which it came.[6] Whig propagandists and satirists were busy with their broadsides, and the London arts scene had taken on a particularly political hue. Two plays about Perkin Warbeck, an earlier unsuccessful pretender, were mounted on the London stage, and Shakespeare's *Henry V* was enjoying a popular run. Its depiction of the quick trial and execution of the traitors Cambridge, Scroop, and Grey had a contemporary parallel in the trial and dispatch of the Earl of Kilmarnock and Lord Balmerino in August of '46.[7] Meanwhile, Sadlers Wells performed a ballet called "Culloden," and society whirled to something called "The Culloden Reel."

Perhaps the most lasting example of London's euphoria comes to us through the suggestion of Frederick, Prince of Wales, that the celebrated composer George Frideric Handel write something appropriate in honor of the great victory won by the Prince's younger brother the Duke of Cumberland over the Pretender and his rebels. The Prince's suggestion was Handel's command, and on July 8 or 9, 1746, he set to work on what would become his great oratorio *Judas Maccabaeus*. Handel finished the piece in less than five weeks, on August 11. The world did not hear it, however, for another seven months. In the spring of 1747 another sensational trial caught the public's fancy. Old, fat Simon Fraser, Lord Lovat, had been caught conspiring with the Jacobites and from March 14 to 19 was in the legal fight of his life. He lost, and Handel, the limelight his at last, brought *Judas Maccabaeus* to Covent Garden on April 1.[8] Among his lesser honors, the Duke of Cumberland may have had a flower, the Sweet William, named in his honor, and he was also made Ranger of Windsor Forest.[9]

Most of her biographers tell us that Flora was confined first in the Tower and then in the house of a king's messenger, a Mr. Dick. Mrs. Wylde agrees in part. She puts Flora in the Tower, from which she was "at last released into the house of a private family." The author adds a touch of verisimilitude or of trail camouflage when Flora muses, "It is strange that I have quite forgotten the name of those worthy people to whom I owe a debt of gratitude for sundry little acts of considerate kindness and forethought."[10] Presumably this private family is not Mr. Dick's.

There is no hard evidence of Flora's having done Tower time. Did the government follow the recommendation of General Campbell and Commodore Smith? Henrietta Tayler, reviewing the tour of duty of Lieutenant-General Williamson as Lieutenant-Governor of the Tower, mentions some of the Jacobite celebrities held in the Tower (e.g., Kilmarnock and Balmerino) but does not place Flora there.[11] Sir Walter Scott moves Flora from the Tower directly to the house of Lady Primrose without pausing at Mr. Dick's.[12] J. P. MacLean and the Reverend A. MacDonald say that because the government was worried about public opinion against Flora's being treated like a common prisoner, she was transferred to a messenger's after a brief Tower stay.

Again *Caledonian Mercury* offers a clue. On January 5, 1747, it quotes from the London *Gazette* of December 30 that

> The famous Miss Flora Macdonald, who has so often been mistaken by the Town for Jenny Cameron, was last Week very particularly examined as to her Conduct in relation to her harbouring and secreting the young Pretender, after the Battle of Culloden, and recommitted into the Custody of a Messenger. She is a young Person of some Fortune in the Highlands, and affects great Humanity and Benevolence, certainly a good Share of Sense, and her Deportment is very modest and reserved.[13]

If "recommitted" to the messenger's custody, had she then come from a messenger's custody? Or was she "recommitted" to custody, this time a messenger's, as opposed to being set at liberty? If the former, it would appear that she spent virtually no time in the Tower, for this piece appeared less than a month after Flora's arrival in London. If the latter, then at most she spent only three weeks in the Tower.

The passage is further interesting because it is one of the few contemporary references to Flora in London that have come down to us. The description of Flora sounds rather introductory, not the way one would describe someone already in the public eye. The passage may support the idea that Flora's fame in London, at least at this early date, stems from her having been frequently mistaken for Jenny Cameron.

How much of Flora's fame arises from this mistake in identity cannot immediately be assessed, but it is clear that Jenny Cameron attained quite a reputation. A. Francis Steuart ranks her second after Flora "in the annals of Jacobite women of the '45," and thus ahead of Lady Clanranald and "Colonel Anne" Farquharson, Lady Mackintosh.[14] As such, of course, she was fair game for the Whig satirists. She appeared as a character in *The Harlequin Incendiary, or Columbine Cameron*, a musical pantomime performed at Drury Lane in 1746 and in *The Rebellion*, an epic poem in five books published in 1749.[15] In the former, the principal characters are Miss Cameron, the Devil, the Pope, and the Pretender; in the latter, Miss Cameron at Culloden takes up arms and takes on one Colonel Rich of Barrel's Regiment thus:

> But when he saw the fair one's beauteous face,
> Her charmful eyes, her mien, her every grace,
> Back he some steps retreated, sore amaz'd,
> And on the fair with admiration gazed;
> Urg'd by success she follows him apace
> And thought her sword had conquer'd, not her face;
> Still she pursues, and with one furious blow,
> Lops the left arm of her yet wond'ring foe;
> Far stream'd the blood from out the gushing wound,
> And the lopp'd limb lay quivering on the ground.[16]

Her success, alas, was short-lived, and the '45 was over:

> The Cameronian maid long strove to fly,
> And when surrounded begg'd in vain to die.
> Thus in one day Rebellion vanquish'd fell,
> And her rapacious sons were sent to hell.[17]

Seventeen forty-nine was a big year for Jenny Cameron in literature. She also appeared in *Tom Jones*, from which it is clear that Flora is not alone in being mistaken for Mistress Cameron. In Book 11, Chapter 2, Sophia Western suffers the same fate.

The Misses Cameron and MacDonald appear together in a cartoon popular in Whig circles of the time. It may have first appeared as the frontispiece to an early edition of *Ascanius*, and consists of three miniature-like portraits—an unidentified figure presumed to be the Prince in the center, with Jenny and Flora, both identified, on the left and right respectively. Beneath the Prince's portrait is a couplet from *Beggar's Opera*:

> How happy could I be with Either
> Were t'other dear Charmer away.[18]

Without tracing in detail the precise stages by which this kind of Whig propaganda was imperfectly noted and passed along from one generation's ear to the next over the course of two centuries (becoming increasingly garbled in each successive transmission), it is possible to imagine a descendant of this satiric snippet eventually reaching the ear and entering the mind of the teacher on the train.

Walter Biggar Blaikie, who should know, identifies two possible Jenny Camerons in history. One was present at Glenfinnan and was later a prisoner in Edinburgh Castle; the other was an Edinburgh milliner who visited a relative in the Prince's army during the siege of Stirling.[19] In *The White Cockade* Baron Porcelli gives us an engaging view of the former.

> Dressed in a sea-green riding habit, with scarlet lapels trimmed with gold, and her hair tied behind in loose buckles under a velvet cap with a scarlet feather, she rode at the head of her men on a bay gelding decked with green "furniture", fringed with gold, and carried a naked sword, instead of a whip, in her hand. She was a handsome woman with pretty eyes and jet-black hair, and riding up to the Prince she gave him a military salute, saying that "as her nephew was not able to attend the Royal Standard she had raised his men and brought them to His Highness, since she believed them to be ready to hazard their lives in his cause". Then her men marched past the Prince, who spoke to her in graceful terms. She did not, however, follow the army when it eventually moved, as has sometimes been suggested.[20]

This Bellona-like figure may explain "The Harlequin Incendiary," but does not explain the mistaken identity with Flora. The dashing woman at Glenfinnan was actually "a middle-aged widow." Blaikie is sure that neither Jenny Cameron was mistress to the Prince and blames the growth of the legend around Jenny on James Hogg and others. But obviously a Jenny Cameron was something of a legend in London before James Hogg went to work on her, and famous enough for Flora to be mistaken for her.

At least by December 30, then, Flora's confinement was in the house of Mr. Dick, King's Messenger. Messengers used their houses to quarter minimum-security prisoners. Like any other group, they were rated by their clients. A Mr. Carrington was reported to be the "least amiable." Mr. Dick "catered for a class different from those in the custody of Carrington."

> His clients included Flora MacDonald, Aeneas M'Donald, the banker, and many of the most distinguished Jacobite ladies as well as men; and residence under his custody, though irksome no doubt, generally meant ultimate unconditional release.[21]

Bed and board at Mr. Dick's were not cheap. Aeneas MacDonald seems to have been paying 6s 8d a day. He and Flora were about to take a trip out to Richmond when he was moved to New Gaol, Southwark.[22] Perhaps these jaunts provided occasions for the public to spot Flora and make the mistaken identification. Evidently, Flora was not doing "hard time." Still, Charles MacDonald Smith may have been a bit hyperbolic when he wrote that "the young girl's cell was turned into a gay reception room."[23] Allan MacDonald does agree that while a prisoner at Mr. Dick's house, Flora "received great attention from all ranks of society in the capital, and even Frederick, Prince of Wales, visited her."[24]

As MacDonald tells it, Prince Frederick asked why she dared to assist a rebel; she gave him the tried and true response that she would have done the same thing had she found him in distress. If this exchange actually occurred, and many writers assert that it did, we see Flora showing that consistency of position that Smith and O'Neill had urged her to maintain.

Margaret Williamson claims that Flora was presented to the Prince "at court."[25] Alexander Nicholson says His Royal Highness visited her "after her release," and goes on to report that "It is said he was so charmed with her answer that he filled her hand with gold."[26] The enthusiastic and independent Charles Smith says the meeting took place in the Tower and that the Prince of Wales "was so impressed with her beauty and dignity that he set about to procure her release, and when she left the Tower it was in a state coach."[27] James Browne concurs, adding that "according to family tradition" Flora was released "at the special request of Frederick, Prince of Wales...."[28] Mrs. Wylde says only that Prince Frederick visited Flora at the house of the "private family," curious to meet "the Pretender's Deliverer, for such was [her] designation at the Elector's court."[29]

Sir Walter Scott puts the famous quotation about doing the same for anyone in a somewhat different setting and in the mouth of a different speaker. According to Scott, when Prince Frederick's wife expressed some concern at Lady Margaret MacDonald's having been presented at court given her role in the Pretender's escape, His Royal Highness said to her:

> And would you not have done the like, madam, had the unfortunate man appeared before you in such calamitous circumstances? I know — I am sure — you would.[30]

If there was a chance that his public association with such harmless rebels as Lady Margaret or Flora MacDonald would have annoyed his father the King, it is certainly reasonable to believe that Prince Frederick would have seized the moment.

In his *London in Jacobite Times,* J. Doran sums up what was known about Flora in London thus:

> The arrival in London of the most interesting of all the Jacobite prisoners in 1746, and her departure in 1747, are left unrecorded, or dismissed in a line, by the journalists.... After her release... Flora is said to have been the favoured guest of Lady Primrose, in Essex Street, and the *lionne* of the season. Tradition says she owed her liberty to the Prince of Wales, and the romance of history has recorded a visit paid by the prince to the guest in that Jacobite house, and has reported all that passed and every word that was uttered when Flora was thus 'interviewed.' Imagination built up the whole of it. The only known fact is that Flora was captured and released.[31]

The release of the rebels did make the papers. *Caledonian Mercury*, for example, on Monday, April 6 (1747) reports, "the discharge from Messenger's hands last Friday of Dr. Burton, the eminent physician of York" [and early recorder of Flora's story]. On June 4, it reports that "on Thursday last" Mr. Dick was ordered to release Roger M'Neal of Barra, "who had been detained for some Time on suspicion of Treasonable practices." On June 22, it carries a report of the release from Mr. Dick's custody of some twelve men, "who were ordered three guineas each and passage to Scotland." Still no word of Flora. Had she been overlooked? In its June issue, *Gentleman's Magazine* reports on the 20th "all rebel prisoners....discharged from the custody of messengers." And on the 25th, *Caledonian Mercury* carried this item:

> A list is ordered to be given to His Majesty's Secretary of State of all Rebel Prisoners now in the several Prisons of the Kingdom and in the Custody of H.M. Messengers, in order to their being further discharged.

Perhaps Flora's name turned up on one of these lists. It is interesting, however, that her release is not as newsworthy as that of other rebels. More likely under the Act of Indemnity of July 4, 1747 than as a result of royal intercession, Flora was released, and in W. D. Norie's account, fancy fills in for fact:

> When permission to depart was at length tardily accorded, London refused for some time to part with her; she became the *lionne* of the season, the talk of the whole town, and as the honoured guest and protege of the newly widowed Lady Primrose of Dunipace, the artless Highland maid was daily visited by personages of the highest rank in society, who extolled her virtues in such inflated language, and poured so many exaggerated compliments into her ears, that the poor girl, quite at a loss to understand why so much fuss should be made over what she, in her modesty, considered a simple act of humanity, soon began to long more than ever for the quiet of her northern home.[32]

That Flora was on good terms with Lady Primrose seems clear, unless of course Her Ladyship was annoyed at the traffic jams Flora was creating in Essex Street. Chambers reports that "family tradition" has as many as eighteen coaches lined up outside Lady Primrose's.[33] Joseph Seawell Jones raises his principal British source and puts the number at twenty.[34] Whatever the carriage count, at Lady Primrose's Flora was visited by crowds of the fashionable world who paid her such homage as would have turned the heads of ninety-nine out of a hundred women of any age, country, or condition.[35] Flora's head remained on straight, however. Though she had already seen such adulation in Leith Road, she is said to have been surprised at so much fuss over conduct which "never appeared extraordinary to herself till she saw the notice taken of it by the rest of the world."[36] What Flora did, then, she terms a simple act of charity, an act of disinterested humanity. As such, it clearly appeals to a greater audience than would the action of some partisan zealot. Put another way, "It is not so easy to be heroic on the cool wave of human brotherhood as on the hot wave of political enthusiasm."[37]

If Flora is being true to herself in following the avuncular advice of Smith or the pragmatic advice of O'Neill, and it is reasonable to believe that she is, then the Jacobite heroine transcends the politics of the moment and facilitates her universal acceptability as an exemplary embodiment of admirable virtues.

Lady Primrose did, on behalf of partisan Jacobites, take up a collection for Flora that eventually amounted to some fifteen hundred pounds, and she provided a post-chaise in which Flora, accompanied by Malcolm MacLeod, made the journey to "the quiet of her northern home" with some stops along the way.

Despite her understandable but happily unfounded fears of what might befall her in the Sassenach capital, Flora was eventually released unscathed. In all, she had been held in captivity for almost exactly one year without ever being brought to trial or even charged with anything. In this regard she was by no means alone. In their study of the records of the eighteen Jacobite women who took a prominent part in the rebellion and another fifty-six "regimental women," all of whom "found their way into captivity," Sir Bruce Seton and Jean Gordon Arnot found that none of the women was brought to trial.[38]

Robert Chambers in 1840 protested that Flora's detention occurred at a time when the Habeas Corpus Act of Scotland had not been suspended. Thus to him it was a violation of the liberty of the subject which seems to have been passed over unnoticed, in the Terror with which the recent bloody triumphs of Government had inspired the people, or which was perhaps rather owing to the maxim then apparently paramount in the public mind of England, that all natives of Scotland had forfeited their rights as British subjects, and were now slaves subject to military law.[39]

Chambers makes a valid point of law and perhaps a valid if embittered social comment as well. But in violating Flora's civil rights, the British government accomplished something else that it may never have intended. It provided the occasion for the creation of a legend that probably hastened considerably the process of reconciliation between the once opposed forces. Today we may find it surprising that such a transformation could have taken place so innocently and unconsciously. No protests, no slogans, no lawyers or public relations consultants, no appearances on TV talk shows, meager media coverage: under such conditions it is unlikely that we could bring it off.

Still, the reduction of what can be said with certainty about Flora in London to the single assertion that "she was captured and released" helps to counteract the romantic effusions and speculations of some of the nineteenth-century writers and is, strictly speaking, accurate. If Flora had become a celebrity, why, as Doran has noted, did the London press pay so little attention to her that her ultimate release from captivity went unreported? One answer is that in the category in which she rose to celebrity—that of Jacobite heroine, she was probably not terribly newsworthy at the time. If a look at contemporary periodicals doesn't turn up much for the Flora scrapbook, it does show us what was on the public mind or, at least, what the editors saw fit to put before the public. First, remember that there was a war on; British troops were still engaged on the Continent in what the history books call The War of the Austrian Succession. Far more often than not, the lead story in the periodicals summarized the latest news from the combat zone in Europe. Probably next in order of importance during the period of Flora's confinement were accounts of the trials and punishments of the rebels. Lord Lovat's aforementioned legal maneuvering to keep his head made good reading, as did the account of his losing it.

Then there were all those other Jacobites with whom the government was dealing far more harshly than it was with Flora. News of deportations and vivid accounts of executions at Carlisle and York and on Kennington Common and Southwark's St. Margaret's Hill seem to have had more reader appeal than Flora's planned trip to Richmond with Aeneas MacDonald or what and whom Lady Primrose had for tea. The steadfastness, undisputed virtue, common humanity, and generous disinterestedness of a woman in non-threatened restraint, however admirable, are not likely to sell a lot of papers.

Chapter 8

The Portraits

Here, too, the beauteous Flora's taught t'assume,
Than ere the goddess knew a brighter bloom.
The faithful canvass softens with her smile,
Who in the royal youth preserv'd the Isle.

—"From the Latin of
Dr. King"[1]

IF THE PAPERS OF 1747 don't give Flora as much space as her fans might like, another medium does provide the means by which to measure her celebrity. During her London captivity Flora was the subject of a number of portraits. Dr. Burton was the first to report Flora's sitting,[2] and Mrs. Wylde provides elaboration when she tells us that a portraitist sought out Flora in the Tower to request the honor of a sitting. Mrs. Wylde has Flora say that she would have refused had he not looked so sad. She summarizes thus:

> So if hereafter a picture of my wonderful self should ever be forthcoming from perhaps some pawnbroker's shop, of a disconsolate-looking damsel in a dark russet gown, with a white rose in her hair, named on the back "Miss Flora Mac-Donald, pinx. 1746," the finder will, I hope, consider he has got a treasure.[3]

So far the world's pawnshops have not yielded up a portrait answering that description or bearing that date. If the chronology of Flora's journey from Leith Road to London is accurate and she reached London a week into December, the portraitist would have had to work fast indeed to intrude, persuade, paint, and date all before the end of the year, even with the extension provided by "Old Style."

85

But let's give Mrs. Wylde, writing some 124 years after the fact, some latitude. There are records of at least four painters who painted Flora in 1747. Two of these, Thomas Hudson and Richard Wilson, seem to have painted her "ad vivum"—from life; about the other two, LeClare and Markluin, we know little, but when we compare their portraits with those for which we can assume Flora sat, it seems unlikely that either LeClare or Markluin painted her from life. Still the June 6, 1747 date of publication of a copy of Markluin's adds to the evidence of Flora's popularity at the time.

Just how many portraits of Flora Thomas Hudson did we do not know, but apparently he did quite a few. The one most frequently reproduced is actually a mezzotint engraving by John Faber (see p. 99). Hudson's original has vanished, perhaps to the dusty corner of the pawnshop alluded to by Mrs. Wylde. The mezzotint depicts Flora as the eighteenth century thought a Jacobite shepherdess ought to look, holding a crook and a locket bearing the Prince's picture and wearing a low-cut billowing gown trimmed with tartan ribbon. The mezzotint bears the notation "painted ad vivum 1747."

In 1838, Charles Kirkpatrick Sharpe[4] was pleased to have acquired a Hudson portrait of Flora. As he wrote to a friend,

> When I bought the picture of Miss Flora, with Hudson's name on it (she certainly sat to him when in the tower) my mother declared that it did not at all resemble her. This set me a-scolding. However, I must confess that the rose in her hair is red—a shocking blunder, if it be one.[5]

Sharpe says that his mother had known Flora well, "having met her often in the Horse Wynd at her uncle's." He goes on:

> My mother told me that Mrs. Macdonald...could never have been tolerably handsome. She had good eyes and eyebrows, but high cheekbones, a snub nose, and a very large mouth, with thick lips: item, a bad complexion....My mother had a mean notion of her mental capacity. Her phrase was, "I thought her a stupid Highland wife."[6]

Sharpe's reference to the rose in Flora's hair indicates that this is not the portrait from which Faber made his mezzotint. But there was another portrait the public exhibition of which was last recorded in

1867,[7] and in the Jennings Collection at the Yale Center for British Art is a reproduction of a portrait attributed to Hudson showing a young lady in a dark dress with a flower in her hair. Is this Sharpe's? Is it the portrait to which Mrs. Wylde perhaps fictitiously refers despite the apparent discrepancy of the color of the hair-borne rose?

So busy was Hudson with portraits of Flora that one client complained about the delay in the completion of his own portrait, noting that Hudson

> is in vast vogue and particularly one lady will be a sort of a fortune to him; its the famous Miss Flora Macdonald, numbers of her copies are bespoke; you will know their way of thinking when I tell you she is the very lady who assisted a certain person in his escape from Scotland.[8]

So in 1748 Jacobites were clamoring for portraits of Flora. Is this an early expression of the guilt to which Sir Walter Scott would refer eighty years later? Ellen Miles, Hudson's biographer, suggests as possible commissioner of the 1747 "mezzotint" portrait one Watkin Williams-Wynn, an MP from Denbigh well known in his constituency as a Jacobite and himself the subject of a Hudson portrait at about this time.[9] The connection is certainly noteworthy. The peripatetic Thomas Pennant, who twenty-five years later would travel to the Hebrides in search of Flora, tells of having met her in 1747 at the London house of Watkin Williams-Wynn.[10]

As puzzling as the Hudson portraits of Flora are those by Richard Wilson. The one now in the Scottish National Portrait Gallery and dated 1747 (see p. 96) is generally accepted as a true rendition. It is certainly among the most frequently reproduced. There is general agreement among the historians that Flora sat to Wilson in London, but whether she sat in his studio, the Tower, Mr. Dick's house, or Lady Primrose's seems lost to us now. There is also a bit of disagreement over who commissioned the portrait. Burton and subsequent conventional wisdom have held that Commodore Smith asked to have a portrait done as a souvenir; another school holds that Flora had the portrait done and presented it to the commodore as a token of appreciation for his kindness and advice.

The picture itself only clouds the issue. On the back of the portrait is the following inscription in ink:

> This portrait of Flora MacDonald was given by herself to
> Sir Nigel Gresley/Captain in the Royal Navy who captured
> her in her flight from Scotland to France/& from whom she
> experienced every civility & as a mark of gratitude pre-
> sented him with this picture 1747.[11]

Remember Gresley? The above inscription is the only place in
which Gresley is mentioned in connection with Flora's capture. It is
also the only reference to Flora's flight to France. The inscriber is
almost certainly wrong on both counts. Gresley did not capture
Flora, though he was a member of the ship's company when she was
brought aboard the *Eltham*, and there is nothing to suggest that
Flora intended to flee to France. Still, in linking this Wilson portrait
to Gresley, the inscriber of the note has done posterity a notable
service. In all likelihood, Flora saw more of Gresley than of Commodore Smith during her shipboard detention. As chief of all naval
operations in Scottish waters, Commodore Smith must have had a
great deal more on his mind than the maintenance of the pretty
young rebel. Enter Gresley. Here was something the twenty-year-
old midshipman could do while Smith directed the Royal Navy in
search of the royal fugitive and in defense against the several at-
tempts to rescue the Prince being launched from France. Though
attending Flora was not as exciting as combat against the French,
Gresley was probably well suited for the task. After all, he did come
from a good family, bringing with him the requisite social skills to
attend Miss Flora and to monitor the visiting ladies of Edinburgh.
When Flora was transferred from the *Eltham* to the *Bridgewater*,
young Gresley went with her.[12] If Flora owed a debt of gratitude to
Commodore Smith, it was for his advice and for the definition of
her treatment, but it was in all probability to Nigel Gresley that
Flora owed gratitude for the day-to-day execution of the commodore's orders.

Commodore Smith was a friend and patron of Richard Wilson,
and Wilson painted at least four portraits of Smith. But Sir Nigel Gresley, sixth baronet, also sat for Wilson, the result of which at last report
hung in National Museum of Wales in Cardiff.[13] Gresley doesn't draw
a lot of attention from Flora's biographers, but it seems clear that he de-
serves a place in her story. When he died in 1787, a memorial was

placed in Bath Cathedral. In a letter written in August of 1956, A. E. Haswell-Miller says that Nigel Gresley "may be the young man who had [Flora's] portrait painted."[14]

Wilson's biographer quotes an editor of Boswell as saying that a portrait of Flora was given to Smith, but that he, the editor, couldn't trace the picture. The same source also reports that "Flora's youngest son or son's nephew had a miniature of the picture."[15] It is tangentially interesting to note that Flora's youngest son John did own what is supposed to be the last picture Wilson ever painted.[16]

But wherever the painting went, who initiated its creation? Under the conventional wisdom theory, Flora sat at Smith's request. Such a gracious accession to Smith's request seems eminently in keeping with what we know of Flora's demeanor at this time. Mrs. Wylde deftly picks up the wry amusement with which Flora contemplates sitting to a famous portrait-painter in her self-consciously ironic remark about "my wonderful self."

On the other hand, if Flora commissioned the portrait to give to Smith or Gresley as an expression of gratitude, she gives us a somewhat different picture as well—a picture of a woman aware of her new-found celebrity and magnanimously ready to reward one attentive gentleman or the other with a portrait. Such a portrait, whether commissioned as a souvenir or as a token of gratitude, was a treasure indeed. Around the middle of the century, Ramsay, Hudson, and Reynolds were getting twenty-four guineas for a waist-length portrait, a substantial sum.[17] While we don't have Wilson's fee schedule, it is reasonable to assume that he could command the same kind of money for his work. Could Flora have afforded to have her portrait done? History is quiet on her finances, except for the attention given to the purse collected by Lady Primrose, which Flora does not seem to have received until later. We don't even know if she paid for her own room and board at Mr. Dick's. As a well-born Highland lady did she have in London means of her own or was she dependent upon financial aid from without?

There is at least one other portrait of Flora by Richard Wilson. Less well known and less frequently mentioned than the one in Edinburgh, it hangs in the National Portrait Gallery in London (see p. 97). Little information seems to be available about this portrait. The card beside it on the wall simply says it was painted in 1747 after Flora's release from prison. Wilson's biographer does not mention it. Clearly, though, both the sitter and the painter of the two portraits are the same. Did Flora sit for both portraits or did Wilson do one from the other? Did Flora resolve the Smith/Gresley controversy before it began by giving one portrait to Smith and the other to Gresley?

The questions surrounding the Hudson and Wilson portraits are typical. Eighteenth-century portraits alleged to be of Flora abound, but here, as with other facets of Flora's life, the modern inquirer must proceed with caution. That Allan Ramsay, son of "the gentle shepherd," painted her seems clear. Biographers agree that Flora probably sat for Ramsay during a return visit to London in 1749. That portrait (see p. 98), which has been in the possession of the Ashmolean Museum at Oxford since before 1840, is frequently reproduced to illustrate books or articles about Flora. The Scottish National Portrait Gallery in Edinburgh also has a Ramsay portrait of Flora, but, despite the frequency of the Oxford portrait's reproduction, neither the Oxford nor the Edinburgh Ramsay seems to be held in particularly high regard by the art world. In his biography of Ramsay, Alastair Smart says "The Flora MacDonald in the Ashmolean Museum shows him almost at his worst."[18] Earlier, A. E. Haswell-Miller, then Keeper of the Scottish National Portrait Gallery, had questioned both the authenticity and the quality of the Ramsay portraits when he wrote

> The only portrait of Flora we consider a real work from life is that by Richard Wilson. The so-called Allan Ramsay is, in our opinion, a work of not quite satisfactory documentary reliability. As a Ramsay it seems to be also a little doubtful. The Edinburgh version is, I think, a better one than that at Oxford....The Edinburgh one, I should say, hardly looks like a painting from life, and I have always considered it to be a copy of another one which might have been done from life. The Oxford one is even more unlike the original.[19]

Given this criticism of the Ramsay portraits of Flora, it is interesting to note the triumph of enduring popularity. The Ashmolean portrait was included in the Stuart Exhibition of 1889[20] and, more recently, was chosen by *British Heritage* to illustrate its announcement of the Allan Ramsay exhibition at the National Portrait Gallery in London during December and January 1992–93.[21] And to commemorate the 250th anniversary of Flora's adventure, the British artist Jane Lightburn Dowds paid Ramsay the sincerest form of flattery when she presented to the world her meticulous copy of the Flora portrait.[22]

The Witt Library collection shows three other portraits attributed to Ramsay titled "Flora MacDonald"; and in 1995, St. Andrews Presbyterian College in North Carolina learned of another portrait said to be by Ramsay and of Flora. Though some art historians are reluctant to attribute the portrait to Ramsay, its proponent says that this portrait was done in 1749, and that the more familiar Ashmolean portrait was in fact done in 1747, while Flora was detained in London. Furthermore, says the proponent, it is likely that this portrait was once in the house of Lady Primrose.

Another portrait of Flora done in her lifetime is one in pastel over pencil by Catherine Read,[23] called by some "the English Rosalba" and one of the leading female artists of her time. A year younger than Flora, she was born in Forfarshire, studied in Paris and Rome, and worked in London. Of her early life in Scotland there is little record, but she can be placed in Jacobite circles. An uncle is said to have "suffered the extreme penalty for his adherence to the Stuart cause in 1746,"[24] and among her friends were the engraver Robert Strange and Isabella Lumisden, sister of the Prince's secretary and later wife of Robert Strange. In Paris, Miss Read studied pastels under Maurice Quentin de la Tour. Among her other famous subjects are two of the three beautiful Gunning sisters.[25] Miss Read closed out her career in India and died at sea in 1778. In her will she stated her wish to be buried in Madras. When she did the portrait of Flora and whether Flora sat to Miss Read have yet to be determined.

Related to Miss Read's pastel is one attributed to Rosalba (Carriera) or Francis Cotes (see p. 102), perhaps the other outstanding exponents of the medium in Britain in the eighteenth century. As with so many other portraits of Flora, unfortunately, information about the creation of this pastel is not available.

Mrs. Wylde, who opened this discussion of Flora in art, reenters in connection with another portrait. On April 13, 1883, the Town Council of Glasgow took up a letter from Mrs. Wylde in which she offered to the Corporation Gallery of Paintings the portrait of her grandmother painted in 1750 by William Robertson (see cover). Mrs.

Wylde's only object in doing so was "a desire that the likeness of such a well-known historical character should be in a good public gallery of her own country." Upon examination of the portrait, the council agreed to accept it. It was hung

> at one end of a long row of large-sized portraits of Kings and Queens. At the other end of the row, in a position corresponding exactly with Flora's portrait, is one—about the same size—of Her Majesty the Queen, painted by Sir David Wilkie in 1841.[26]

The Flora in the portrait by William Robertson seems younger and softer than the Wilson Flora. Robertson's portrait bears the notation "ad vivum pinxit 1750." Robertson, who seems to have flourished around 1745 and was partial to Jacobite subjects, also did a small whole-length portrait of Prince Charles Edward Stuart to which he similarly affixed "ad vivum pinxit."[27] This painting, too, was shown in the Stuart Exhibition of 1889.

Among the paintings of Joseph Highmore (1692–1780) are two alleged to be of Flora MacDonald. The one that hangs in the North Carolina Museum of Art in Raleigh (see p. 100) seems to have been done sometime around the middle of the eighteenth century. Like the Robertson portrait, this one may at one time have been in the possession of one of Flora's granddaughters, Mrs. Benjamin Cuff Greenhill, of Knoll Hall, Bridgewater, a sister of Mrs. Wylde.[28] Though reluctant to call the portrait Flora's, a Highmore biographer says it is "one of Highmore's more individual female portraits, and has an introspective air partly created by the half-smile and soft treatment of the features."[29] The other Highmore portrait (see p. 101), the provenance of which is unclear, shows a somewhat younger woman in a red dress. In the left background is an arched bridge in an unidentifiable landscape. While judging the painting "a handsome and typical later female portrait," Alison Lewis states that "the identification of the sitter as Flora MacDonald is surely wrong."[30]

Indeed, there is no clear evidence that Flora ever sat to Highmore and some to suggest that she didn't. Citing Highmore's portraits of the Gunning sisters as examples, another biographer says "Even when he drew real people...he resorted to memory and imagination, without flesh and blood sitters."[31] Lewis questions the authenticity of both portraits on the grounds that "No contemporary evidence mentioned any portrait of Flora by Highmore, and no portrait by that name was offered for sale by Highmore in 1762."[32] In addition she points out that there are none of the usual identifying trappings such as tartan, a locket, or a boat in the background. Highmore did not title either painting and apparently did not always paint "ad vivum." Under those circumstances it seems as hard to prove the portraits aren't of Flora as it is to prove that they are.

Another seldom seen portrait worthy of note is one said by some to be of Flora and by Hogarth. Copies of the picture do show up from time to time. There is one in the Jennings Collection at Yale, and one appears as an illustration in Donald Chidsey's 1928 biography of Bonnie Prince Charlie.[33] In an article in *Art Journal* in 1899, J. Penderel-Broadhurst bases the case for the legitimacy of the portrait on its provenance. Central to the argument is the assertion that the painting was in the possession of Flora's London benefactress Lady Primrose when she died in 1775. It was then purchased by Mr. John Law, who passed it on to his son, Mr. William Law, in 1852. That Mr. Law left it in 1891 to John Rendall, Esq., of Hays Lodge, Loughborough Road, Brixton, in whose possession it was at the time the article was written. Given the "clear and unquestioned pedigree," argues the author, there can be little doubt that it was one of the pictures painted during Flora's stay in Essex Street.

To counter the objections of those who find in this portrait "smoother handling" and "softer textures" than those usually found in Hogarth's work the author points to Hogarth's portrait of his wife and several of his Peg Woffingtons for examples of similar handling and texture. Finally, the author notes that this portrait served as the model for Mr. Andrew Davidson's Inverness statue of Flora. But the author of the article does affix a kind of caveat in telling us that Ramsay's Ashmolean portrait of Flora "was not painted until long after she was married."[34] In point of fact, of course, it was painted in the year before her marriage.

From collections in the Scottish National Portrait Gallery, the Yale Center for British Art, Aberdeen University Library, and the Frick Library gaze countless images of Flora. In addition to pictures attributed to the above-named artists, one can find works said to be by Bardwell,

Cotes, Rosalba, Pickering, and, aptly enough, the ubiquitous "Unknown."

All the portraits said to be of Flora do not give us a composite image of what Flora really looked like. The Ramsay Flora doesn't much resemble the Wilson Flora; the Wilson doesn't much resemble the Robertson, and so on. Those who saw Flora and wrote about her are in greater accord in their descriptions but still leave us short of positive identification. Boswell: "She was a little woman, of a mild and genteel appearance, mighty soft and well-bred." Dr. Burton: "Miss Flora is about twenty-four years of age, of a middle stature, well-shaped, a very pretty agreeable person, of great sprightliness in her looks...." J. Drummond: "She is a young person of about 20, a graceful person, a good complexion, and regular features: she has a peculiar sweetness mixed with majesty in her countenance;...." Bishop Forbes calls her "well-enough shaped." Dr. Johnson sees "a woman of middle stature, soft features, gentle manners, and elegant presence." Flora's daughter Anne, who looked like her mother, told an interviewer that her mother had a small but neat figure and provided an anecdote to suggest that it was possible to recognize Flora's features if one happened to run into them on the street. In London one day Anne had paused before a picture of her mother in a shop window. As she stood there, no less a person than General John Burgoyne happened along and "was so struck with the resemblance that he accosted her and taxed her with the relationship." As Anne explained it, "Her mother's escape with Charles Edward was then an event sufficiently recent to render her an object of considerable curiosity."[35]

Behind the roses, lockets, tartans, shepherdess attire, and seascape backgrounds that make up the recurrent iconography of the portraits, Flora the sitter remains shrouded in mystery, and though we cannot, apparently, approach her any more closely through her pictures than through her biographies, the plethora of portraiture does attest to the contemporary celebrity of our lady.

Flora's birthplace, South Uist, Outer Hebrides. Photo courtesy of Carver Collins.

Floddigary, Isle of Skye. Once the home of Flora and Allan, now an inn. Photo by Irene Toffey.

"Flora MacDonald" by Richard Wilson (1747). Scottish National Portrait Gallery.

"Flora MacDonald" by Richard Wilson (1747). By courtesy of the National Portrait Gallery, London.

"Flora MacDonald" by Allan Ramsay (1749). By courtesy of the Ashmolean Museum, Oxford University.

"Mrs. Flora MacDonald" a mezzotint by John Faber of Thomas Hudson's 1747 portrait. Scottish National Portrait Gallery.

Portrait by Joseph Highmore of a woman said to be Flora MacDonald. North Carolina Museum of Art, Raleigh. Purchased with funds from the North Carolina Art Society.

Copy of a portrait by Joseph Highmore of a woman in a red dress. Some say the woman is Flora MacDonald. Photo by The Snap Shop, Great Barrington, MA.

A pastel portrait of Flora MacDonald attributed to Rosalba or Cotes. In the collection of the Earl of Wemyss.

THE AGREABLE CONTRAST.

Shews that a Greyhound is more agreable than an Elephant, & a Genteel personage
More agreeably Pleasing than a Clumsey one, a country Lass is better y.ⁿ a town trollop
and that ... a ... is better ... than ... is bound at the author in Cromford Street.

"The Agreeable Contrast," a pro-Jacobite cartoon showing Flora admiring Jacobite plenitude while rejecting the Duke of Cumberland and establishment inadequacies. By permission of the trustees of the National Library of Scotland.

Statue of Flora MacDonald at Inverness. Photo by the author.

Stained glass window, St. Columba's Church, Portree, Isle of Skye. Photo by Ernest Allsop, courtesy of St. Columba's Church.

The graves of the children in Red Springs, NC. Photo by the author.

The re-burial of children alleged to be Flora's at Flora MacDonald College, April, 1937. Courtesy of St. Andrews Presbyterian College Archives.

Flora's grave, Kilmuir, Isle of Skye. Photo by Irene Toffey.

Chapter 9

The Middle Years

At Kingsborrow The third day of December jmviic and fifty years It is agreed and matrimonialy Contracted betwixt the parties following vizt., Allan Macdonald Eldest Lawfull son of Alexander Macdonald of Kingsborrow with consent of his father on the one part and Mrs Flory Macdonald only Lawfull Daughter of the deceast Ranald Macdonald of Miltoun now his spouse with the Consent of Angus Macdonald of Miltoun her brother on the other part in the manner following....

—FROM THE MARRIAGE
CONTRACT OF FLORA AND
ALLAN MACDONALD

"I CAME UP TO LONDON TO BE HANGED, and now I am returning in a post-chaise with Miss Flora MacDonald!" With this oft-quoted line exuberantly uttered by Malcolm MacLeod, most historians ring down the curtain on Flora's London adventure, and some leave it down during a matrimonial intermission of twenty-six years. It rises again as Samuel Johnson and James Boswell find Flora and provide posterity with a new batch of quotations with which to work. Only recently has the work of Hugh Douglas and others brought light upon the quarter of a century that separates the two events.

Despite what sentimental biographers would have us believe, Flora did not speed from London over land and sea to Skye. She and Malcolm stopped off in York to see Dr. Burton, who had been released from Mr. Dick's some two months before Flora. From York they continued north, reaching Edinburgh early enough in August for the Reverend Robert Forbes to interview MacLeod on the seventh. The Jacobite story was by this time starting to come together through the enthusiastic efforts of Dr. Burton and the Reverend Mr. Forbes. Like Dr. Burton, Mr. Forbes had been detained for nothing more than being sympathetic to the Jacobite cause. And although Forbes is now the more well known through the eventual and posthumous publication of *The Lyon in Mourning*, it was really Dr. Burton who started to interview the Jacobites during and just after their release from custody, and thus to tell the story of the '45 with a Jacobite spin. Forbes's commitment to the lifelong project of compiling the Jacobite stories probably grew out of his having read in manuscript form a draft of Burton's work. Burton published first; Forbes was apparently in no hurry to wrap up his story and print it, continuing to hope that some day the Prince would come back again. While that hope lived, it was probably prudent not to illuminate lives or actions of shadowy Jacobites.

Though she had given her story to her one-time fellow inmate, Flora seems to have been a bit reluctant to tell it to Forbes. Having read the account she had given to Burton, Forbes asked Burton to put certain questions to Flora, to which she gave enigmatic and evasive answers. Forbes wanted to know how Flora had met Captain O'Neill (he had stopped at her brother's place at Milton several times during the Prince's skulk); whether Hugh MacDonald of Armadale, Flora's stepfather, had met the Prince while the latter was in hiding (no, but he was the first to greet the Prince when he arrived on the mainland of Scotland); the contents of the passport on which Flora had traveled from Uist to Skye (she demurred, having previously answered that); the songs the Prince had sung during their crossing ("The King shall enjoy his own again" and "The Twenty-ninth of May"); and whether Lady Clanranald had given the Prince bottles of milk (yes, which he drank straight from the bottle and shared with the boatmen, but he retained some wine lest Flora need fortification against the cold).[1]

Forbes did not meet Flora until January of 1748, by which time, as John Gibson has pointed out, her story had changed, assigning to both her stepfather and MacEachain larger roles than she given them in her first reports. One plausible explanation for the change is that when she first told her story, she had realized that in fact she was in no great peril of dire punishment. Therefore, she could safely take upon herself and give to Felix O'Neill, who as a foreign military officer would be treated as a prisoner of war and not as a traitor, responsibility that actually belonged to the other two men. It is worth noting in this regard that Flora's stepfather, while commanding a company of militia in search of the Prince, certainly participated in, if in fact he didn't design, his quarry's escape. Yet he was never taken into custody.

Whatever else Flora was doing in Edinburgh in that fall and winter of 1747–48, it was at this time that she undertook her study of writing with Mr. David Beatt, though she might well have received this instruction from any number of people anywhere. Her activities in Edinburgh remain at this distance unclear. The adulation that was hers a year earlier seems to have died down. It is possible, of course, that Flora was in no hurry to return to Skye because people there were resentful of her and the attention paid her.[2] Many of her friends and relatives had lost much as a result of their harboring of the Prince. Flora, on the other hand, suffered nothing more than a year's required accommodation and in the process acquired fame and something of a fortune. The hardscrabble residents of Skye might be less adoring than the young ladies of Edinburgh or the closet Jacobites of London had been. For this reason and the fact that Sir Alexander MacDonald was already dead, it is extremely unlikely that he threw for Flora upon her return to Skye the large party of which Alexander MacGregor speaks in his biography.[3]

In the spring of 1748, Flora finally left Edinburgh to return to Skye. As several biographers tell it, Flora and her traveling companion and acquaintance from the Leith confinement, Peggy Callander, narrowly escaped death when their boat hit a rock. Flora was saved by the intervention of "a clever Highlander."[4] Noting that Allan MacDonald, younger of Kingsburgh, came to Edinburgh five days before Flora left and that there he paid a visit to the Reverend Mr. Forbes, Donald MacKinnon wonders if Flora's future husband had perhaps come to town to escort Flora back to Skye and whether he, in fact, was the "clever Highlander."[5] At any rate, by July of that year, Flora was back on the island visiting her mother. Sketchy details of Flora's movements over the next couple of years come to us largely through letters. She seems to have gone back to London in the summer of 1748 and again stopped to visit Dr. Burton on the way back north. She was in London again in late spring of 1749, perhaps on business related to the Primrose purse and at the same time to sit for the better known and more likely authentic of the Ramsay portraits, the one that hangs in the Ashmolean Museum at Oxford.

Before we marry Flora off and consign her to a period of domestic anonymity, we should pause over a letter Flora received from Neil MacEachain written in Paris on February 28, 1749, and first published in MacGregor's *Life*.[6] In it MacEachain shows that he knows quite a bit about his cousin's comings and goings—more, in fact, than those closer to Flora seem to know. He calls her "Florry" and writes cryptically to her as to a colleague in some clandestine venture. He speaks of the Prince as "the person you once had the honour to conduct" and as "somebody" with whom he and Clanranald had dined "the day they [the antecedent is "somebody"] were took" by King Louis's officers outside the Paris opera. He also commends to Florry the bearer of the letter, Colonel Henry Goring, and asks Florry to "exert [her]self among the honest and worthy, to help him dispose of some valuable toys he has on hand."

These toys are in all probability souvenirs of the Prince—relics, if you will—which Goring sought to sell in Britain to raise money for the Prince in France. In his discussion of the letter, Alasdair Maclean suggests quite reasonably that many of these relics today cherished as family heirlooms with their attendant legends of having been presented by the Prince himself were in fact purchased at one of Goring's fundraisers.[7]

The relic market seems to have been strong. Mr. Carmichael had a brisk business in strikingly realistic replicas of the Prince's disguise, and John MacLeod told Boswell that Flora herself had dabbled in the market on at least one occasion. It seems that she received from Mac-Donald of Kingsburgh the brogues that the Prince had worn with his Betty Burke costume and that she in turn sold them for twenty guineas.[8]

Neil MacEachain is a figure in the story of the '45 whose role has been obscured by the sequence in which the story has come to light. Treated by most historians as a bit player in the events of June 20–July 1, 1746, MacEachain, through the research of John Gibson and Alasdair Maclean, has in the last decade or so begun to get the attention he has long deserved.[9] As has already been seen, the accounts of Flora and Felix O'Neill play down the importance on MacEachain for quite different reasons. Felix O'Neill's reasons, were largely self-serving: he was disinclined to spread credit around and, besides, in his attraction to Miss Flora he was perhaps a bit jealous of MacEachain. On the other hand, Flora's downplaying of MacEachain's role was her deliberate attempt to draw attention away from him, knowing that he was engaged in other covert operations in Scotland. Just as the early histories of the '45 drop Flora upon her parting with the Prince, so do they drop MacEachain. Where he was and what he was doing over the next two and a half months might make another fascinating story. Significantly and without fanfare, however, Neil MacEachain was aboard one of the two ships that rescued the Prince in September 1746.[10]

It was largely through MacEachain's story of the Prince's wanderings that Charlie's darker side becomes visible. Under the traditional romantic view of the handsome, charismatic young Prince enduring great hardships and trusting his life to his beloved Highlanders one begins to see a less engaging side of someone given to heavy drinking, wild swings of mood, and a frequently recurring fear of betrayal by the very Scots who were risking their lives to protect him.[11]

As Alasdair Maclean tells us, "Neil MacEachain, the Prince's companion, is well known in folk memory, but his actual identity is extremely vague."[12] Originally from Uist, MacEachain studied for the priesthood at the Scots College at Douai, in France. By 1738, when he returned to Scotland, he was something of a stranger to his native land. He is often described as a schoolmaster on Uist at the time of the Rising, but he may well have been doing other things in the service of France as well. When he left Scotland in 1746, he adopted the name of MacDonald. He married a French woman and fathered four children, one of whom rose to fame in the French army and was made Duke of Tarentum and a Peer of France by Napoleon. Few who have held such titles have had names like MacDonald. MacEachain's marriage was not a particularly happy one, and he lived out his life rather meagerly. In 1768 and again in 1770 he wrote to Charles to ask for financial help, but Charles remained consistent in ignoring those who had helped him in his time of greatest need. MacEachain died in 1788 without ever seeing Scotland again because he "did not take advantage of the amnesty extended by the English government in 1784 to those exiled in similar circumstances." In 1982 Alasdair Maclean told his story and wrote this touching epitaph:

> In his sixty-nine years this remarkable man had traveled a
> long way from the stark banks of Abhainn Though in South
> Uist to the lush Val de Loire, student priest, Jacobite agent,
> soldier of France, writer, philosopher, raconteur, and lin-
> guist; friend of gentle and simple, and of royalty, but at the
> end a lonely cripple.[13]

But back to our lady. We know that she was back on Skye in July
of 1750, and of course we know that she married Allan MacDonald,
eldest son of the Alexander MacDonald of Kingsburgh who had
served a year in prison for providing the Prince with a night's hospitality. Details of the wedding are few and contradictory. MacGregor describes with his wonted hyperbole and wanton inaccuracy the wedding
festivities, but Dorothy MacKay Quynn displays research that corrects
the site of the ceremony (Armadale) and the color of Flora's wedding
gown (black, in deference to her recently deceased half-brothers).[14]

Perhaps because they believe that she deserved them or perhaps to
advance her position as a celebrity, many historians like to have large
parties thrown for Flora on whatever occasion might be at hand. Mac-
Gregor sees in Flora's wedding such an opportunity, but Ms. Quynn,
consulting Forbes, argues that it was a rather simple family affair.

It should also be noted that in the same year that Flora and Allan
were married, Prince Charles Edward Stuart entered London—not in
the triumph he might have imagined as he marched towards Derby that
December five years before, but in a manner to which he had become
accustomed in his Continental intrigues: in disguise. Accompanied to
London by John Holker, Charles arrived on Lady Primrose's doorstep
on September 16. A few trusted Jacobites were quickly gathered to
meet him. One, Dr. William King, found the whole thing preposterous.

> If I was surprised to find him there, I was still more aston-
> ished when he acquainted me with the motives which had
> induced him to hazard a journey to England at this junc-
> ture. The impatience of his friends who were in exile had
> formed a scheme which was impracticable; but although it
> had been as feasible as they had represented it to him, yet no
> preparation had been made, nor was anything ready to carry
> it into execution. He was soon convinced that he had been

deceived, and therefore, after a stay in London of five days only, he returned to the place from whence he came.[15]

Ardent Jacobite though he was, Dr. King was singularly unimpressed with what he saw in Charles. He was handsome enough, "but in a polite company would not pass for a genteel man." Dr. King was surprised that the Prince seemed lacking in "the belles lettres and finer arts." He goes on:

> But I was still more astonished, when I found him unacquainted with the history and constitution of *England*, in which he ought to have been very early instructed. I never heard him express any noble or benevolent sentiments, the certain indications of a great soul and good heart; or discover any sorrow or compassion for the misfortunes of so many worthy who had suffered in his cause. But the most odious part of his character is his love of money, a vice which I do not remember to have been imputed by our historians to any of his ancestors, and is the certain index of a base and little mind.[16]

Charles returned to France and Flora married. She and Allan started domestic life at Kingsburgh, but moved to Flodigarry when Allan's father prevailed upon Lady Margaret to give the tack* there to Allan. Some of Flora's Primrose purse went to the fixing up of Flodigarry, and the removal of the previous tenant of long-standing, Martin Martin, fueled a feud between the Martins and the MacDonalds.[17]

Out of the limelight, and quite possibly glad to be, Flora settled into domesticity defined by the vicissitudes of agricultural economy and the raising of a family. Flora's first child, a son, was born in 1751. That he was named Charles is less surprising today than it would have been in the eighteenth century, when family names were bestowed on the firstborn. That Flora departed from strong family tradition to name her firstborn son after the Prince is a bit of sentimentality seldom found in her. That she followed by naming her second child and first

---

*A tack is a portion of an estate leased from the owner. The lessee, called a tacksman, in turn sublets portions of the tack to other farmers.

daughter Anne (1754) is only a little less notable. To be sure, she bears the name of Allan's sister, but in her name may well be an expression of gratitude to Lady Anne Primrose, Flora's London benefactress, as well.[18] Alexander in 1755 and Ranald in 1756 came along and received traditional family names. Then James in 1757, John in 1759, and, finally, Frances or Fanny in 1766.

Around the middle of the last century, there came to light a cache of letters written in 1751 among Flora, Lady Anne Primrose, Mr. Thomas Clerk of London, and Mr. John Mackenzie of Edinburgh. All have to do with the money that Lady Primrose had raised for Flora. More interesting than the financial matters taken up in the letters is the prose style of Flora. Remember that the majority of Flora's biographers have said that she went to finishing school in Edinburgh for three years, in apparent contradiction to which is the evidence that Flora engaged the services of a writing tutor after her release from custody. Here is what she wrote in 1751:

> Sir:—Few days agoe yours of the 26th March came to hand, by which I understand my Lady Primrose hath lodged in your hands for my behoof 627 l. sterling, and that her ladyship had in view to add more, of which you would acquaint me, so as to send a proper discharge to my lady, which I am ready to doe, how soon you are pleased to advise me; and as I am to have security to my friends' satisfaction, on Sir James Macdonald's estate, it's designated the whole should be paid next May to John McKinzie, of Delvin, writer att Edinboro', of which my father-in-law spock to Kenneth McKinzie, attorney, who will give you proper directions; at the same time shall be glad to hear from you as oft as you pleas, in order I may observe such directions as my lady will be pleased to give you concerning me; I was uneasie befor the recipt of your letter that my lady was not well, haveing wrott frequently to her ladyship, but has had no return. Pleas be so good as to offer my humble duty to my lady and Mrs. Drelincourt.
>
> An I am, Sir, your humble servant,
>
> Flora McDonald[19]

Forced, stiff, and artificial as anyone can become when trying to write something businesslike, official, or legal, Flora writes here without the polish that one ought to have picked up in three years of finishing school. As to the value of Mr. Beatt's services as indicated by the letter, one can see that Flora did not owe her tutor much, whatever his bill.

In 1757, giving in to the poor health that had plagued him since his year's confinement, Allan's father retired, and Allan became factor of the estates inherited by young Sir James MacDonald from his father Sir Alexander. When Allan's mother died in 1759 and was buried in the Prince's sheets, Allan and Flora moved back into the house at Kingsburgh. Times were hard, and Allan was not a good factor or business man. He seems to have had good ideas about modern agricultural practices but little success in getting people on the island to implement them. It is whispered that he drank a bit. Allan seems to have tried to gain his release from the position of factor with a debt of £360 owed to young Sir James MacDonald, but for some reason was unsuccessful. In 1766, "After a long and extremely painful illness / Which he supported with admirable patience and fortitude," Sir James MacDonald died in Rome at the age of 24. "The fame he left behind him is the best consolation / To his afflicted family."[20] But there was no consolation for Allan, for shortly after Sir James's death, Allan was dismissed as factor. Removal from the position once held by his father must have been a severe blow to the pride we see from time to time in Allan.

Allan was not alone in his misfortune. Virtually all of Skye was suffering. Emigration to America was increasing throughout the Highlands and Islands. By one account, four thousand emigrated from Skye alone between 1772 and 1791.[21] Dr. Johnson noted the "general discontent" permeating "a great part of the Highlands," and the eroding of allegiance to the clan chief. As Johnson explained it, "...he that cannot live as he desires at home, listens to the tale of fortunate islands, and happy regions, where every man may have land of his own, and eat the product of his labour without a superior."[22] Johnson's sympathy for the Highlanders he met is visible in a number of observations about what he saw and what he arrived too late to see. Perhaps his grimmest observation on the plight of the Highlanders is that "Of what they had before the late conquest of their country, there remain only their language and their poverty." And even the former "is under attack on every side."[23]

Perhaps Flora and Allan had read a pamphlet entitled "Information Concerning the Provinces of North Carolina Addressed to Emigrants from the Highlands and Western Islands of Scotland." The piece was published in Glasgow in 1773 and was writen by someone — probably The Reverend William Thom of Govan — using the pen name of Scotus Americanus. The pamphlet begins with a strong attack on landlords, especially those who held their lands in absentia. In the Highlands and Islands, claims the author, thousands of men and women "without means, without encouragement, at a distance from market, against climate, and soil too, in many places" were expected to "cultivate and enclose wide extended heaths, rugged mountains, and large barren morasses." Ignoring these handicaps, the author adds, "the owners raised rents and then complained of emigration."[24] The pamphleteer goes on to extol the virtues of North Carolina, calling it "of all our colonies the most proper for Highlanders of any degree to remove to, if they want to live in a state of health, ease, and independence." The poor could travel as "redemptioners," who could be disposed of by the ship's captain to pay for their passage. Still they would work off their indebtedness under contract as free men. Finally noting the relatively low cost of acquiring unpatented land, Scotus Americanus summarizes North Carolina thus: "Upon the whole . . . the best country in the world for a poor man to go to, and do well."[25]

On Raasay one night Johnson was entertained with some songs sung in Gaelic, to which the Doctor "listened as an English audience to an Italian opera, delighted with the sound of words which I did not understand." Upon inquiring what they meant, he was told that one was a love song and the other "a farewell composed by one of the islanders that was going in this epidemical fury of emigration to seek his fortune in America."[26] *Dod a ah'iarruidh an fhortain do North Carolina*, as the popular Gaelic song of the times goes. Boswell speaks of another entertainment in which

> We performed, with much activity, a dance which, I suppose, the emigration from Sky has occasioned. They call it 'America'. Each of the couples, after the common involutions and evolutions, successively whirls round in a circle, till

all are in motion; and the dance seems intended to shew how emigration catches, till a whole neighbourhood is set afloat. Mrs. M'Kinnon told me, that last year when a ship sailed from Portree to America, the people on shore were almost distracted when they saw their relations go off; they lay down on the ground, tumbled, and tore the grass with their teeth. This year there was not a tear shed. The people on shore seemed to think that they would soon follow.[27]

A letter of May 9, 1771 reports that "2000 emigrants are preparing for their departure from the Isle of Skye to some part of the foreign settlements.... They are all of the estate of Sir Alexander MacDonald, who may chance to be a proprietor of land without tenants."[28] A year later Thomas Pennant found that high rents were driving many tenants to seek relief across the Atlantic. He relates in romantic terms suggestive of the dance Boswell would later describe the process by which those who had gone wrote to their friends and relations at home so that "their friends caught the contagion: and numbers followed; ...[29]

In a conversation on the subject Dr. Johnson said that "a rapacious chief would make a wilderness of his estate." Mr. Donald McQueen told Johnson that the problem was one of

> landlords listening to bad advice in the letting of their lands; that interested and designed people flattered them with golden dreams of much higher rents than could reasonably be paid; and that some of the gentlemen tacksmen ... were themselves in part the occasion of the mischief, by over-rating the farms of others. That many of the tacksmen, rather than comply with exorbitant demands, had gone off to America, and impoverished the country, by draining it of its wealth; ...[30]

With the death of Allan's aged and infirm father in January 1772 at the age of eighty-three, the last tie holding Flora and Allan to Skye was loosed, and in August of that year Flora sent young John to the protection of MacKenzie of Delvine. Though it would be another two years before Flora and Allan would leave, Flora saw ahead nothing "but poverty and oppression." As a result of devasting livestock losses, including 327 cattle in the last three years, Flora and Allan had hardly enough to enable them to pay their creditors "and begin the world again, anewe, in a othere Corner of it."[31]

Two years later, "out of real necessity" Flora made a pathetic appeal to the Duke of Atholl. She sought "to have one or two boys I still have unprovided for in some shape or other off my hands." In appealing to the Duke, Flora said that she could not ask more of her "known friends Lady Margaret MacDonald and my Lady Dowager Primrose." Anything the Duke could do for Alexander "would be the giving of real relief to [Flora's] perplexed mind."[32] Whatever the Duke's reply, if any, Alexander was not taken off Flora's hands. He accompanied his parents to America.

Boswell tells us that his "heart was grieved, when [he] recollected that Kingsburgh was embarrassed in his affairs, and intended to go to America." To assuage his grief, however, he "pleased [him]self in thinking that so spirited a man should be well every where." At one of the many dances Boswell attended in the Islands, he wondered at the gaiety of the scene surrounded by so much misery. For a moment, he says, he doubted whether unhappiness had any place there. "But," he adds, "my delusion was soon dispelled, by recollecting the following lines of my fellow-traveller:

> Yet hope not life from grief or danger free,
> Nor think the doom of man reserv'd for thee."[33]

Chapter 10

Going to America

Come up to Anson County, and I'll show you a place
with a farm and a mill I bought at Cheek's Creek. Remember the name—Cheek's Creek.

—FLORA IN CAROLINA, I, i.

BY THE TIME JOHNSON AND BOSWELL got to Skye, the last ob-
stacle to the emigration of Flora and Allan had been removed. Flora
and Allan were set to seek their fortune in North Carolina with their
sons Alexander and James. Tradition holds that they were also accompanied by daughter Anne and her husband, the much older Alexander
MacLeod, recognized illegitimate son of Norman MacLeod, 19th
chief of the MacLeods of Dunvegan. Though there is no hard evidence to support the assertion, it is clear that Anne and her husband
went at about the same time to about the same place. Two or three
years earlier, probably as a result of the brutal lingering winter of
1771, Flora's stepfather, the enigmatic and presumably widowed Hugh,
Flora's half-sister Annabella and Annabella's husband Alexander Mac-
Donald, 5th of Cuidreach and another Skye tacksman, had decided to
emigrate.

Of the four MacDonald children who did not accompany Flora
and Allan, eldest son Charles was by now a lieutenant in the service of
the East India Company, and third son Ranald was a lieutenant of
Marines. The two youngest children remained in Scotland: John in
high school in Edinburgh under the care of MacKenzie of Delvine,
and Frances with family friends.

Historians generally agree that Flora and family sailed from
Campbeltown, Kintyre, sometime in late summer or early fall of
1774. In the absence of historical confirmation, this was a plausible
port of embarkation, given Flora's maternal kinfolk in that part of

119

Scotland. And clearly this was the best time of year for emigrants to begin their journey. They would thus arrive when the harvest was in and food was plentiful, and in time to find and clear land before the next spring's planting. Most historians have given the name of the ship that carried Flora and her family as the *Baliol*. However, no one has as yet found any record of a ship by that name carrying emigrants from Scotland to the American colonies at that time. Hugh Douglas makes a strong case that the *Baliol* was in fact the *Balole*, citing Alexander Campbell of Balole as active in the emigration movement at this time. Douglas also notes that at least ten other ships on record might have carried Flora and her family, and that the lack of a record is not unusual.[1]

By whatever vessel, Flora and her family first saw the New World at the mouth of the Cape Fear River below Wilmington, North Carolina. By various vessels, of course, Flora's story had preceded her to America as it had to Leith and London. Highland Scots had been coming to North Carolina in large numbers since 1739. Among those who came in the months and years immediately after the Rising of '45, many of whom were Flora's kinsmen or had been her neighbors, Flora's story had been passed by word of mouth. In that form it made a pleasant piece of the old country to bring to the new world, and it was much easier to pack than a book. It is clear that in its early years Flora's story traveled far by word of mouth before the written accounts ever reached publication. Indeed, it is worth keeping in mind that Americans with ties to North Carolina had Flora's story in print before any full-length book was written about her in her native Britain. Remember, too, that the first of the Americans to write down Flora's history in the nineteenth century still had the same important resource that Flora's contemporary scribes in Britain had had: people who had actually known Flora. We shall look at the contribution of one of these presently; meanwhile, it is fitting that the American historians take over the telling of Flora's story in America.

Conventional biography tells of a great ball held in Flora's honor in Wilmington, though research cannot substantiate it. We also find allusions to lesser fetes as Flora and Allan moved up the Cape Fear River to Cross Creek and beyond, seeking their new homesite. This kind of anecdote reflects both the tendency of biographers to honor

Flora and the perhaps embellished recollections of people who claimed to have known Flora and were still living when Joseph Seawell Jones and William Henry Foote wrote.

The Reverend Mr. Foote first settles Flora and family in Cross Creek and then moves them west to Cameron's Hill, where Flora became a member of the Barbecue Church congregation. A Mrs. Smith was still living at the time Foote wrote, and he cites her as a source "from whom much information respecting Flora was derived." Mrs. Smith remembers in her youth seeing Flora at church, "a dignified and handsome woman to whom all paid respect." In the 1896 *Clan Donald Journal*, a "Rev. Professor Moore of Boston" says that in Fayetteville in 1849 there lived "an old Scottish lady, 87 years of age," who remembered Flora as

> not very tall, but very handsome and dignified, with a fair complexion, sparkling blue eyes, the finest teeth, with hair slightly streaked with white, and nearly covered with a fine lace cap. "Her voice was sweet music, and Oh!," exclaimed the lady, "how the poor and the church missed her when she went home after experiencing much trouble here. She was often at my mother's house, when she first came, and I almost worshipped her, because of her beauty and goodness."[2]

Foote tells us that the family moved farther up country into Anson County where, presumably, they expected to make their permanent home. But the blast of war was blowing, and in February 1776, Allan answered Governor Martin's call for Highlanders to take arms. Tradition holds that Flora was a firebrand, assisting in the recruiting of troops and exhorting the assembled Highlanders. Jones says that "The enthusiastic spirit of Flora forgot that it was not for 'her Charlie' that she was warring," and he attributes to "tradition" the idea that "she was seen among the ranks, encouraging and exhorting them to battle." Foote gives Flora an important role in rallying the Carolina Highlanders in support of the crown. Her husband and their family and friends were "animated by the spirit of this matron, who now, on her former principles, defended George III, as readily as she had aided the unfortunate Prince Charles about thirty years before." Foote also attributes to tradition the notion that Flora accompanied the Highlanders as they started towards Wilmington and "communicated her own enthusiasm to the assembled Scotch."[3]

Writing in 1899, J. P. Maclean enlivens the account of Flora's activities thus:

> The war spirit was stirred within her. Night after night she and Anne attended meetings, addressed the men in her native Gaelic, and urged them to enter the King's army. . . . She used her persuasive powers to excite the slow, the indifferent, and doubtful to action.[4]

And ten years later he cites this incident as an example:

> On the public square [at Cross Creek] near the royal standard, in Gaelic, she made a powerful address, with all her power, exhibiting her genius, she dwelt at length upon the loyalty of the Scotch, their bravery, and the sacrifices her people had made. When she had concluded, the piper asked her what tune he should play. Like a flash she replied, "Give them 'Leather Breeches,' . . . "[5]

The same old lady who almost worshipped Flora remembers "seeing her riding the line on a large white horse, and encouraging her countrymen to be faithful to the King."[6]

Foote and other historians go to some lengths to resolve the Highlanders' willingness to take up arms for King George III after opposing George II thirty years before. In fact, of course, many of these Highlanders had been in the service of the crown in the '45. Flora's step-father certainly had been, and Allan writes of his own service to the government in that rising. It is also helpful to remember that more Scots remained loyal to the crown than took up Charlie's banner. In the '45 which side one fought for was determined by what the clan chief said; in the colonies a generation later, to the extent that the tight clan system had been eroded, one's allegiance was more a matter of individual choice.

Furthermore, as Bruce Lenman has pointed out, the choosing of sides in North Carolina had a great deal to do with how long a Scot had been in the colony. Old timers had more on which to base their feelings about independence. The newcomers had probably had to swear a loyalty oath which they were not ready to break.[7] As Joseph

Jones wrote, "The truth is, the countrymen of Flora MacDonald were incapable of appreciating the value of our revolution."[8] But Scots who had followed Charlie were quite capable of understanding the consequences of backing a loser against the crown. Having been burned once, they were not likely to fly into the next fickle flame to flare up. So once again they were unable to pick a winner. Above all, there was the growing tradition of Scots entering military service. Even before the '45 Scots made up a significant part of the British army, and afterwards, as times were tough at home and as the government recognized both the fighting prowess of the Scots in combat and their role as convenient, non-English cannon fodder, it waged an immensely successful recruiting campaign.[9] All five of Flora's sons entered the service of the crown, and both her daughters married military men. Such was probably not unusual among Scottish families in the late eighteenth century.

James Banks writes that upon her arrival in North Carolina and her approach to Cross Creek, "the capital of the Scotch settlement," Flora was greeted with a "Highland welcome" that included "the strains of the Pibroch and the martial airs of her native land."[10] It is to Banks that we are indebted for the first recorded telling of this anecdote:

> On visiting Mrs. Rutherford, afterwards Mrs. McAuslin, who lived at that time in a house known as the Stuart place, north of the Presbyterian church, [Flora] saw a painting which represented "Anne of Jura" assisting in the Prince's escape. "Turn the face of that picture to the wa'," said she, in her clear, soft accents, "never let it see the light again; it belies the truth of history, Anne of Jura was na' there, did na' help the bonnie Prince."[11]

In his 1919 history, until recently unpublished, Governor McLean passes along the same anecdote. It is interesting for a couple of reasons. First, of course, because it alleges the existence of a painting, however fanciful, of another female helping the Prince. Famous though Flora was for her exploits, was there someone else to whom credit was (wrongly) given? Where does the idea of "Anne of Jura" come from? None of the Prince's biographers makes any mention of such a person. No one has placed Charlie on the isle of Jura during his skulk. The Kenneth Black family, whom Flora certainly knew in North Carolina, had roots in Jura, but from this fact to the alleged picture the route remains unmarked. Obviously Flora's fame preceded her to North Carolina and had been allowed to grow unchecked for a generation before her arrival. But the implication that the legend of Flora's heroic assistance was somehow mixed up with that of another Hebridean woman is puzzling. Was there indeed such a picture that Flora might have seen? If so, is it evidence of another case of mistaken identity similar to the one we saw in London, where Flora was, at least by some, mistaken for Jenny Cameron?

The other interesting contribution of the anecdote is that it has Flora speaking in the Scots dialect. Those biographers who do resort to dialogue—Mrs. Wylde, MacGregor, Jolly, and Banks most of the time, for example—give to Flora the gift of cultured speech. The point here is not what Flora was actually speaking when and if she spoke to Mrs. Rutherford—it may well have been Gaelic; rather, the point is how the tellers of the tale want us to see Flora. Banks, remember, was writing at a time when Sir Walter Scott, James Hogg, and Robert Burns had made Scots dialect acceptable and popular in polite literature. The later biographers prefer to present Flora more formally. Flora's use of dialect plays a part in another piece of the Flora legend, as shall be seen later.

Exactly how influential Flora was in recruiting and rallying Highlanders to the loyalist cause is unclear. A letter written in April of 1776 does tell of a speech that was made to the loyalist troops before they marched off to their defeat at Moore's Creek Bridge. The speech encouraged the men

> to consider the glorious cause they engaged in & in serving their King & being the instruments of relieving this Country from Tirannical oppression it now groans under.... [and] if any amongst them was so fainthearted as not to serve with that resolution of conquering or dying, this was the time for such to declare themselves, upon which there was a general huza for the King except from about 20 men of Col Cottons Corps who laid down their arms & declared their courage was not warproof.[12]

Unfortunately, the writer of the letter does not identify the orator. If it was not Flora, perhaps repeated word of mouth references to such a speech eventually attributed it to Flora.

One North Carolina historian believes that Flora and her extended family—her husband Allan, her two sons James and Alexander, her daughter Anne and son-in-law Alexander MacLeod, her stepfather Hugh MacDonald, her half-sister Annabella and Annabella's husband Alexander MacDonald—formed something of an isolated colony among the longer-settled Scots in what are now Richmond and Montgomery Counties, and he maintains that "this group had great influence among their more lowly-born country-men." Indeed,

> had they not arrived upon the scene at that crucial moment, the Highlanders would never have risen, but instead, would have joined the American cause or at least remained aloof during the fast approaching conflict.[13]

Banks does not have Flora stirring up the Highlanders before the battle; instead she "embraced her husband, and tears dimmed her eyes as she breathed a fervent prayer for his safe and speedy return to her new home at Killiegray."[14] Allan, however, was taken prisoner, and he and Flora began a lengthy period of separation and hardship.

In the various accounts of what happened next, fact and legend diverge markedly. Let us look first at the facts, and let Flora herself relate them. First she reports that her husband "and about 30 other gentlemen were draged from goal to goal for 700 miles, till lodged in Philadelphia Goal, remaining in their hands for 18 months befor exchanged."[15] Her property was confiscated, and Flora lived for a while with friends. Some years later, writing chiefly in the third person, Flora remembered that wretched time this way:

> Mrs. Flora MacDonald being all this time in misery and sickness at home, being informed that her husband and friends were all killed or taken, contracted a severe fever, and being dayly oppressed with straggling partys of plunderers from their Army, and night robbers, who more than once threatened her life wanting a confession where her husbands money was—Her servants deserting her, and such as stayed, grew so very insolent, that they were of no service or help to her. When she got better of her fever, she went to visit & comfort the other poor Gentlewomen whose Husbands were prisoners with Mr. MacDonald, as they blamed him as being

the outhor of their misery, in the riseing the highlanders and in one of those charitable visits, fell from her horse and brock her right arm, which confined her for months; the only phisishtian in the collony being prisoner with her husband in Philadelphia Gaol haveing no comforter but a young boy her son, the oldest Alexr., being prisoner with his father. She remained in this deplorable condition for two years, among Robers, and faithless servants, Untill her husband, and son in law, major Alexr. McLeod obtained a flag of truce from Sir Henry Clinton and Admirall How, which brought me, my daughter, and her Children, from wilmingtown in N. Carolina to New York.[16]

Foote and Banks, remember, did not have Flora's memorial to draw upon. Foote passes briefly and generally over the above before reuniting the family and sending them directly back to Scotland.

After the release of her husband from Halifax jail, the place of confinement for the officers taken in the battle, having suffered much in their estate from the plunderings and confiscations to which the Royalists were exposed, they with their family embarked on a sloop of war for their native land.[17]

Banks has the story another way. He has a Whig Captain Ingram grant Flora a passport by which she went to Fayetteville, then to Wilmington and on to Charleston,

from which port she sailed for her native land, leaving her husband a prisoner in Halifax jail, and her five sons actively engaged against the Whig cause. This step she took at the entreaty of her husband, whom she was not permitted to visit, and for the benefit of her daughter's health.[18]

These two early accounts of Flora's Carolina tribulations, though wrong by Flora's own testimony, are pretty sparing of detail. Later, however, the accounts of Flora's hardships without Allan and of her departure picked up some additional ornamentation. Governor McLean, for example, recounts an incident said to have occurred after Flora's plantation had been confiscated. In it Flora and her daughters

Anne and Fanny are stopped by Col. Wade, who "allowed his men to take their swords and spilt open the dresses of the two daughters in order to secure jewels which he conceived they had concealed on their person."[19] Dramatically illustrative of the hardships that Flora had to bear in Allan's absence though this anecdote is, there is no evidence that such an event befell Flora or her family.

Another folktale is one on which Rassie Wicker was raised and which he passes along with appropriate caveats. The story goes that once during this same period of difficulty it became necessary for Flora to leave the place where she was staying, but she was delayed in doing so because a servant, Dan McDonald, was acutely ill with small-pox. He could not travel, and Flora would not leave him. "To solve this dilemma, she, in desperation, smothered what little life remaining, with a blanket, and with the help of other women servants, dug a grave and buried him." The meticulous Wicker accepts none of this story except that a Dan McDonald was indeed buried in a certain grave marked "a few years ago" by a sassafras tree.[20]

Perhaps the most celebrated of the folktales about Flora in North Carolina also involves graves. Precisely where the story of Flora's two dead children originates we do not know. Banks mentions them in his 1857 essay, and Angus McLean, who draws heavily from Banks, fills in his version of the details. He says that sometime after Allan's capture, while she was faced with all the other difficulties which she herself has described, Flora "was called to grieve the loss of a son and a daughter, aged respectively eleven and thirteen, who died of typhus fever and were buried at Killiegrey." He adds that although their names have not been preserved, their graves have. A subsequent owner of Killiegrey "fenced the graves, erected a small monument to mark the spot, and cared for the place up to the breaking out of the Civil War." Governor McLean relates a report that in 1886 "the graves were in good condition, enclosed by a rail fence, though covered with brush and weeds." Unfortunately, "no names or dates could be deciphered on the wooden headboards."[21]

At the time he was working on his history, Governor McLean must have been aware of some doubts about these being Flora's children. He offers in evidence the affidavit of W. R. Coppedge, Superintendent of Schools of Richmond County, who in turn presents statements of six long-time local residents all of whom agree that the graves are those of Flora's children. A couple of these suggest how far back the story might go. Terrell Poole, who bought property "within half a mile of the graves," learned their identity from John Alred, "an elderly man who had lived all of his life within half a mile of the graves." Mr. D. M. Morrison, who had "for a long time known these as the graves of Flora MacDonald's children," stated that the late Isaac Alred, "who died years ago at an advanced age," had told him.[22]

Dr. Charles G. Vardell, president of the women's college that had stood in Red Springs since 1896, first as Red Springs Seminary, then as Southern Presbyterian College, and then as Flora MacDonald College, learned of the graves while attending a meeting of the Fayetteville Presbytery in the early teens. Though he had recently studied the influence of Flora MacDonald on the Scots in that part of North Carolina, he was unaware of the story of the graves of Flora's children.[23] Dr. Vardell was a man who liked to do things thoroughly and in a big way. In 1917 he was able to persuade the North Carolina legislature to pass an act permitting the removal of the bodies in the graves so that they might be reburied on the grounds of the college that bore the name of their alleged mother. However, the actual removal did not occur until 1937. Meanwhile, Leonard Tufts, son of Pinehurst's founder, wanted to do something to commemorate the children, and in 1922 marked the site thus:

> Graves of
> Flora MacDonald's
> Children
> Her Estate of
> Killiegray
> Was Located Here[24]

While all this was going on, however, and as early as 1914, Rassie E. Wicker was conducting his own research into Flora MacDonald's life in North Carolina. After some forty years, Mr. Wicker presented a persuasive case that the property that Flora lived on was not in fact where these children were buried, nor for that matter where other historians had placed it. He placed the MacDonald holdings over on Cheek's Creek in Anson County and some five or six miles from the traditionally accepted site. Mr. Wicker concludes that the estate called

"Killiegray" was not owned by the MacDonalds but by an Alexander MacLeod, not the Alexander MacLeod who was Flora's son-in-law. Down through the years the confusion over the different Alexander MacLeods is understandable. Even so, there seems to be no solid reason for the MacDonalds to have named their estate "Killiegray," after an island off the Scottish coast with which they had no particular connection. As Wicker points out, it would make much more sense for Allan MacDonald of Kingsburgh to name his place in North Carolina after the one he held in Scotland.

Paul Green's account of the discovery of Flora and Allan's homesite is delightful. Green, Malcolm Fowler, Rassie Wicker, and two others left Wicker's home in Pinehurst to continue Wicker's quest. Aided by ancient maps and eighty-one-year-old Daniel Poole, they found the remains of a mill dam along Cheek's Creek. After a digression to the little town of Pekin for a quick lunch and a look at the fifth game of the World Series on one of Pekin's few television sets, they returned to the creek. They worked their way north along the ridge west of the creek, until they came to "a very old home site — with scraggly walnut and locust trees growing about.... In a tangle of briars, plum bushes and honeysuckle, [they] found a couple of rock piles—ancient collapsed chimneys—about twenty-eight or thirty feet apart. [They] figured this to be the dwelling site." Fowler and Wicker agreed that everything checked out. As for Green and the others,

> The rest of us were all ready to agree with these two authorities that after many years of searching around we had at last found the plantation of Flora MacDonald, the home site, the mill site, and the spring.[25]

Green was much taken with the mill stone. "I got to have that rock," he said. When Fowler asked him what he would do with it, he said,

> I'll take it home and keep it. Maybe some day there will be a Scotch museum or something like it in Fayetteville or somewhere and I can present it to the museum. In the meanwhiletime I'll take care of it the way I did that Virginia Dare marble statue....[26]

There is a museum in Fayetteville and at last report the stone still sat in the yard of Paul Green's former house in Chapel Hill.[27] In 1960 the North Carolina Society of the Colonial Wars marked with an inscribed stone the site of Allan and Flora's plantation, but subsequent explorers have found evidence which places the actual site south of the 1960 marker.

With the location of Flora's property newly corrected, the graves were, of course, no longer on the family land. Why would Flora have buried her children on someone else's property? That is the least of the questions about the authenticity of the graves. Why would Flora, in enumerating the misfortunes she experienced while her husband was away, make no mention of the deaths of two of her children? Certainly such a loss would rate right up along side insolent servants and a broken arm in her list of priorities. Nor does Allan mention the loss of two children in his various appeals for compensation during his captivity and after the war. In fact, in a letter from Reading Gaol in 1777, Allan accounts for all seven children. And why is there no mention of the births of these children in Scotland? If they died in 1777 at eleven and thirteen, they would have been born in 1766 and 1764. Seventeen sixty-six was already taken; Frances was born in that year, and, as previously noted, she did not accompany her family to North Carolina. In her 1774 letter to the Duke of Atholl, Flora accounts for all of her seven children.

To be sure, there is another letter in which Flora seems to mention young children. It appeared as part of an article in the *American Historical Record* in 1872. Governor McLean quotes it as follows:

February 1, 1776.
Dear Madam: Allan leaves tomorrow to join Donald's standard at Cross Creek, and I shall be alone wi' my three bairns. Canna ye come and stay wi' me awhile? There are troublous times ahead I ween. God will keep the right. I hope all our ain are in the right, prays your good friend,
Flory MacDonald[28]

Unfortunately, the article is unsigned, and the letter, which McLean says was preserved in Fayetteville in 1852 is now nowhere to be found. The text itself is "troublous" because of the use of dialectal words like "wi'" and "bairns" and "canna" and "ween" and "ain."

With the exception of the "Anne of Jura" anecdote, Flora does not speak Scots; and with the minute exception of an "ane" in her 1789 memorial, Flora does not seem to write Scots-isms. If we are to believe Mrs. Vining, remember, "Flora learned to speak at home well, like others of her class, without Scottish accent."[29] Why then would she write with one? After all, why was Flora sent to Miss Henderson's high-class school? Or why did she engage the services of Mr. Beatt, the writing tutor? The authenticity of the letter seems worth questioning. Another cause for question is that at least one version of the letter has it addressed to "Maggie,"[30] perhaps the same "Maggie" at whose fictitious suggestion Mrs. Wylde has Flora relate her autobiography.

Still the graves continued to attract attention. On a visit to Red Springs in 1923, Cameron of Lochiel and his lady sought out the graves and stood bareheaded while the chief's piper played Flora's "Lament" and "Flowers of the Forest."[31]

Dr. Vardell went ahead with his plans to exhume and re-bury the children. He had been present on Skye in 1922 to pronounce the invocation at the unveiling of the monument that currently stands over Flora's grave. While there, he was able to procure the pieces of the plaque from the 1912 monument smashed in a violent windstorm. These pieces he had brought to Red Springs and reassembled at the new gravesite to display Dr. Johnson's famous tribute to Flora. Also set in the marker was a piece of Balmoral granite, a gift to the college from King George V in Flora's memory. At noon on April 28, 1937, the reinterment took place at the college with considerable flourish and fanfare. The principal address was given by Mrs. Edith Magna, daughter of Col. Walter Scott and a past president of the Daughters of the American Revolution. Correspondence shows that the 17th Field Artillery Band from Ft. Bragg would be present "to take part in patriotic exercises." A photograph (see p. 105) shows the procession forming up: faculty in academic gowns, young ladies of the college in tartan skirts, plaids, white blouses, and Glengarry caps. Four girls, all said to be named Flora MacDonald, carry the remains.

The college has merged and moved. On the Red Springs grounds is now a school which bears the name "Flora MacDonald Academy." The grave site and marker remain. Those who care can pause before the marker and reflect upon what it represents in the lore and legend of Flora MacDonald. It reads:

Here Rests
The Remains
of
Two Children
of
Flora MacDonald
interred
Richmond Co. N. C.
1777
Reinterred
April 28, 1937

It brings to mind the earlier quotation, "How powerful is the sway of the irrational over human beings."

Chapter 11

Homeward

For me and mine there's nothing to do now but to deny this land and turn our faces back to the old world, there to — die.

—FLORA IN *The Highland Call*

GOVERNOR MCLEAN CITES "State Records of North Carolina," Vol. XIII, as evidence that Flora, accompanied by Anne, left North Carolina in March 1778 under a flag of truce arranged and brought by her son-in-law.[1] However, rather than have her go to New York to join her husband, which in fact she did, McLean adds details to the legend narrated first by Banks that Flora made her way directly from Carolina back to Scotland. The governor mentions the intercessions of Captain Ingram. He goes on to explain that, being short of funds in Wilmington, Flora had to sell her silverware in order to pay for passage to Charleston and on to Scotland. The popular belief is that most of this silver was presented to Flora by her admirers in Lady Primrose's London circle. McLean reports that the silver was bought by Richard Quince, a Wilmington merchant. Somewhere along the way the set was broken up, with parts finding their way onto the sideboards of several different Carolina families. The governor points out that while there is evidence that Quince did indeed own silver believed to have been Flora's, there is none that he actually bought it from Flora MacDonald herself.[2]

Rassie Wicker suggests that whatever silver of Flora's turned up in the Carolinas was more probably stolen in raids on her house than sold by her to pay for a voyage which in fact she did not take. In support of his theory Wicker cites Allan MacDonald's claim of £500 for "the value of Books, plate and furniture plundered by the enemy."[3]

Whether the silver was sold by Flora or stolen from her and then sold, the legend persists that these old family heirlooms were once Flora's, and from there it is easy to accept the tradition that at least some of the silver was given to Flora by Bonnie Prince Charlie. Once again, history gives us no reason to believe that Charlie ever gave Flora anything except, perhaps, garters from his Betty Burke get-up, the half-crown he owed her, and maybe a lump of sugar. A commemorative silver service stands not within the prospect of belief.

Back to facts. Flora tells us that she sailed from Wilmington to New York to join Allan. She says that for most of the voyage she and Anne were "in danger of our lives by a constant storme." In New York Allan "commanded a Company of Gentlemen Volunteers, all scotsh Refugees from Carolina & Virginia; with them (all dressed in Scarlet & blew) ...." Subsequently Allan was ordered to Nova Scotia to take a commission in the 84th regiment, and Flora "was obliged, "tho' tender, to follow, and was very nigh death's door, by a violent disorder the Rough sea and long passage had brought on." Flora was allowed to remain in Halifax for eight days because of her "tender state," before setting out on a five-day journey "throu woods & snow" in "one of the worst winters ever seen there" to join Allan at Windsor "on the bey of minos." Though Flora says they nearly starved, they did survive the winter, but she by "ane accidentall fall the next summer dislockated the wrist of the other hand, and brock some tendons, which confined [her] for two months, altho [she] had the assistance of the Regimental Surgeon." Enough was enough. Flora had understandably had it with the new world.

> I fixed my thoughts on seeing my native Country, tho in a tender state, my husband obtained a birth in the Lord Dunmore, Letter of mark ship of 24 guns, I and three other young ladys and two gentlemen, sett sail in octr. But in our passage spying a sail, made ready for action and in hurreying the Ladys below, to a place of Safety, my foot sliping a step in the trap, fell and brock the dislockated arm in two. It was sett with bandages over slips of wood, and keep my bed till we arrived in the Thames.[4]

Flora's account of this oft-reported naval engagement differs significantly from others'. Two commentators say that the incident occurred when Flora and her family were westbound aboard the *Baliol*. A composite of most of the other versions has Flora refusing to seek safety below. Instead she remains on deck, in some versions pacing the quarterdeck, but from whatever exposed position, exhorting the gunners to give it their best shot. Some do acknowledge that she broke the arm in a fall; one says she slipped on the "bloody deck"; others assert that she received a wound. Whichever, Governor McLean speaks for most commentators when he says that Flora "refused to leave her post, and continued to animate the sailors."

In the fall of 1789, ten years after her return from the new world and five months before she died, Flora wrote and sent to Sir John MacPherson, "Late Governor General of India," two memorials. One focused on her activities with the Prince in 1746, the other on her life in North Carolina and her return to Britain. The latter memorial concludes as follows:

> Those melancholy strocks, by the death of my Children who, had they lived, with Gods assistance, might now be my support in my declining old age brought on a violent fitt of sickness, which confined me to my bed in London, for half a year, and would have brought me to my Grave, if under gods hand, Doctor Donald Munrow, had not given his friendly assistance. The cast in both my arms are liveing monuments of my sufferings & distress—And the long goal confinement which my Husband underwent, has brought on such disorders, that he has totally lost the use of his legs—So that I may fairly say we both have suffered in our person, family, and Interest, as much if not more than any two going under the name of Refugees, or Loyalists—without the smallest recompense.[5]

In a postscript to the cover letter she adds, "I am always oppressed with the Rhumatism &c &c since I saw you—god bless you."

Here, then, are Flora's last words on these two periods of her life which have fascinated posterity on both sides of the Atlantic and given rise to history, legend, song, and story. That these last words are so melancholy and querulous is, though understandable, sad indeed. She seems to pile grief upon grief here, compressing events as she does so. It sounds as if she learned of her sons' deaths while in London, and that the resultant collapse left her bedridden there. In fact, however, in a letter written in July of 1782 she mentions that "Ranald is Captain of Marines" and she still holds out hope for Sandy, though he is "a-missing."[6]

We can understand, too, the hopes she might have had for Alexander as a comfort and support in her old age. Ranald seems to have been something of a different story, however. It was actually John, the youngest and seemingly the most successful son, who provided most if not all of the financial support. The eldest son, Charles, gets mixed reviews. Chambers notes that he was "a captain in the Queen's Rangers" and "a most accomplished man." Chambers goes on to quote "the late Lord Macdonald," who, on seeing Charles lowered into his grave, said, "There lies the most finished gentleman of my family and name."[7] A dissenting opinion has Charles taking after the Prince whose name he bore, earning a reputation as a profligate drinker and spender and adding notably to his parents' financial woes. "A fine young fellow for whom I have the sincerest regard," writes Captain Alexander MacDonald, a cousin, in Nova Scotia to Allan in New York, "he is very Clever when Sober but rather unhappy when he is anyways disguised in Liquor." Because of his capacity for going through money, "the income of a General Offr wd be rather small for him if he could get it."[8] The cousin hopes that Allan's presence "might be the means of altering & putting a Stop to it." Charles may also be a bad influence upon Ranald. Asking for anonymity, the cousin urges Allan "with the power and authority of a parent [to] Command Ronald [sic] at his peril to tell you the truth of all he knows Concerning Charles & his Behaviour."[9] This is clearly not the stuff of which twilight comfort is made.

John, as noted above, turned out well, and he shall be mentioned later. James, too, had a solid career in the military. About the daughters we know somewhat less. Anne, the elder, married before the emigration. Her husband, Alexander MacLeod, was of her parents' generation. She shared with her mother the hardships of the new world and returned to Skye where she died in 1834. Frances, the youngest child, stayed behind in Scotland (North Carolina tradition to the contrary not withstanding), married, and eventually emigrated to Australia.

What about Allan? What sort of a man was he? It is quite possible that with Allan, as with Prince Charles, there was less than met the eye. Boswell seems to have been taken with the man upon meeting him. He deems him "hospitable" and commends "the most respectful attention" with which he greeted Dr. Johnson and "supported him into the house." He describes him thus:

> Kingsburgh was completely the figure of a gallant high-lander, exhibiting 'the graceful mien and manly looks', which our popular Scotch song has justly attributed to that character. He had his tartan plaid thrown about him, a large blue bonnet with a knot of black ribband like a cockade, a brown short coat of a kind of duffil, a tartan waistcoat with gold buttons and gold button-holes, a bluish philabeg, and tartan hose. He had jet black hair tied behind, and was a large stately man, with a steady sensible countenance.[10]

Impressive, indeed, but even as Boswell describes Allan, he recognizes and regrets that Allan has not been able to make a go of it on Skye and will soon uproot and separate his family in an effort to make a new start. Steadily beset by bad timing, bad luck, and bad debts, Allan was unable to succeed in Scotland or in North Carolina. No one has really looked into the impact of his wife's fame upon him, and from this distance, no one is likely to be able to. Neither Scottish nor eighteenth-century reserve allows for unseemly outpourings of one's innermost feelings. Still, commentators have invented, conjectured, and speculated about so much else in Flora's life, why not a little on Allan? Could not his male ego have been a bit bruised at his wife's celebrity?. What else was there for him to do when Pennant or Boswell and Johnson came to call upon his celebrated spouse but dress up and cut a handsome figure while his guests—Boswell and Johnson, at least—fell all over themselves in their attention to his wife.

Maybe the flight from Skye to Carolina had for Allan more than economic incentives to it—a fresh start where he could establish himself. With the choosing up of sides and taking up of arms in his new land, Allan had a chance at a military career. As he states in one of his memorials, in the '45 he had served as a "Lieut of an independent Company of Highlanders under the Duke of Cumberland and Lord Loudon."[11] In a letter recommending a commission for Allan, Governor Martin calls him a man "of great worth and good character" with "most extensive influence over the Highlanders here."[12] Allan says that he was instrumental in raising for the Crown 1,500 fighting men from among "the Highlanders &c of North Carolina." He also says in one of his memorials that he had command at Moore's Creek Bridge. This claim is not supported by facts. At the same time, while Allan was highly thought of by the governor and was among the principals in raising the Highlanders in North Carolina, he was given only the rank of captain. And contemporary accounts of the events of February 1776, make slight, passing reference to him.

Did Allan command respect by means of his own qualities of leadership, or was he merely the recipient of the deference that accrued to the spouse of the legendary and revered Flora? We shall probably never know. Allan's opportunities to lead men were limited indeed. He was a soldier of the King in Scotland, North Carolina, New York, and Nova Scotia, and we know next to nothing about his service. In North Carolina, about which we know most, less than a month after taking up arms, he was ordered to put them down, and he spent the next seventeen months being walked from jail to jail or in writing letters to John Hancock and others in authority pleading for freedom and compensation. Did he want more, or was he content to be just "the figure of a gallant Highlander?"

Allan remained in Nova Scotia for four years after Flora left. For three of these he continued to serve as a captain in the 84th Royal Highland Emigrant Regiment. When the regiment was reduced in the fall of 1783, he settled on and tried to work a piece of land along the Kennetcook River. In January 1784 he submitted from Nova Scotia to the Board of Commissioners in London the first of two petitions seeking compensation in the amount of £1086 for his "losses Sufferings and Service." Later that year he sailed for London to pursue his claim. In early 1785 he presented his second petition, in which the value of his losses had risen to £1341. He sought speedy resolution to his case so that he could return to Nova Scotia. He asked that the board

> look to and commiserate the misfortunes of an old Gentleman worn out with fatigue and service and who lost the strength of his Family in the cause of his King & Country and his Estate, the only means of supporting himself and Old wife and daughter in his latter days and as his looking after some recompence for his lose's on Government service

in America, the only inducement which brought him over, he wishes as soon as possible to return and Cultivate and Cutt down on his Regimental Grant of Lands where he has already built a little hutt, and cleared a few acres of ground, but was obliged to give up his little improvements for want of cash which hurt him much, as he has no other place of Residence or Abode.[13]

Finally in 1786 he received a settlement of £440, meager recompense indeed for what he calls his "losses Sufferings and Service," and insufficient, apparently, to permit a return to Nova Scotia, even if Flora had been willing to recross the Atlantic. Allan's statement that he had "no other place of Residence or Abode" and references to Allan and Flora as "late of Kingsburgh" support the idea that at this time they had lost their former home on Skye. Probably for that reason upon her return to Scotland Flora settled with or near her brother at Milton on South Uist, and when Allan finally joined her, they continued to live there until 1787. Then Allan seems to have succeeded in leasing or buying an estate at Penduin, in northern Skye, to which they moved and where they remained.

The fanciful MacGregor omits considerable travel and discomfort in looking only at a brighter side as he describes Allan's return to Flora and Skye.

When peace was eventually restored, Flora's husband was liberated from Halifax jail, and he made as little delay as possible in returning to Skye, as Captain on half-pay. On his arrival at Portree, he was met by his affectionate wife, and a numerous party of friends, to welcome him. He made no delay in reaching Kingsburgh, which during his absence in America, was left open for his return. For eight or nine years Flora and her husband lived comfortably and happily in their old residence, until both were removed by death, within less than two years of each other.[14]

Most of the writers of the nineteenth century display this same desire to give Flora and Allan a happy issue out of all their afflictions, if indeed they acknowledge any afflictions at all. Flora's nagging poor health, Allan's incapacity, their long separation, the deaths of two sons, and the prolonged and largely unsuccessful efforts to recover financial losses are ignored or dismissed by virtually all writers in the nineteenth and early twentieth centuries. To be sure, they may not have been aware of the last memorials of Flora and Allan, and thus did not see the definitely forlorn side that these documents reveal. To the reader who has seen the memorials, however, the Pollyanna-like tone of many of the writers seems to suggest that among these writers the notion prevails that a woman of Flora's caliber should not be so beset, nor should the husband of such a woman.

Though we are told from time to time that Flora was a woman of some means in the Highlands, there are other indications that money was tight towards the end. A fitting finale to Flora's life might have been a pension to ease the burdens of mounting years and declining health, but none was awarded. The money raised by Lady Primrose was long since gone, and the small sum from the settlement of Allan's claim did not go far or last long. In 1822 King George IV did grant a pension of fifty pounds a year to Flora MacDonald,[15] but the recipient Flora was "the grand-daughter of the illustrious Flora MacDonald," one of three of her granddaughters to bear her famous name.

One of these, the tantalizing Mrs. Wylde, brings up the possibility of a pension from another source. She has Flora tell Maggie and her readers that Henry, Cardinal of York, younger brother of Prince Charles, made inquiry after her and would have provided a pension of any sum she would name if Flora would renounce her Presbyterian faith and become a Catholic. She firmly and graciously declined:

> No, had I been starving, I would not have accepted the Cardinal's favour. Yet I believe his Royal Highness meant kindly; so viewing the matter in that light, he has my thanks and gratitude for the recollection of a simple body in a far-off country.[16]

Given Mrs. Wylde's use of fictional license, can we give any credence to this story? Before we dismiss it altogether, let us consider an envelope in the Macbean Collection. In a hand not unlike the one that signed Flora's marriage contract, the envelope is addressed "A Son Altesse Roiale Monseigneur le Cardinal, Duc Dyorck. A Rome."

Written across the envelope in another hand is "De la part de Flora MacDonald et sa fills" and then what appears to be "C.th." The envelope is empty, and no explanatory notes accompany it. Did Flora indeed write to the Cardinal? If so, when? What was the subject—her son who was named after the Cardinal's brother? Did she initiate the correspondence, or did this envelope once contain Flora's reply to the offer of a conditional pension? Is the envelope even legitimate, or is it part of some manufactured memorabilia? While we continue to see if time, "that great revealer of secrets," will lead us to answers, we must again ask if Mrs. Wylde writes better biography than her detractors have been willing to admit.

"Flora...retained to the last that vivacity and cheerfulness which distinguished her in her youth," wrote "E. E. G." in *Gentleman's Magazine* in May 1868.[17] For this assertion the initialed author seems indebted to Chambers, who had earlier written that she "retained to the last that vivacity and vigour of character which has procured her so much historical distinction."[18] Even Eric Linklater wraps up Flora summarily when he tells us that when Allan came home, he and Flora "went back to the old house of Kingsburgh"[19] until Flora's death in 1790.

In any event, on March 4, 1790, after a sudden and short illness, Flora died. Most writers agree with MacGregor that Allan died in 1792, though one has him predecease Flora, and another has him live until 1795.

Chapter 12

Death and After

The canonization of Flora MacDonald is reaching an acute stage.

—Miscellanea Jacobitiana

IF THE BIOGRAPHERS AND HISTORIANS who have written about Flora achieve unanimity on anything, it is that Flora had an enormous funeral—"the most numerously attended of any of which there is any record of having taken place in the Western Isles," one calls it.[1] Estimates of the number of mourners in attendance run to three and four thousand. The funeral procession is said to have stretched for at least a mile, and anywhere from seven to a dozen pipers were placed throughout the cortege. Three hundred gallons of whisky were consumed along with other suitable refreshments. People of all ranks came to pay their last respects to the Highland heroine. In his *History of the MacDonalds and Lords of the Isles* of 1881, Alexander Mackenzie describes another, later funeral, that of a MacDonald known locally and lovingly as "The Taightear." Mackenzie provides logistical details which are remarkably similar to those of Flora's funeral. He says the procession of mourners stretched for two miles with six men abreast and seven pipers interspersed to play the funeral coronach. He, too, mentions three hundred gallons of whisky "and every other description of refreshment in proportionate abundance."[2] Mackenzie then adds that the only other Skye funeral to resemble it was Flora MacDonald's, "which was about as numerously attended."[3] It is probably true that Flora was given an heroic funeral, but as with so much else about Flora, we wonder if the specific details may have come later and from other sources describing similar events.

By way of commenting on her death, Malcolm Fowler calls Flora "one of the unluckiest women of history." Noting that "Misfortune dogged her steps all the days of her life," he adds that "Even in death she was denied a normal burial. A violent storm began raging the day she was to be buried and it was three days before her body could be committed to the earth." Earlier, Angus McLean had commented upon a night "of inky darkness, save when relieved by the lightning's red glare. The thunder rolled with terrific peals, and the rain fell in torrents." The "stalwart youths" carrying Flora's coffin found the stream ahead of them "swollen from bank to bank." As he tells it,

> Some proposed to return, but others declared that she whose body they were carrying had never flinched when alive from any duty which she had undertaken, neither would they in performing the last rites to her mortal remains.[4]

Needless to say, they did press on and safely bore their burden to the other side. McLean then has Flora lie in state at Kingsburgh for a week before being carried sixteen more miles to burial in the churchyard at Kilmuir.

Given general agreement about an epic funeral for our lady, it is surprising to discover how little attention the outside world paid to Flora's passing. In his multivolume compilation of the obituaries of noteworthy eighteenth-century figures, Sir William Musgrave lists only three places in which notice of Flora's death was published: *Scots Magazine*, *European Magazine*, and *Gentleman's Magazine*.[5] The first reads in its entirety: "March 4 At the Isle of Skye, Flora Macdonald, spouse to Capt Allan Macdonald, late of Kingsburgh."[6] The other two also are terse. *Gentleman's Magazine* agrees with the March 4 date and adds "in the Isle of Skye Mrs. Flora Macdonald, famed in the annals of the late Pretender."[7] *European Magazine* gives the date as April 4, but otherwise is almost identical to *Gentleman's*, only substituting "famous" for "famed" and adding a reference to Boswell's Tour.[8] Indeed, it is interesting to note that *Gentleman's Magazine* gave more space to Flora in its two-page obituary of her son John in January 1832, than it did in announcing her death.[9] In giving her such short shrift, the national press maintained the same level of indifference it had displayed during her captivity in London.

Flora's winding sheet has received a great deal of ink over the years. According to tradition, for almost forty-four years Flora had cherished the bedding in which the Prince had slept that night at

Kingsburgh, presumably carrying it with her to North America and back because it had been her ardent wish ever since that night to be buried in the very sheets that had once enveloped the Prince. However, in her memorial of October 1789, Flora has this to say on the subject:

> The sheets he lay in were by Mrs Macdonalds order taken of the bed and carefully laid up with injunctions to her Daughter never to be us'd or wash'd till she dy'd and then put about her body which accordingly was done.[10]

John MacLeod of Raasay corroborates Flora's statement in his account of the Prince's escape written in 1775 for James Boswell:

> It cannot be pass'd in Silence that old Mrs Macdonald after her guest had left the house, took the sheets in which he lay, and having carefully folded them up and laid them by, told her daughter, that no other person shou'd ever ly in them, or serves any other purpose, than as a shroud to be put about her body, unwash'd as they were, after her death, and accordingly when she dy'd, in obedience to her will, that very use was made of them.[11]

Boswell includes the report in his *Journal,* but does not say whether he got it from Flora as well as from MacLeod. He does say, however, that old Mrs. Kingsburgh's "will was religiously observed."[12] Tradition not withstanding, we must question the idea that Flora was buried in bedding once slept in by the Prince. Even had old Mrs. MacDonald been willing to share her treasure with Flora, it is unlikely that Flora as we know her would have been interested in preserving the sentimental shroud.

It was James Banks who in his 1857 Fayetteville lecture opined that Allan had died a few years before Flora; thus she was buried "within a square piece of brick wall, which encloses the tombs of the McDonalds of Kingsboro'," where

> she sleeps well by the side of him, whom in life she honored with her hand, and on whom for thirty-six years, she lavished all her wealth, and generous impulses of a truly noble loving heart, . . . [13]

Banks is further moved to observe that

> though it is from characters such as hers that Scotland's
> grandeur springs, which makes her "loved at home, revered
> abroad," yet to Scotland's shame be it spoken, not even a
> simple stone marks the last resting place of the gentle
> Flora....[14]

Gaining momentum and modifying a phrase from Gray's *Elegy*, he
closes out the thought:

> and though no sculptured urn or animated bust ever should
> rise to point the traveller to her lonely grave, yet her charac-
> ter and virtues will lead millions o'er those heath-clad hills,
> upon a solemn pilgrimage, to that sacred shrine....[15]

"E. E. G." was one of the pilgrims Banks foresaw. When he visited
Skye in 1868, he was appalled to discover at Flora's grave "a complete
harvest of nettles, some three or four feet in height." The clergyman
who was showing him the burial ground expressed regret "that as yet
no monument had been erected to Flora's memory," and added that
"there was some talk a short time ago about having one put up, but
the idea has never been carried out."[16]

So when E. E. G. walked and ruminated seventy-eight years after
perhaps the largest funeral ever held on Skye, Flora lay in an untended
grave, covered by a marble slab but without suitable monument. Actually, there had been a marker once, but it did not last very long. As the
visitor tells it, two of Flora's sons, Charles and James, brought "a fine
marble slab ... to be placed over their mother's grave." It had been provided for in a provision of their younger brother John's will, specifically:

> I wish my surviving brothers to take the trouble (gratifying
> it must be) of seeing a plain tombstone erected over the
> grave of their parents—a marble slab—and is to have the
> following epitaph inscribed:—"Underneath are deposited
> the remains of Captain Allan Macdonald, and of his spouse,
> Flora Macdonald, a name that will be mentioned in history;
> and if courage and fidelity be virtues, mentioned with hon-
> our. She was a woman of middle stature, soft features, gentle

manners, and elegant presence." "So wrote Dr. Samuel Johnson."[17]

This report raises some questions, however. Though the will to which E. E. G. refers is dated 1 November 1794, John, in fact, lived a long and extremely productive life until his death at Exeter in August 1831, by which time Charles had for thirty-six years been dead and buried in the family mausoleum along with other family members including James.

If not by Charles and James, however, John's wishes were carried out by someone. Unfortunately, though, the monument was broken in transit, and at the time of E. E. G.'s visit, nothing remained of it, "admiring tourists having carried away its minutest fragments to preserve as mementos of their visit to this interesting spot."

In a 1926 letter to Dr. Vardell in North Carolina, Alexander MacDonald of Kilmuir, Skye, dates John's monument from 1826 and agrees that it had been chipped away by enthusiastic relic-seeking pilgrims. The talk, about which the clergyman had spoken, of having another monument put up must have been soon revived. In 1871, a twenty-five-foot granite monument was raised by public subscription and placed over a marble slab covering the graves of Flora and Allan. This one blew down in 1873, "and shortly after, the present one [was] erected."[18] In 1912, a marble tablet was inserted in a niche in the monument, and two years later it was broken into fragments in a violent gale. These are the pieces that were sent to Flora MacDonald College in Red Springs, North Carolina, and reassembled at the new grave of the mysterious children. In 1922, as part of the bicentennial celebration of Flora's birth, the present tablet was set in place and ceremoniously unveiled by Miss Emily Livingstone, "a descendant": specifically a granddaughter of the above-mentioned James, late of Flodigarry on Skye, and thus Flora's great-granddaughter.

In one of the fourteen volumes of *Miscellanea Jacobitiana* that are a part of the MacBean Collection at the University of Aberdeen is an 1896 clipping the first sentence of which makes an arresting observation:

> The canonization of Flora MacDonald is reaching an acute stage. One of her descendants is placing in St Columba's Church, Portree, where she took leave of Prince Charles, a

gorgeous stained glass window in her memory. The subject is Queen Esther's self-sacrifice, and bears the words "If I perish, I perish." And now another descendant has left £1000 for a statue to be erected in Inverness.... [19]

Another clipping in the same collection identifies the donor of the money for the statue as Captain John Murray Henderson MacDonald and says also that the town council had chosen Andrew Davidson's design for the statue.[20] The April 1895 issue of *Scottish Notes & Queries* mentions receipt of a letter from the executors of the estate of the late Captain John Murray Henderson MacDonald, 78th Seaforth Highlanders, "intimating the death of his widow and consequent availability of £1000 which he left to erect a statue of the heroine." Captain MacDonald went on to stipulate that the statue "shall be of bronze, and that upon the pedestal Dr. Johnson's famous and oft-quoted description shall be engraven." The pedestal also bears the Gaelic inscription, "Fhad's a dh' thasas flur air machair,/Mairidh cliu na h-ainnir Chaoimh." [While the flowers bloom in the meadow,/The name of the fair maiden shall endure.]

This statue, which now stands before the Inverness town hall, was unveiled in ceremonies held on July 26, 1899, by a Mrs. Fraser, "wife of Francis Fraser and only daughter of the late Captain J. M. Henderson MacDonald of the 78th Highlanders, who had put up the money."[21]

Yet another clipping in the MacBean Collection reports that Flora's memorial window, displaying the words of *Esther* 4:16, was done by a local artist, "Mr. Taylor of Berness Street." The window was placed in the church by "Fanny Charlotte, widow of Lieutenant-Colonel R. E. Henry and daughter of Captain James Murray Macdonald." Thus she was a granddaughter of Flora's son John.[22]

Eighteen-ninety was, of course, the centennial of Flora's death and therefore an appropriate time to promote retrospection and to mount a campaign for canonization. The Inverness statue (see p. 103) and the Portree window (see p. 104) are two prominent signs of an organized effort to keep Flora in the eyes as well as the hearts and minds of her countrymen. Mrs. Wylde's fictional biography in 1870 and 1875 and MacGregor's imaginative one of 1883 (and at least five subsequent editions through 1932) show that Flora and her legend had never passed completely from the scene, and the publication of these books may have sparked interest among relatives who suddenly dusted off and displayed long-forgotten anecdotes and memorabilia.

In 1884, Sir Harold Boulton's words set to Annie MacLeod's adaptation of an old folk song became "The Skye Boat Song," and though Flora appears only briefly in the second stanza, this musical composition may have spread Flora's story more widely than either Wylde's or MacGregor's biographies. In 1887, Charles MacDonald Smith reported that "in one of last season's popular comic operas this Highland heroine appears in a character that is purely fanciful, and has almost no trace of the real story."[23]

In 1891, George Joy painted his impression of "Flora Macdonald's Farewell to Prince Charlie" and exhibited it at the Royal Academy. In 1893, *Scottish Notes & Queries* published an article by "W. T." in which he presents "incidents concerning Flora Macdonald, and the events of the '45, [which were] gleaned from her life by her granddaughter." In so doing, W. T. hoped "that they may induce a study of the history of the period to which they refer, while resting in a Highland clachan during a drenching rain."[24]

In 1895, a reviewer of Sarah Tytler's *The Macdonald Lass* (q.v.), described the book as Flora's "adventures gathered from a little book by the late Mr. MacGregor..." whose "information was [in turn] derived from one of Flora's grand-daughters."[25] Actually Mr. MacGregor used two of Flora's granddaughters as resources. He had used Mrs. Wylde's book as a source, and he knew Mary of Stein, Anne's daughter, on Skye. Mary died in 1858. A couple of years later, in 1897, Margaret Macalister Williamson published in the September number of *Lady's Realm* a piece called "The Real Flora MacDonald." Mrs. Williamson speaks with the authority that comes with being the great-great-grand-niece of Flora's husband Allan. Furthermore, she was the current custodian of a piece of the punch bowl that Charlie and Kingsburgh broke that June night in 1746. Mrs. Williamson also refers her readers to the oft-reported marriage proposal that Captain O'Neill made to Flora to protect her good name during her association with the Prince. Though it is unlikely that anyone (except perhaps the wishful O'Neill) took the proposal seriously, Mrs. Williamson explains that Flora did not accept it because she was already engaged to Allan. *Scottish Notes and Queries* called the piece "very well-informed" and "valuable for its beautifully reproduced illustrations of prints of the period." Mrs. Williamson's article is just one of many that appeared in the last decade of the century. In the months leading up to the dedication of the statue, the Inverness *Courier* carried a St. Valentine's Day article on Flora's burial and grave site and a week later a piece on her family.

On the more scholarly front, the close of the nineteenth century marked the publication at long last of Henry Paton's three-volume edition of Bishop Forbes's *The Lyon in Mourning* (1896) and of Walter Biggar Blaikie's companion piece *Itinerary...* in 1897. Thus fortified, history could begin to catch up to legend.

Chapter 13

Flora in Literature

A Song in Praise of Miss Flora MacDonald

Flora, virtuous, faithful maid,
  Thou pointed out by Heav'n!
To guide the hero in his way;
  To thee that trust was given.
Wreckt was our hope, thy charge and thee,
  And cruel death the fate;
Had not a powerful hand sent down
  Protection to thy boat.

Sure refuge to great Charles and thee,
  And darkness to those men,
Who sought for price the heir to kill,
  And watch'd a time to sin.
In state that powerful hand exerts
  Its attributes on high,
By secret means works out its ends,
  Withdrawn from human eye.

The mist which blinded William's fleet
  To you gave safety there.
A ray directive shone for you
  And led you where to steer.
O Happy nymph! thou sav'dst the Prince;
  Thy fame be handed down.
Thy name shall shine in annals fair
  And live from sire to son.[1]

THIS POEM, WHICH ROBERT FORBES ACQUIRED in 1748 and published in *The Lyon in Mourning*, is an indicator that Flora's fame had spread from the street to the drawing room and coffee house. We know that as the personification of virtue and fidelity, Flora was already enjoying bipartisan celebrity in London and Edinburgh. It seems, however, that those writing verses about her in the first years of her fame were Jacobite sympathizers. From 1749 Forbes includes four lines in Latin, which he renders into English thus:

> Vex'd with bad servants, thus old England said
> Prithee, dear Flora! let me have thy maid.
> Take her, says Flora, If I know my Burk,
> She is the girl to do Old England's work.[2]

Another example of Flora in verse is a poem "By Dr. King of Oxford upon seeing Miss Flora MacDonald's Picture." Dr. King, remember, is the ardent Jacobite who presented so unappealing a report of his 1750 meeting with Prince Charles at Lady Primrose's London residence. He is also the expert who pronounced Donald Roy MacDonald's ode on his wounded foot "quite respectable Latin." At this distance, we cannot identify with certainty the portrait which prompted Dr. King's paean to Flora. The poem is, of course, in Latin. It hails "pulcherrima Flora,/ Nata Donaldorum, servatrix Principis," and concludes "Semper amata/Semper honorata, insignissima Virgo, manebis."[3] Forbes provides a somewhat free translation in "From the Verses of Dr. King":

> Here, too, the beauteous Flora's taught t'assume,
> Than ere the goddess knew a brighter bloom.
> The faithful canvass softens with her smile,
> Who in the royal youth preserv'd the Isle.
> She led thro' treach'rous firths and ev'ry storm
> The hero lurking in the handmaid's form.
> O born to Better fate! O Heaven design'd
> To succour nations and preserve mankind.
> So to her son, as thro the wilds he stray'd,
> The Cyprian goddess shone a hidden aid.
> A veil of thick'ned air around she pours
> And safely lands in Carthage lofty towrs.

What thanks, O wondrous maid, to thee we owe!
As long as verse shall soar or canvass glow
So long thy name, thy praises shall remain,
The pencil's labour and the poet's strain.[4]

Flora lived some forty-four years—about two-thirds of her life—after her adventure with the Prince. Though thousands attended her funeral, the press gave her one-sentence obituaries; and as we learned from E. E. G., not until John's death did Flora's grave receive a proper monument.[5]

In the nearly eighty years between Flora's fame-producing action and John's monument, attitudes changed. The changes were not really in attitudes towards Flora, but towards the events in which she played a cameo role. Nowhere are these changed attitudes more clear than in the literature of the first half of the nineteen century. That Sir Walter Scott not only felt them but asserted them is virtually everywhere visible in his writings. As Ian Jack puts it,

> In the Jacobites Scott found the modern equivalent of the spirit of chivalry which he had admired as a boy in the pages of Froissart. It was for reasons imaginative rather than political that he loved to look back at those brave men "who did nothing in hate, but all in honour."[6]

In the introduction to *Redgauntlet,* Scott gives us this portrait of the Jacobites:

> Their love of past times, their tales of bloody battles against romantic odds, were all dear to the imagination, and their little idolatry of locks of hair, pictures, rings, ribbons, and other memorials of the time in which they still seemed to live, was an interesting enthusiasm; and although their political principles, had they existed in the relation of their fathers, might have rendered them dangerous...yet, as we now recollect them, there could not be on the earth supposed to exist persons better qualified to sustain the capacity of innocuous and respectable grandsires.[7]

There is the change: those who had once taken up arms against the established government of Britain were no longer "dangerous," but with their quaint "little idolatry" were "innocuous and respectable." "Dear to the imagination" does Scott find "their love of past times," and their love was his love and, for that matter, the love of Scott's romantic age.

Flora's son John described his view of the change in an article that he wrote for *Gentleman's Magazine* in November 1828:

> I well recollect my arrival in London, about half a century ago, on my way to India; and the disapprobation expressed in the streets of my Tartan dress; but now I see with satisfaction this variegated Highland manufacture prevalent as a favourite and tasteful costume, from the humble cottage to the superb castle. To Sir Walter Scott's elegant and fascinating writings we are to ascribe this wonderful revolution in public sentiment.[8]

Scott sold to the English the notion that the "bare-ars'd lousy pack" of "thieves and rogues" were all gone away and things Caledonian were "in." In 1789 Prince George had actually worn highland dress to a masquerade ball, and "great ladies affected the lofty plumed bonnets and short military coats of the highland regiments now so visible in the streets of London."[9] Although as far back as the 1380s the chronicler John Fordun noted the same Highland-Lowland divisions that prevailed into the early and middle eighteenth century,[10] in their haste to bestow this new respectability on the Scots, the English tended to lump together all of their neighbors to the north. After what one writer measures as "centuries of derision and contempt,"[11] the Highlander came to represent all of Scotland. As Flora's son John put it, writing from England,

> In this country, the Scottishman and the Highlander are always confounded, while in fact they are as distinct as speaking a different language, and having different manners and customs, can constitute a difference.[12]

Flora's son greatly admired Scott for what he has done to bring the English and the Scots together in the years following the '45.

> He, with an uncommon felicity of style peculiarly his own, and with a happy display of the heroic incidents and charac-

ters found in the histories of our Island, has so conciliated feelings formerly at variance, and has, with admirable talent, created so much mutual sympathy and relative estimation, that the effect has been complete, not only in eradicating the sad prejudices that unfortunately long prevailed, but in substituting an increasing and reciprocal esteem.[13]

Later in the article John wrote about the "captivating charm and grace" of Scott's "finely-imagined female characters," like "the gentle, but heroic, Flora Macyvere," a character in *Waverley.*

Apparently Scott was drawn more to the martial Jacobite women as fictional characters than he was to Flora, for she is mentioned but once in all of his novels: in the first chapter of *The Surgeon's Daughter* (1827), when a character refers to those dangerous days of yesteryear and the Jacobite ladies of quality who, though charged with "high treason," were "all favourably dealt with—Lady Ogilvy, Lady MacIntosh, Flora MacDonald, and all."[14] Scott also, of course, recounts as history Flora's role in the flight of the Prince in *Tales of a Grandfather* (1827–28).

Despite this single allusion to Flora in all his fiction, Scott seems to have retained an awareness of Flora and her developing role in the legends of Sir Walter's Scotland. At one point, he apparently planned to build around "The Lady of the Lake" a setting in which the poem would be told "for the amusement of the Young Pretender," and to include among the characters in the supporting framework "the heroic Flora MacDonald."[15]

Actually, Flora MacDonald had already appeared as a principal character in a work of imaginative literature before Scott took her up. On February 18, 1802, there was "acted for the first time at Paris" a play entitled *Charles Edward Stuart, The Pretender in Scotland, or, The Misfortunes of an Exile.* According to the title page, the play was "interdicted and suppressed by the command of Buonaparte after the second night." It was "brought forward again by His French Majesty's Company of Comedians, June 9, 1814, and acted repeatedly with applause at Exeter, this season." It was first performed at Exeter on Monday, April 7, 1823.[16] In the British Museum catalog, John MacDonald, son of Flora and a resident of Exeter after his army career, is listed as the author; in The University of Aberdeen's MacBean Collection, however, he is listed as translator of a play written by Alexandre V. Pineux-Duval.

The piece, in three short acts, presents another meeting between Flora and the Prince, this time at the hall of the Duke and Duchess of Athol. The Prince arrives by way of a shipwreck and once again escapes just as Cumberland comes upon the scene. Flora observes, remembers, and converses with Charlie and with the Duke and Duchess. This time the Prince's savior is the choric and comical servant Thomas. Songs like "Lochaber No More" and "Auld Lang Syne" set the mood, and a chorus of fishermen presents antecedent action.

John MacDonald was a prolific writer on such diverse topics as history, military tactics, Napoleon, telecommunications, Ossian, natural science, decorum of public worship, and magnetism. For his treatise on diurnal variation of the magnetic needle he was elected a Fellow of the Royal Society in 1800.[17] Sadly, though, he never told us much about his mother. He left that task to his daughter, and she, too, chose to keep Flora behind a scrim of fiction.

Whatever John's thought's about his mother, Mrs. Grant of Laggan suggested some in these lines which she addressed to Flora's youngest son:

> Let those of wealth and empty titles proud
> Dazzle with idle pomp the vulgar crowd;
> 'Tis thine a nobler ancestry to boast
> For courage famed, for virtue honoured most.
> Calm fortitude in female graces drest
> Adorn'd the generous Flora's dauntless breast,
> With ev'ry milder charm that sweetens life, —
> The tender mother, and the virtuous wife, —
> And all that loyal truth and courage claim,
> Such honours deck the gentle heroine's name,
> Who now to thee bequeaths her well-won fame.[18]

Most of Flora's 19th-century literary appearances were, of course, in verse. In the early part of the century, collections of Jacobite poems and songs were quite popular. Indeed, we must remember that many of the songs most likely to appear on a list of Jacobite hits—tunes like "Skye Boat Song," "Jacobites by Name," "Come O'er the Stream Charlie," "The Hundred Pipers," "Wae's Me for Prince Charlie," "Who'll be King but Charlie," and, fairest of them all, "Will Ye No Come Back Again" were all written long after the '45.[19] In 1817, the

Highland Society of London commissioned James Hogg, "the Ettrick shepherd," to compile a definitive collection of the old songs, which he did, claiming that in the process he did not purify or refine his material.[20]

It is in these collections gathered during the height of the British Romanticism that Flora is put forward. A frequently used vehicle is that in which words of lament are put into Flora's mouth. "The Lament of Flora MacDonald" (published by Hogg as "Flora MacDonald's Farewell") "Flora's Lament," and "Flora's Lament for Charlie" are illustrative.[21]

As might be expected, another common device was to put words about Flora into Charlie's mouth. In one such piece published by Andrew Lang and entitled merely "A Song," the Prince remembers "But one poor maid, with gown and plaid,/Convoy'd me through the isles;..."[22] The best and best known of this genre, of course, is William Aytoun's "Charles Edward at Versailles," with its famous lines:

> Give me back my trusted comrades—
> Give me back my Highland maid—
> Nowhere beats the heart so kindly
> As beneath the tartan plaid.[23]

In the following final twenty-four lines of the poem, Aytoun has the Prince address Flora directly:

> Flora! when thou wert beside me,
> In the wilds of far Kintail—
> When the cavern gave us shelter
> From the blinding sleet and hail—
> When we lurked within the thicket,
> And, beneath the waning moon,
> Saw the sentry's bayonet glimmer,
> Heard him chant his listless tune—
> When the howling storm o'ertook us,
> Drifting down the island's lee,
> And our crazy bark was whirling
> Like a nutshell on the sea—
> When the nights were dark and dreary,
> And amid the fern we lay.

Faint and foodless, sore with travel,
Waiting for the streaks of day;
When thou wert an angel to me,
Watching my exhausted sleep—
Never didst thou hear me murmur—
Couldst thou see how now I weep!
Bitter tears and sobs of anguish,
Unavailing though they be,
Oh! the brave-the brave and noble—
That have died in vain for me![24]

Flora receives recognition for having shared with the Prince more
hardships than in fact she did, but at the same time she is apart from
the action; she is "an angel," someone to watch over him, a personified
abstraction to which the long apostrophe is addressed.

A dissenting view of Charlie's memories of Flora is expressed at
the end of "On the Beach of Portree, Skye, 30th June, 1746":

...Across the sea,
   In sunnier lands, where hearts beat not more true,
The Maiden lived not in the memory
   Of him whose life to her fond zeal was due.
Forgotten all the goodness and the grace—
   Has gratitude for ever taken wing?
Forgotten that kind sympathetic face—
   Ingratitude forgetteth everything![25]

"Prince Charles and Flora MacDonald's Welcome to Skye" engag-
ingly describes "Two bonny maidens,/...Come over the Minch,/

There is Flora, my honey,
So dear and so bonny,
And one that is tall,
And comely withal;
Put the one as my king,
And the other my queen,
They're welcome unto
The Isle of Skye again.[26]

And MacGregor offers this variation on the theme of "The Skye Boat Song":

> 'Tis midnight: a lone boat is one the sea,
>   And dark clouds gather, but no thoughts of fear
> Chill those brave hearts! A princely refugee
>   Disguised—a faithful maiden sitting near,
> Upon whose cheek anon there falls a tear—
>   Fond woman's pledge of sympathy. A crew,
> Trusty and gallant, labour at the oars.
>   The shifting wind white showers of spray uprears
> Like incense heavenward; the water roars,
>   While from huge murky clouds the lurid lightning
> pours![27]

Another "Song" published and described by Lang as an "artless ditty about Flora" opens with an echo of Hogg's "Lament" before turning to our lady:

> There, fair Flora sat complaining,
>   For the absence of our K - - g,
> Crying, Charlie, lovely Charlie,
>   When shall we two meet again?[28]

In the middle stanza the poet combines Flora's musical talent with her politics:

> Fair Flora's love it was surprising,
>   Like to diadems in array;
> And her dress of tartan plaidie
>   Was like a rainbow in the sky;
> And each minute she tuned her spinnet,
>   And Royal Jamie was the tune,
> Crying, C - - - - -s, Royal C - - - - -s,
> When shalt thou enjoy thy own?[29]

One of Flora's laments bears attention because of its suggestion of a sexual relation between Flora and the Prince that forms a minor part of the legend but, as the teacher on the train showed and as shall be seen in more detail shortly, carries forward into this century. "Flora's Lament for Charlie" eschews the passion of the Jacobite cause and presents instead an unrequited and abandoned girl who has perhaps been "row'd in a plaidie" and left to resolve her grief alone.

> Why, my Charlie, dost thou leave me,
>   Dost thou flee they Flora's arms?
> Were thy vows but to deceive me,
>   Valiant o'er my yielding charms?
> All I bore for thee, sweet Charlie,
>   Want of sleep, fatigue, and care;
> Brav'd the ocean late and early,
>   Left my friends, for thou wast fair.
>
> Sleep, ye winds that waft him from me;
>   Blow, ye western breezes, blow—
> Swell the sail; for I love Charlie.—
>   Ah! they whisper, Flora, no.
> Cold she sinks beneath the billow,
>   Dash'd from yonder rocky shore;
> Flora, pride and flower of Isla,
>   Ne'er to meet her Charlie more.
>
> Dark the night, the tempest howling,
>   Bleak along the western sky;
> Hear the dreadful thunders rolling,
>   See the forked lightning fly.
> No more we'll hear the maid of Isla,
>   Pensive o'er the rocky steep;
> Her last sigh was breathed for Charlie!
>   As she sunk into the deep.[30]

Even given poetic license this seems highly fanciful. As an antidote, albeit similarly fanciful, there is "Flora MacDonald's Love Song," in which her thoughts are not with the Prince, but with her husband.

> Allan, would that thou wert with me!
> Allan donn, my dear, my treasure,
> Heavy load of love I carry
>   Allan, would that thou wert near me!
>
> Harp nor fiddle e'er can lift it,
> Nor shrill pipes with lilting chanter.

Allan, would that thou wert near me!

Sad, each day for thee I'm longing,
Gone with thee all joy and gladness.
    Allan, would that thou wert near me!

In deep groves and leafy woodlands,
Fain would I with thee be wandering.
    Allan, would that thou wert near me!

Allan of the curling ringlets,
Sweet to me thy honey-kisses.
    Allan, would that thou wert near me![31]

Flora MacDonald: A Tale of Freedom and Loyalty is a long poem (eighty pages, two thousand or more lines) that appeared in America in 1870.[32] The poem begins with a dialogue between Warthe and Egan, two guests at Flora's funeral and moves to a three-stanza elegy, "Sleep, cherished one, the night is dark,..." The scene and time shift to the first settlement of North Carolina at Roanoke Island, and brings in, among others, Raleigh, Hobart, and Manteo, and features another elegiac song, "Farewell—if e'er a vision blest/The wayward pilgrim in his path,..." Part III moves into the eighteenth century and the mountains of North Carolina, introducing the Regulators and Governor Tryon, and a Song of Freedom, "Speed ye, ye valiant..." sung by Howel, a poet. In Part IV—The Battle, Flora arrives and engages in a dialogue with Letia about danger and duty.

If danger threat, I would not, therefore, shrink,
Because 'tis such; nay, rather on the brink,
E'en seek it, when it must by some be met:
Tho' safer 'twere, delay, 'tis no regret,
T'ave come, nor ill-timed, do I ween the cast;
If soon, 'twere o'er, who knows how long 't may last?[33]

Letia remains unconvinced and rails against the ill fortune that has put her there. Flora replies,

.... Nay, Letia, 'tis a glorious boon,
To be so opportune placed, t'obviate harm:
Be not concerned, then, 'tis a blest alarm,

> More than the contrary, some strife is nigh,
> Just when there's most to fear, that I am by.[34]

The strife o'er, the battle lost, Flora returns to Scotland contemplating all that has happened.

> But Flora stays apart, absorbed in thought;
> Which many a recollection recent brought.
> The prospect fades, the landward view is lost,
> The ocean's visual boundary is crost;
> To Flora's mind, her brief sojourn, 'twould seem
> A various, yet no incoherent dream.[35]

Benjamin Herre, the author, concludes with what begins as a classical tag and settles into anticlimax.

> The minstrel rose, and his spent state restored,
> Warthe, Egan, followed at th'adjoining board;
> Their eye toward the antique timepiece cast,
> The Tocsin tolls, — it is their day's repast![36]

Herre knows the basics of Flora's legend. He includes references to the winding sheet and the naval engagement in which Flora broke her arm. The verse throughout is pretty rough, as these sample passages show, and the reader must bring to the poem curiosity and stamina.

In these poems of the eighteenth and nineteenth centuries as in many of the other presentations of the Flora legend, we see little of Flora as a real person. She remains apart and largely stylized in description and sentiment. Finally, it is perhaps appropriate to close this survey of Flora in verse with mention of a couple of collections in which, surprisingly, she does not appear.

One is the Jacobite poems of Caroline Oliphant, Lady Nairne. Born in 1766 and named after the Prince, Lady Nairne wrote several of Scotland's best-known traditional songs. Nowhere in her staunchly pro-Jacobite verses—not in "Will ye no come back again" or "Charlie is my darling" or "The Hundred Pipers"—does Flora appear. Perhaps Lady Nairne found it unnecessary to share her Prince with another woman.[37]

The other collection in which Flora does not appear is the poems of her kinsman Alexander MacDonald (Alasdair MacMhaighstir Alasdair). His "Oran Araid" (A Certain Song) is a dialogue between the Prince and the Gaels in which Am Prionnsa (The Prince) thanks the MacDonalds for their assistance: "Beannachd gu leir le Clann-Domh-nuill,"

> My whole blessing on Clan Donald,
>   In my peril you were my aid,
> Both on islands and on mainland
>   Ever willing followers were;
> Many the hill and sea and moorland
>   We travelled on the course of death,
> But God has saved us from the danger
>   Of the bloodhounds at our heels.[38]

He misses a good spot in which to commemorate Flora. Perhaps to put things right, when the Reverends A. Macdonald and A. Macdonald, DD ("both joint authors of *The Clan Donald*") published their bilingual, annotated edition of the *The Poems of Alexander MacDonald*, they wrote:

To the Undying Memory
of
Flora MacDonald
Cousin of the Bard
Daughter of Ranald MacDonald of Milton,
And 5th in Descent From
Allan 9th Chief of Clanranald,
Whose Noble and Heroic Rescue of
Prince Charles in the Crisis of his Fate
Shed imperishable glory on her name,
Her Clan, and her Country,
This Volume, which abounds in
Devotion to the Royal House of Stuart,
Is reverently dedicated by her Clansmen,
The Editors[39]

It is with fiction that we shall round out our consideration of Flora in nineteenth-century literature. Mrs. Wylde's *Autobiography* of 1870 was, of course, a full-length novel about Flora. The repeated references during this period to information supplied by Mrs. Wylde make it clear that the lady was held in higher regard in the first two decades after the publication of her book than subsequent biographers have seen fit to ascribe to her. Even MacGregor, whose biography was for many years "definitive," displays dependence on her despite his disapproval of the fictional coating she gave her work. Mrs. Wylde was, however, not just another amateur dabbling in family reminiscence. She had already published *The Tablette Book of Ladye Mary Keyes* in 1861. She followed with the "autobiography" of her grandmother in 1870. In her next work, in 1873, she stuck to the genre of facsimile autobiography with *The Life and Wonderful Adventures of "Tatty Testado," an Autobiography*. The final work of which we have record is *The Widow Unmasked; or The Firebrand in the Family, a Novel*, which she produced in 1875. It seems reasonable to assume that Mrs. Wylde knew what she was doing when she chose the autobiographical genre for her book about her illustrious grandmother. To someone trying to work back to Flora, far more disappointing than the choice of genre is the fact that Mrs. Wylde leaves us without a guide to her sources.

At the close of the century came another full-length novel about Flora: *The MacDonald Lass*, written in 1895 by Henrietta Keddie under the pen name of Sarah Tytler. Tytler's novel covers Flora's life from her meeting with the Prince to the eve of her marriage to Allan, a span of about four years, and about 60 percent of it treats those ten days in June 1746.

In the course of the novel the author suggests that "O'Neal" was one of the seven men of Moidart, that Flora was arrested on Uist and, that she went to a school in Edinburgh run by the Misses Henderson. We also hear that among Flora's gentlemen callers while she was in captivity on the *Bridgewater* were Lord President Duncan Forbes, poet and "gentle shepherd" Alan Ramsay, and husband-to-be Allan MacDonald. Flora meets "O'Neal" on the *Bridgewater*, but she does not slap his face. Among the details of Flora's London sojourn, Sarah Tytler includes entrance to the Tower through Traitors' Gate, the oft-recounted visit with the Prince of Wales, and the equally familiar departure for the north in the company of Malcolm MacLeod.

According to the author, Flora saw the Prince whom she helped to escape as "little else than a hapless young man," and the one she saw four years later in London as besotted with "shameless profligacy" and accompanied by his mistress Clementina Walkinshaw, who had "fed and fatted herself on him."[40]

Sarah Tytler appends to her novel a three-chapter epilogue giving "briefly, in narrative the particulars which have been preserved of Flora MacDonald's later years." The first chapter she devotes completely to the Johnson-Boswell visit of 1773, the second to the North Carolina years, and the third to Flora's death on Skye. Among the notable particulars touched upon are the deaths in North Carolina of two unnamed children, Flora's return from Carolina directly to Britain, and the traditional broken arm during a naval battle on the voyage homeward bound.

Though Sarah Tytler brings Flora's time with the Prince into largely unromanticized perspective, she follows conventional, unsubstantiated legend in her retelling of the North Carolina story. Here, in this telling of Flora's story a little more than one hundred years after her death, elements of the old biographical order blend with those of the new.

Chapter 14

Twentieth-Century Imaginings

"Courage is our history and our heritage. Courage we have brought from our misty isles, from our glens and mountains. Let us show it here in our new home."

—INGLIS FLETCHER,
THE SCOTSWOMAN

SHE WAS "BEAUTIFUL, WITH UNRULY DARK HAIR, big brown eyes mirroring her gentle loving soul." She could remind one of the picture of "Diana of the Uplands." So wrote Emmuska, Baroness Orczy of Flora MacDonald in the September 26, 1934 issue of *The North China Herald*.[1] The paper had been running a series of pieces— "special articles," it called them—under the general title of "Royal Romances." The Baroness, creator of the Scarlet Pimpernel, Lady Molly of Scotland Yard, and a couple of other detective types, served up "Flora and the Bonnie Prince" in terms that by the standards of the times fairly sizzled. This was the piece that moved Allan R. MacDonald "to vindicate [Flora's] character" in the last article that he wrote before the posthumous publication of *The Truth about Flora MacDonald*.

The Baroness begins, as would befit such a tale, with the continental version of the meeting. Flora is riding her pony; the Prince stops her; she recognizes him, dismounts and, of course, falls on her knees. She kisses his hand, which the Baroness says was merely "soiled," as opposed to covered with scabs and festering sores. They hit it off immediately: "The rapture of lying in one another's arms must have outweighed for the young lovers the sorrows of the past and the terrors of the future." Obviously she was resolved to save her beloved. But how? "With the play of her lovely eyes she subjugated a Captain of militia

167

and obtained a permit" to cross to Skye with Betty Burke. The Baroness seems uninterested in the fact that this captain of militia whom Flora vamped was her stepfather. On the crossing to Skye, the Baroness rhapsodizes, "The Prince and his young lover were alone save for the silent ignorant boatmen—alone in their ship of dreams." After all, "They were young and loved passionately."

As readers well knew, the couple reached Skye safely. What they did not know is that

> On that very day, tradition or perhaps legend tells, the Prince sent imperiously for a priest, and was joined in holy wedlock to the beautiful girl whom he had loved and to whom he owed his life.

According to Baroness Orczy, Kingsburgh and his wife witnessed the ceremony. The newlyweds part with noble restraint. Flora is subsequently arrested, taken to London, tried for treason, condemned to death, lodged in the Tower awaiting execution, and pardoned by King George.

The Baroness confides that rumors of the marriage eventually got around, but Flora always denied them strenuously. Not because in 1750 she had married the son of the witnesses, mind you, but because she did not wish to interfere with any politically expedient marriage that might come the Prince's way. In later years, we are assured, Flora thought back to her Prince and

> those wild days in Portree, when heedless of danger and laughing at the thought of pursuit, he lingered in the house of Kingsburgh by the side of his exquisite young bride, his 'Flower of the Isles.'

Having brought her readers squirming to this point, the Baroness writes the bottom line: "This, at least, is a fact, that when Flora died, her winding sheet was one which had been on the bed at Portree on her wedding night." (Over Mrs. Kingsburgh's dead body!)

A year later, in 1935, Carole May Anima Lenanton published *Over the Water*, a well-researched and engaging piece of historical fiction. Familiar names take on credible shapes. Felix O'Neill is "that hooknosed little captain." Nigel Gresley, "an enormous boy with a face as pink as a carnation under his white bob-wig," gives up his cabin on the *Bridgewater* for Flora. The author puts Flora in the Tower under the supervision of "elderly, ungenial" Colonel [sic] Williamson. The meeting between Flora and the Prince of Wales occurs at Mr. Dick's house. Lady Primrose, a forty-year-old widow of six years, had let her house in Essex Street for the summer and hired a more attractive house in Bolton Row. As to the parting of Flora and the Prince at Portree, after the crown/half crown exchange, "A terrible pain contracted Flora's bosom. With a sudden movement the tall figure above her bent and kissed her twice, hotly and quickly." After the Prince has gone, Flora and Neil MacKeckan sob in each other's arms. Of Allan, the author has one of the characters observe what several who know Flora's story may have thought as well: "[Allan] won't be content to spend the rest of his days glorying in the knowledge that he's Miss Flory Macdonald's husband."[2]

On November 20, 1939, playwright and outdoor dramatist Paul Green introduced to the audience in the Lafayette Opera House in Fayetteville, North Carolina, *The Highland Call*, "A Symphonic Play of American History in two acts with hymn tunes, folksongs, ballads, and dance."[3] Here for perhaps the first time we see Flora in a different light—as representative of the old order newly synthesized. The swearing of allegiance with which the play opens buries the broadswords of Jacobite resistance to the de facto crown. In the list of characters, Green describes Flora as "a Scotch heroine and British loyalist," and when she is about to address the Highlanders at Cross Creek, she is introduced and synthesized as the "preserver of Bonnie Prince Charlie, loyal daughter of the empire and ward of his majesty, King George the Third." Thus, at the end of the play, with her new cause lost, Flora sounds a bitter and cynical note when she predicts the aftermath of American independence.

> You'll see the meaning of this liberty—how the states will quarrel among themselves, civil war will be bred and the land overrun, how the rich will oppress the poor because they'll have the power to do it. How greed and avarice will flourish, waste and confusion, because they are free to. And the voice of the people will be bought and sold like cattle in the marketplace. And the land will be gutted and ruined and the treasures of the mountains and forests rooted up as if by

swine—and this nation of liberty and free men you talk of
will become a land of demagogues and office seekers and
bloated slave drivers. And so it's ended now. All the old days
are ended....And for me and mine there's nothing to do
now but to deny this land and turn our faces back to the old
world—there to—die.[4]

It remains for the comic drover and local legend in her own right, Jennie Ban MacNeill, to see a different future in the younger generation,
"so fresh and young and hopeful."[5]

While most of the play's material is drawn from historical facts,
Green acknowledges that four characters are "entirely imaginary," as
are the two children referred to in the last scene. These he attributes to
legend, not fact. Girls from Flora MacDonald College in nearby Red
Springs appeared as Highland dancers in that first production, and
Charles Gildersleeve Vardell, the son of the college's president-emeritus
and head of its music department, wrote the play's two organ preludes.

In 1965 Green reworked his material, reducing it to one act and
removing the music, and called it *The Sheltering Plaid*. He retained
much the same tone and the idea of the old order yielding place to the
new, and Flora as synthesized representative of that old order. In the
list of characters, Flora has changed from "Scottish heroine and British
loyalist" to "the famous Scottish heroine."

In 1975 he brought out a revised edition of the original play as
part of the Cumberland County bicentennial celebration. This he
chose to dedicate to the memory of Flora MacDonald, noting that he
had dedicated the first edition to another Flora, his mother. The 1975
version retains the two-act structure of the original, but adds another
scene to each act. Flora, too, changes. This time she is listed after Allan
as simply "his wife." Her bitterness is softened somewhat as well.

The long speech quoted above undergoes interesting modification.
The prophecy that opens the speech is gone. Perhaps the prophecy was
too Cassandra-like for a nation's or even a county's bicentennial celebration. The "great and glorious empire of English men and women"
becomes a "great and glorious union of English men and women."
The new version of the speech then concludes as did the original:
"And for me and mine there's nothing to do now but to deny this land
and turn our faces back to the old world, there to—die.[6] And Jennie

Ban sees freedom in "the symbol of Flora McDonald," but still turns to the next generation to see what is "fresh and young and hopeful."[7]

The Highland Call was not Flora's first depiction on the musical stage. C. M. Smith tells us he saw a comic opera during the 1886–87 season. And in London in 1900, S. M. Lyne brought out *The Rose of Sleat or, The Days of Prince Charlie*, "An Historical Drama Cantata" in three brief acts intended, the author says, for school groups and other amateur performers. The cast of characters is familiar: the Prince, Captain O'Neil, Neil MacEachin (identified as Flora's manservant), Kingsburgh and Lady Kingsburgh, Lady Margaret MacDonald, Flora's servant Katie, and "boatmen, soldiers, peasants, fishwives, girls, etc." The play opens at Flora's birthday at Milton, but Flora won't dance; her heart is too heavy. It ends at Portree with a chorus of fishwives singing "Caller Herrin'."

On a somewhat grander scale, around 1900 an article appeared stating that the Scottish composer Learmont Drysdale was "engaged in throwing the story of Flora MacDonald into operatic form."[8] According to the article and confirmed by notes in Drysdale's own hand, the original plan had the opera consisting of three acts, with principal episodes set in a "cave near Ormaclade in South Uist, Kingsburgh in Skye, and the Pass of Glenmoriston."[9] Drysdale, however, says that these scenes will follow one "laid in Holyrood during one of the receptions held by Prince Charlie...at the zenith of his glory after Prestonpans." Drysdale intends to keep the opera "as historically true as we can without ignoring theatrical license and opportunities for picturesque and dramatic effects."[10] The work remains unfinished, retaining its loose ends. Below the list of characters in the front of the libretto, Drysdale notes that "the opera is historical, but not history." The Holyrood scene mentioned in Drysdale's notes does not appear in the libretto. In correspondence that may date from 1908 are letters from Andrew Lang, apparently in reply to Drysdale. In one Lang says, "...We can look at the scenario, but my verse is very unpopular, and I know nothing of music though I know plenty of Prince Charles...."[11] Was Drysdale seeking the services of Scotland's reigning man of letters as a lyricist, or was he merely consulting him as an authority on the subject? Lang had published his elegant biography of the Prince in 1903.

In 1940, a year after *The Highland Call*, Inglis Fletcher gave Flora a cameo role in one of her several novels tracing the history of white settlement of North Carolina. *Raleigh's Eden* treats events leading up to and beginning the revolution. At a party honoring the newly arrived Highland heroine, the novel's principal female character, on seeing Flora for the first time, describes her as "...a proud woman, so composed and tranquil she seems almost lifeless."[12] A little later the same character observes that "Whatever Flora had in her secret heart, the face she showed the world held the tranquillity and dignity of a great soul." Perhaps stereotypically we think of such a woman as being tall, and so Mrs. Fletcher makes Flora, ignoring thereby every eyewitness description of our lady. Nevertheless, in emphasizing Flora's tranquil and dignified composure, Mrs. Fletcher has read Flora well, and to her credit, has not sought to insert behind the mask qualities that do not belong there, perhaps with one exception. Following tradition, Mrs. Fletcher does have Flora at the Highlanders' camp near Moore's Creek come "out of the night, [and] grasping the scarred battle flags she roused them to pledge themselves to follow the Macdonalds to death or victory."[13]

Mrs. Fletcher works some ironic foreshadowing into her tale when, soon after their arrival, Flora and Allan gaze at their star and predict happiness in North Carolina.[14] After the rout at Moore's Creek Bridge, Flora extends her hand "in a gracious gesture" to a character and of what has just happened says, "...it is my evil fate which will always pursue me and mine." She then goes off to be near her prisoner husband "in his dark hour."[15]

Fourteen years later Inglis Fletcher returned to Flora when she made her the title character in *The Scotswoman*, a novel that centers on Flora and her extended family from just before their departure from Skye to just after Allan's capture at Moore's Creek Bridge. Flora remains true to the characterization that Mrs. Fletcher had previously given her. She is not a zealot burning with a martial spirit; she is certainly no Hanoverian and cannot understand Allan's desire to support that House. In fact, throughout most of the novel, she seeks to remain neutral and is concerned by Allan's yielding to political pressure. We see her going for advice to Hugh MacDonald her stepfather, who had settled nearby, and we listen with her as her minister Mr. Bethune argues that neutrality must be active. To stay out of the rebellion, he says, one must oppose the rebellion.

In the end, of course, Flora supports her husband. Mrs. Fletcher describes the scene in which, under a mighty oak, Flora addresses the assembled Highlanders. She wore a dress of the MacDonald tartan, but for the occasion she

> had laid aside her favourite and customary ancient hunting plaid. To her it was a symbolic act: she hoped her men would encounter no prey on this journey. At the sight of her a great shout went up.[16]

General MacDonald quieted the throng and introduced "Flora Mac-Donald, saviour of Prince Charlie in the '45...." In a voice that "was fire and ice," she talked to them. Some of the fire:

> What Highlander has hung back when his chief called? What mother or wife has grudged her sons or husbands when strong arms and brave hearts were needed? Courage is our history and our heritage. Courage we have brought from our misty isles, from our glens and mountains. Let us show it here in our new home.[17]

The next day as the army marched off to war, Flora watched them pass in review. She

> sat stiffly erect on her white horse under the spreading crown of the great oak and watched the Highlanders stride by. Her heart swelled as they passed her, their faces quiet and determined, their kilts swaying to the rhythm of their step. Young faces and old blurred as her eyes filled with tears. With a great effort, she sat firmly erect as each line of men proudly saluted their beloved Flora.[18]

On her way to these climactic scenes Mrs. Fletcher gives us some refreshing glimpses into Flora's earlier life. In describing the first meeting of Flora and the Prince, for example, Mrs. Fletcher offers a variation on the Cordara/Voltaire version of the meeting It seems that every night since Culloden Flora "had been praying to the good Lord for [the Prince's] well-being." Upon realizing that the "golden lad" standing before her was her Prince, her lost King, "I sank to my knees and thanked God I'd seen him safe with my own eyes."[19] Mrs.

Fletcher also gives us the refrain and two stanzas of a song that she says Flora had written. She tells us that the room in which the Prince had slept was a secret room. She has Flora's faithful Katie say that no one had been allowed to use the room until "that fat London man who wrote the books, him and his friend," slept there. And she has Flora say that she will take the Prince's sheets with her to America.[20]

In the mid-fifties, two novels about Flora were published for younger readers. Elizabeth Coatsworth's *Aunt Flora* (1953)[21] deals with the North Carolina period by focusing on Nepsie MacQueen, Flora's niece. Here, as in Green's treatment, the young girl personifies the spirit of the new country against the loyalist predilections of her famous aunt. A year later, Lillian De La Torre, who elsewhere turned Dr. Johnson into a detective and Boswell into his investigator,[22] brought out *The White Rose of Stuart, The story of Flora MacDonald, heroine of the '45*,[23] a well-researched, well-written account of the tale.

In 1948 Alexander Korda set out to film *Bonnie Prince Charlie*, with David Niven in the title role, Jack Hawkins as Lord George Murray, and Margaret Leighton as Flora MacDonald. Lovers of the legend like the film better than do film critics. Niven calls it "one of those huge florid extravaganzas that reeked of disaster from the start." Though Clemence Dane is credited with the screenplay, Niven says there was never a completed script and that the writers were never more than two days ahead of the actors.[24]

Most of the familiar characters are present. One invention is a character called Donald of Eriskay, a shepherd, piper, and factotum substituted for Neil MacEachain and resembling a Highland Gabby Hays. Despite the film's glaring historical inaccuracies, Flora comes across admirably. Though we believe her when she says she is non-partisan, as the picture opens she is playing and singing a popular air about "somebody" over the water in Italy. On their way to Portree, Flora says to Charlie,

> A week ago I had my life snug and warm about me as a furred cloak with naught in it but kind memories and clear hopes. Then you come, like a high wind, and blow my cloak away. Where's my past? Emptied out of my mind! Where's the future? Blown away to nowhere.... I'm no question mark on the page o' history. I'm just the one whose cloak was blown away.

Traditional scenes and dialogue are woven into the picture's story line, though not where students of the legend might expect to find them. When Charlie arrives in Scotland, Kinlochmoidart anticipates Lady Nairne by a good many years when he tells the young Prince, "Better lo'ed ye canna be; nevertheless, in the name of sanity we say to you 'Go home'". This sets up Charlie's "I am home." About 110 minutes later, Flora watches Charlie sail for France while a chorus sings "Will Ye No Come Back Again."

In addition to Paul Green, three dramatists have brought Flora to the stage in the twentieth century. In 1945 Clare Johnson Marley, an alumna of Flora MacDonald College, wrote the verse drama *Flora MacDonald Preserver of Prince Charles* as her thesis for an M. A. in dramatic arts at the University of North Carolina. At Chapel Hill she studied under Professor Frederick Koch, founder and director of the Carolina Playmakers and mentor of Paul Green. In fact, Professor Koch suggested that Marley write her thesis play about Flora, "an interesting character" through whom Marley could pursue her interest in Scottish folklore.[25] Dr. Vardell was pleased to include performance of the play in the college's "Semi-Centennial Celebration" in the spring of 1946.

Marley undertakes her task with enthusiasm, but the work is flawed, as assigned topics sometimes are. Literary license gives way to obvious but inexplicable—and thus distracting—inaccuracies. In her first scene, a masked ball in the Edinburgh home of the Countess Eglinton, we meet several celebrities from both sides of the '45. Though the year is 1745, Robert Forbes is already a bishop. The Duke of Cumberland says he has just received dispatches describing the British defeat at Fontenoy; if so, he moved even faster after his defeat than Cope would after his. We learn that George III is already on the throne and that Frederick, Prince of Wales is his son. The dialogue taxes. To Charlie's question, "What say you,/My bonnie maiden— wilt thou sing a merry/Ballad or chant a Celtic lay?" Flora says it will be a lay and then sings "The Bonnie Banks of Loch Lommond" to Charlie while Neil MacEachain, identified as "the tutor," unpacks a picnic hamper, plays the impudent fool in a poor imitation of Shakespeare's Touchstone or Feste, and is repeatedly admonished by his mistress to hold his tongue. Captain Fergusson actually meets Betty Burke, the gangling Irish spinning maid, and even seeks a kiss but doesn't penetrate the disguise. To draw Fergusson's attention away from the Prince, Flora does a Highland fling while singing "The Campbells Are Coming."[26]

In the third act we see Flora and the faithful Kate, who has become an old nurse, in the Tower. Among Flora's visitors are Bishop Forbes, Lady Primrose, and the Prince of Wales. Lady Primrose pushes past Mangy Dick, the guard, to meet Flora and to speak of Commodore Smith's fatherly kindness towards Flora and of his having had Ramsay, not Wilson, paint Flora. She mentions Johnson, Boswell, and Goldsmith, three literary stooges who are trying to gain admittance to the Tower to see Flora. Johnson has already written his famous tribute, Boswell has written down everything Johnson has said, and Goldsmith has written a novel that he can't get published.[27] The Prince of Wales thinks Charlie intended to make Flora Queen of England, but he will spare her life and ship her to North Carolina if she will pledge her loyalty to his father George III. Finally Flora admits reverence for "the English saints" and admiration for "the democratic ideals o' England's writers," but vows to fight until she dies "the scoundrels and the tyrants — at home — or in any land."[28] That's good enough for Frederick; he came to the Tower her enemy but leaves her friend. At the final curtain Flora contemplates the future:

> ...I begin
> To see a new light — a ray of hope in that
> Wondrous new world — where men wi' high resolve
> Make plans born o' faith in the rights o' man —
> A lasting peace-universal brotherhood —
> And now — America — great new land across
> The sea — Scotland I ha'e lost and sae — I'll place
> My faith in thee.

Another play about Flora's American sojourn originated in the Scottish town of St. Andrews, noted for its golf and its university. In 1976, at the suggestion of Steven Watson, then principal of the university, Alex Paterson wrote *Flora in Carolina*. Paterson, whose "life and its influence on the community of St Andrews will be remembered alongside... Andrew Lang," was a journalist and historian widely active in Scottish community theater.[29] Created as a commemorative piece for the American bicentennial, Paterson's play celebrates Scottish ties to America while, by focusing on Flora and her family, maintains the appropriately loyalist position.

The play begins on a ship sailing up the Cape Fear River in August 1774. Sheila, a young emigrant, mentions Flora to Caleb Touchstone, a Carolina river pilot and realtor, and when Flora appears on deck, Sheila says that Caleb already knows all about her. "Not all," Caleb says to Flora, "Just that you saved Prince Charles." Caleb's comment underscores the way in which Flora seems at once known and unknown over these last two centuries. Touchstone, the play's representative of the new world and the new order, continues to help Flora and her family even after politics make them adversaries.

Paterson uses recent research in setting seven of the play's ten scenes at Cheek's Creek, and then makes a point of not naming the new homestead after any place in Scotland. Paterson emphasizes Allan's consistent loyalty to the crown and suggests some mild jealousy on Allan's part at his wife's fame won in a rebel cause. Flora throughout urges neutrality but in the end her loyalty is to her husband. The Highlanders go off to war without a speech from Flora. At the play's bland ending, Flora thanks Allan for letting her go home, to which he replies, "Well, it's a small return for all that you have endured for us." Even as she sails for Britain, however, Flora seems to want to return to America and says she will "pray every day that we shall be back there—dear Carolina!"[30] As the lights dim, Flora's son James reminds us that Flora did not return, but remained "on her beloved home island," where, when she died, "Doctor Johnson's words became her epitaph."

David Pitman's *The Life and Death of Betty Burke*[31] is a short piece in two acts of a single scene each. Written in the early eighties, the play, as the title implies, is not really about Flora. The first act is set at Kingsburgh's house on Skye. The Prince is in bed. Flora enters the room and they talk of many things—Culloden, blame, their relationship over the past few days, and the lock of hair sought by Mrs. Kingsburgh. The second act is set in Rome almost forty years later. Again the Prince is in bed; this time he is ill and his faculties have been eroded by years of abuse. Again a woman is with him in the room. Sometimes she is his daughter Charlotte, as would have been historically plausible; sometimes, though, she is Flora, as the Prince drifts in and out of reality. Pitman has studied his material well and makes good use of allusion to historical fact as he tries to look into the Prince's mind.

In Pitman's short play and Fletcher's later novel Flora seems more lifelike than elsewhere in literary representations. In each work, her character emerges from the author's mixture of historical fact, tradition, and psychological extrapolation. While both characters are convincing, neither character may be the real Flora MacDonald. The observations of Mary in *Raleigh's Eden* and of Caleb in Paterson's play are significant. Flora has remained enigmatic. After the precipitating fact that she preserved or protected Prince Charles, those who seek to depict Flora are largely on their own. Most are more interested in the symbol than in the woman. Thus, it may serve their purposes to make a quiet and reserved woman an exhorter of Hebridean boatmen, Carolina militiamen, and naval gunners. It may serve them to make a short woman tall or a plain woman beautiful. Flora, as symbol, is at their service. And it is perhaps Green who best sees Flora when he compellingly portrays her as the old order bitterly yielding place to the new.

Chapter 15

"A Thistle among the Pines"[1]

An institution that gives women the highest Moral
and Spiritual development, combined with the most
careful mental and physical training, and thus prepares
them for true and earnest service, is doing work of in-
calculable value....

— PAMPHLET OF THE SOUTHERN
PRESBYTERIAN COLLEGE AND
CONSERVATORY OF MUSIC

IN 1907, THE EMINENT CANADIAN Dr. James A. MacDonald, historian, lecturer, author, and for years editor-in-chief of the Toronto
Globe, published an account of his travels to Scotland to explore the
roots of which he was so deeply proud. In that account he tells of
standing with William McKay before the statue of Flora MacDonald
on Castle Hill in Inverness. "You must go to the glen," McKay told
him. "It's only ten miles' sail down Loch Ness, and you must go." The
glen was Glen Urquhart, and for many years it "had been sending
Grants, MacDonalds, MacMillans, McKays and men of many other
clans to London and to India and to Canada." At Drumnadrochit,
where the glen opens into Loch Ness, an innkeeper, also named Mac-
Donald, asked the Canadian visitor if he had seen the local school. The
innkeeper spoke glowingly of the "mere glen school" that was preparing more scholars for university than any other academy in the country.
"O yes, it costs money," he is quoted as saying, "...but it is worth all
that it costs.... The only thing we have to export is educated people."[2]
Dr. MacDonald had long been interested in the migration of his
ancestors and their countrymen to Canada, and the discovery of the

179

small school in the glen producing educated people for export touched him. Later, while in Chicago for a speaking engagement, he came across an article about the North Carolina Scots, to some of whom he knew he was related. The article mentioned Flora's sojourn in the state, a fact of Flora's life of which Dr. MacDonald had been unaware. Incredulous at first, he resolved to go to North Carolina and settle the matter. There, of course, he found Flora's legacy. He also found that in Red Springs there had been since 1896 a seminary "for the intellectual, moral, and religious development and training of young ladies."[3]

Before long, Dr. MacDonald made a proposal to Dr. Charles A. Vardell, DD, president of the institution which by this time had grown in name from Red Springs Seminary to Southern Presbyterian College and Conservatory of Music. "Dr. Vardell," he said, "I want you to join me in a petition to the governing bodies of this college that they change the name of this institution to Flora MacDonald College."[4] MacDonald went on the enumerate his reasons:

> First, after careful investigation I judged the college to be worthy of the name of my great country woman; second, she lived in this region, and it is but right that her name be perpetuated; third, that her splendid example might be an inspiration to the fine young women, most of them of Scottish ancestry, who enter these doors; fourth and most important, the naming of this college after our heroine will be a great and sympathetic link between Great Britain and this country.[5]

At the time, Dr. Vardell reports, he scarcely knew more about Flora MacDonald than that she was "just another heroic woman." Realizing that changing the name of the college would be no small undertaking, he set about to discover how the woman was regarded, not only in Scottish North Carolina, but in other parts of the United States and Scotland as well. The response was overwhelming. Typical is the comment of the Marquis of Graham, from the Isle of Arran:

> ...We have everything to be proud of in our land,—great men, grand women, glorious country and good blood; and all you may do in America to enhance our history has the unqualified approval of Scotsmen at home.[6]

Dr. Vardell agreed to effect the name change.

In May 1914, the Scottish Society of America met in Fayetteville. Standing by the stump of the very oak under which Flora is said to have watched the Highlanders pass in review on their way to Moore's Creek Bridge, Dr. MacDonald, the society's president, spoke of his vision, now become reality:

> The most worthy memorial of Flora MacDonald would be an educational institution bearing her name, that would offer to hundreds of girls and young women in these Scottish communities the advantage of a college education, which Sir Alexander MacDonald...gave to Flora herself when he sent her for three years to a ladies' college in Edinburgh.[7]

Here and elsewhere in his remarks about Flora's life and accomplishments, it must be noted, Dr. MacDonald follows conventional accounts. He had read Dr. Foote's famous comparison of Flora, Pocahontas, and Lady Arabella, and his indebtedness to William Jolly's *Flora MacDonald in Uist* has already been noted. If the connection between Flora's improbable Edinburgh education and a college bearing her name in North Carolina does not ring true historically, it appeals emotionally. Dr. MacDonald wanted the college, with adequate endowment and broader scope, to change its name "so as worthily to bear the name of the Scottish heroine, herself a Presbyterian, a college graduate, and a noble example of Christian womanhood."[8]

In his remarks on that day, Dr. MacDonald followed the story line of the time in referring to Flora's having lived at Killegray. Most ironic, however, is his observation that Flora never visited Canada.[9] Instead, he joined his contemporaries in having Flora and her daughter Fanny go to Wilmington and Charleston and then directly back to Scotland.

At the time, remember, Flora's 1789 memorial had not come to light, and no one knew any better. The conventional details as the world knew them were perfectly acceptable. And besides, the details weren't what Dr. MacDonald's message was about. He continued the educational parallels:

> Like very many Scottish girls in the Carolinas and Virginia, Kentucky, Tennessee, and Alabama, [Flora] inherited good

blood, good character, but not even a competent portion of worldly wealth. War and reverses of history have made for the Southern States what similar influences did for our forefathers in the shires and islands of Scotland. And what MacDonald of Skye did for his young kinswoman, our Scottish-American democracy might surely do for generation after generation of our young women, who, like her, have high ambitions and a worthy desire to fit themselves for useful lives and helpful service. Therefore, it is, that I propose a Flora MacDonald College.[10]

To express his faith in the great venture, Dr. MacDonald challenged the membership of the Scottish Society of America and all Scottish people in North America to support the cause. When the endowment reached $100,000, Dr. MacDonald promised that he would add $10,000 of his own and that he would continue to raise funds "until the endowment shall be worthy of the cause, worthy of Scottish traditions, and worthy of the 'Flora MacDonald College.'" He then brought his speech to stirring conclusion:

And so, on this historic ground of North Carolina, here where once they parted, I raise again, in its larger meaning and with its world significance, Flora MacDonald's own rallying slogan to the clans: "*Clanna nan Gaidhael ri Guillibh a chiele*": "Sons of the Gael, shoulders together."[11]

The following winter, on February 12, 1915, Dr. Vardell wrote to the trustees of the college, polling them on their support of a resolution changing the name of the college. The reason Dr. Vardell gave is that the name "at present is too long, and either does not express enough or expresses too much."[12] The trustees approved the new name.

The Scottish Society of America held its 1916 meeting on May 21–24, on the campus of Flora MacDonald College in conjunction with the college's graduation exercises. The highlight of the festivities was the ceremony combining the graduation of the senior class and the dedication of the college.

As Dr. MacDonald began his address to the assembled crowd, he found it singularly appropriate that commencement and the dedication should take place on Victoria's Day, celebrated throughout the British

Empire. "The thing that we do today will carry a message and a meaning around the world," he said.

> For all time to come, this college and all who bear its name will hold an essential and abiding place in one of the rarest and greatest romances in all history. This name in American academic lists will link coming generations of Americans with their historic past.[13]

The portion of the ceremony devoted to the dedication of the college included the presentation by the Scottish Society of America of a portrait of Flora and an engraving of a painting by Thomas Duncan, depicting a scene in Flora's life.[14] Between the two presentations came this "Toast":

> Fine is the name of you,
> Lovely the face of you;
> Over the sea of years
> Reach we our hands to you
> Asking your blessing.
>
> Mists of the drifting years
> Almost would cover you:
> Could we, forgetting you,
> Dare speak of loyalty
> Or of true courage?
> No! We drink now to you
> All glasses high to you,
> Long and right heartily
> Drink to your memory
>   Flora MacDonald![15]

The importance of the college to the local community is seen in two distinct areas. Financial support was largely local. Of $150,000 raised around the time of the name change, all but $4000 was raised within North Carolina and "by far the larger part...from within a radius of fifty miles of the college."[16] The mission, both Dr. MacDonald and Dr. Vardell believed, was provide an education that the women who came to it could afford. "...the doors shall be closed to no worthy girl whose only bar is poverty," said MacDonald.[17]

How the leaders of the college saw its mission is interesting. Early on Dr. Vardell wrote that

> In the United States one woman out of every five over six-teen years old works for wages. One out of every seven of these is a married woman, and one out of every six is a widow. There is little demand for untrained, uneducated workers and their wages are pitifully small. WOMEN WORKING FOR SMALL WAGES HAVE MANY AND GREAT TEMPTATIONS. Should we not protect our daughters from these temptations? We can do this by edu-cating them.[18]

"One of the greatest banes of the cotton belt is hog and hominy—the everlasting, enervating succession of fried pork and fried chicken, of fried bread and fried potatoes," wrote Ralph Page in 1916. Thus, to Page, the principal value "of the country college for country girls is in the thorough and practical training they receive in the essentials of home life." Page saw the college as not only educating but training.[19]

Clearly the practical side—the training—was important. But a metaphysical nurturing was from the outset as much a part of the education of these young women as was their learning about balanced diets low in fat. The Christian woman was frequently seen at this time as the conduit of Christian values. The principles on which Dr. Vardell presented the college's mission were these:

> ...that the most desirable thing in the world was a cultured Christian woman; that men have the making of civilization, but that women have the making of men; that the chief el-ements in any community are its homes and its primary schools; that they are made by women; that no State which will educate its mothers need ever fear for its future;[20]

The 1921-22 catalogue put it this way: "The aim of this institution...is the carefully developed and thoroughly educated Christian woman... prepared to do her life work successfully in the home, the school room or wherever duty may call her." "Do you know," asked another fund-raising pamphlet, "that the stability, growth and dissemination of Christian principles, both at home and abroad, are lodged chiefly in the hands of pious women?"

If to modern tastes the emphasis on home and primary school seems a bit repressive and stultifying, consider what some of the young women who graduated from the college in the 1920s projected as duties to which they might be called. In the class of 1922, for example, several young women saw themselves as future missionaries in this country or abroad; at least three were projected to be concert and operatic stars; there were a surgeon and an ambassador, a mayor and the first congresswoman from her state. Those pursuing careers in education did not see themselves limited to the primary-school classroom, however important it may be. Members of the class aspired to be college professors, heads of major university libraries, and directors of state or municipal education departments. In the class of 1928, a bank president, a governor, more legislators, a concert violinist, a tennis champion, owners of a business franchise, authors, lecturers, a director of pediatric nursing, and educational administrators took their places beside wives and mothers.[21]

To be sure, class prophecies, long mainstays of yearbooks, often contain bits of irony and topical allusions lost over time and distance to researchers seeking sociological trends. Still, it seems that Flora MacDonald's graduates in the 1920s saw before them opportunities beyond the examples used in the college's literature. The perception of these examples as limiting stereotypes would not occur until later.

Dr. Vardell retired as president in 1930 but remained active in the affairs of the college until his death in 1958 at the age of ninety-eight. In the decade of the 1930s enrollment doubled. On the occasion of the college's fiftieth anniversary, Angus L. MacDonald, Premier of Nova Scotia, was the featured speaker and Clare Johnson Marley's play was performed. In 1947, students sought and obtained permission to have social dancing on campus. The inexorable march of modernism continued when a few years later students petitioned for and were granted an end to compulsory weekly chapel attendance.

In September 1953, Dame Flora MacLeod of MacLeod came to visit the Cape Fear Scots. On September 27, fifteen hundred of them gathered at Bethesda Presbyterian Church to attend a worship service and picnic and to hear Dame Flora speak "with confidence and poise" of the links between Scotland and America. The next day, in Fayetteville, she stood by the stump of the oak tree where the other Flora from Skye had allegedly exhorted the Highlanders as they marched off to battle.

A little over a year later, on November 17, 1954, Reginald H. Macdonald[22] accepted the invitation of President Woodson to visit the college and deliver an address. Macdonald was a New Zealander who had retired from the British army as a major and had come to the United States as vice president of a firm of investment and economic consultants. More important, he was Flora's great-great grandson, descended from Flora's son John. In his address to the college, Major Macdonald chose not to re-tell his illustrious ancestor's story. Instead, he talked about "The Forgotten Men and Women of Flora and Allan's family." He spoke of 103 Macdonald descendants (58 males, 45 females) who made up the six generations reaching back to Flora and Allan's children.[23] The major then selected from each generation a representative or two for special mention. The profession of arms, noted in Flora's children, dominated in succeeding generations as well.

Major Macdonald made one intriguing observation about Flora's daughter Anne. He reminded his audience that she had married a MacLeod and that she and their children had accompanied him to North Carolina. He then added, "Perhaps Anne left two of her children here." He did not elaborate on his conjecture. It does, however, pose a plausible explanation of the identities of the children buried on the campus.

A year later, as head of Clan Donald in the United States, Major Macdonald held the first meeting of the clan at Flora MacDonald College. He also placed a marker in Fayetteville to commemorate Flora's alleged address to the troops as they marched off to Moore's Creek Bridge.

In that same year, 1955, the Presbyterian Synod of North Carolina recommended the consolidation of colleges under its control, suggesting that Flora MacDonald College merge with two others. Loyalty to Flora MacDonald was strong, however. As part of the efforts to keep the college in Red Springs and to keep its name, the college in 1956 presented an honorary degree to the Reverend Donald MacKinnon "in view of his eminent scholarship, his devotion to the memory of Flora MacDonald, and his relation to the Clan Donald." Despite all efforts, the merger went through.

At the last commencement at Flora MacDonald College in 1961, Dr. Charles Vardell, the younger, touched the hearts of the audience when he closed the doors of the college thus:

Nor will Flora MacDonald [College] ever be forgotten. She is going to change her name. She is, if you please, going to be married. And we are predicting the marriage will be a success.

Even with the sense of loss that people felt, when they were able to set their emotions aside, they realized that "the health of Flora Mac-Donald [College] had been deteriorating for many years...and [she] would have faced a humiliating death." More hopeful was the editorial in the last issue of *The Skirl,* the college's newspaper:

Through the merger and consolidation..., the name of Flora MacDonald will be lost. But its Scottish traditions and ideals will greatly enrich this new school even as FMC students have contributed greatly to their communities through the years. This is not the end of a great Scottish school. It is the beginning of its finest days.[24]

Flora MacDonald—the woman and the college—were fittingly tied together by Dr. MacDonald, and through the college the woman's name continued to be mentioned with honor, as Dr. Johnson had predicted. Dr. MacDonald had achieved his purpose

to link with this our common country and heritage the name of Her who by her purity of life; her patience in adversity; her unswerving fealty and unfaltering courage, illuminated the dark days in which she lived and has shed lasting glory on the name and fame of Scotland.[25]

Chapter 16

The Company She Keeps

Scotch history flames with gallant and heroic deeds, and thrilling events crowd the records. Each clan has its roster of heroes, staunch and brave, but all clans do reverence to the "Bright and Particular Star," Flora MacDonald.

—Dr. C.G. Vardell

Toby: Modern women have no courage — in olden times women did brave things for their menfolk every day of the week.

Stella: I don't look upon you as my menfolk.

Toby: Think of the girl who put her arm through the latches of the door to save Bonnie Prince Charlie.

Stella: In my opinion a misguided ass.

Toby: I won't hear a word against Flora Macdonald.

Stella: It wasn't Flora Macdonald.

Toby: Don't be so ignorant, of course it was. Flora Macdonald never stopped doing things like that.

Stella: It was not.

Toby: Who was it, then?

Stella: I don't know who it was, but it was not Flora Macdonald.

Toby: I suppose you'll tell me it was Grace Darling in a minute.

....

Stella: I tell you I don't know who it was, I only know it wasn't Flora Macdonald.[1]

Toby and Stella, the impecunious, free-loading husband and wife in Noel Coward's *Ways and Means*, are trying to devise a scheme by which

189

to continue their indolent soujourn in the south of France. The means under discussion requires the wife to display a bit of bravery, and in the course of Coward's crackling dialogue, the names of Flora MacDonald and Grace Darling are ironically invoked as model British heroines.

Here, again, Flora's name is juxtaposed to that of another heroine in the legend that proceeds from her nation's history. Coward was, for his purposes, linking Flora and Grace Darling as Foote in the middle of nineteenth century had done when he said that "Massachusetts had her Lady Arabella; Virginia her Pocahontas; and North Carolina her Flora MacDonald."[2] A closer look at these juxtapositions will mark the direction in which Flora's legend has developed in Britain and in America.

In September 1838, the same year in which Joseph Seawell Jones said of Flora, "The life of no female in the history of any country was ever more deserving of the attention of the historian," Grace Darling, of Bamburgh, Northumberland, was thrust into the eye of adulation when she may have assisted her father, a lighthouse keeper, in the rescue of passengers and crew of the *S. S. Forfarshire* which wrecked on Big Harker Rock. What part Grace actually played in the rescue is unclear; her participation did not come to light until after the initial reports had reached the public. When her name was mentioned, she became an instant sensation. Less than six weeks after the event, Grace's father reported that seven portrait painters had sought her out in the space of twelve days, and two months after the event, Queen Victoria gave Grace £50. Ironically, though she survived the deed, Grace, an unassuming girl, fell under the weight of the accolades heaped upon her and died quietly of consumption in 1842.[3] A year later Poet Laureate William Wordsworth wrote his ninety-seven-line tribute to Grace and published it in 1845 so that it "Might carry to the clouds and to the stars/Yea, to celestial Choirs, GRACE DARLING's name!"[4]

Noel Coward was not the first to link these ladies as folk heroines. Several writers in the nineteenth century had made the connection. An unsigned article on "The Jacobite Heroine Flora MacDonald" in the MacBean Collection says that while "Cleopatra, Boadicea, and Joan of Arc are remembered as great in history, Grace Darling and Flora MacDonald are great in themselves."[5] The syntactical opposition of "in history" and "in themselves" is sharper than the distinction in meaning. Legend overlays the pages of history of the first three women as it does the footnotes to history in which the last two women are found. In legend all five are larger than life. And while agreeing that Flora is indeed great in herself, we must also acknowledge that forces larger than herself—the stuff of history—thrust upon her the occasion from which our awareness of her greatness is derived.

In 1866, Alexander Smith also saw a connection between Flora and Grace, noting that

> Neither at the time [of her adventure with the Prince], nor afterwards, did Flora Macdonald consider herself a heroine, (although Grace Darling herself did not bear a braver heart;) and she is noticeable to this day in history, walking demurely with a white rose in her bosom.[6]

A recent biographer of Grace sees her in terms equally applicable to Flora:

> Grace was unremarkable as a personality, pious, obedient, hard-working, modest. There was nothing to distinguish her from countless other English country girls—except for her fortuitous assistance in the Forfarshire rescue. This single act of great courage was, in a sense, the sum total of her. Thus she became a sort of blank slate upon which the writer could construct his own version of her life, and pursue his own ruminations as to the significance of her story.[7]

In America less than a decade after Grace's precipitating event, Foote linked Lady Arabella, Pocahontas, and Flora MacDonald. In the light of her 1995 quadricentennial celebration and politically correct treatment by Disney, Pocahontas needs little introduction. Lady Arabella is far less well known. With her husband Isaac Johnson she sailed for the New World from Yarmouth on April 7, 1630. She landed several rough weeks later at Salem, in Massachusetts, where she shortly fell ill and died a few weeks later. Her grief-stricken husband went on to found Boston.[8]

Unlike Flora and Pocahontas, Lady Arabella saved no romantic adventurer from barbaric enemies. She just came to America, took sick, and died. But it wasn't what she did that preserved her memory and made her name a household word up and down the East Coast at least until the middle of the nineteenth century; it's what she was:

A shining and delicate shell, cast by the surges of the ocean upon some bleak shore; a tropical plant of rare beauty, flowering and fading amidst the snows of the wintry north; a diamond, or a drop of gold, gleaming among the stern rocks of a lofty sierra—are emblems of the life of high-born Arabella. The records of her life are scattered; but enough may be gathered to present a beautiful contrast of grace and loveliness, with the rugged simplicity of colonial adventure. Her name is a monument of the power of domestic affection and religious principle... and the triumph of these principles over all feminine dread of perils of the sea, and of strange wilderness, made doubly fearful by the supposed ferocity of its savage inhabitants.[9]

Both Pocahontas and Flora MacDonald did, of course, save romantic adventurers, and in so doing opened the floodgates of legendary celebration. In real life they had a bit more in common. Both women married men other than the ones they saved, and with their husbands, both crossed the Atlantic for economic reasons. Both seem to have been the darlings of the London social scene and to have met members of the royal family. Both tried to return to their native lands; one succeeded. Both have vast numbers of descendants—real or imagined.

Though Pocahontas had over a century's head start on Flora, their legends as told in the imaginary treatments of their lives begin at about the same time. Both were the subjects of plays at the beginning of the nineteenth century—Flora in one written by her son John and Pocahontas in one written by George Washington's step-grandson. The two women share at least one dramatist: Paul Green, who had featured Flora in *The Highland Call* (1941), wrote Pocahontas into *The Founders* in 1957.

Both the Highland lass and what one writer called "the pagan, savage, American aboriginal"[10] were seen as having almost all the noble Christian virtues one could ever hope for. Many writers accept the innate presence of such virtues in the noble savage—Highland or Tidewater. Others see the need to gentrify the two women. Just as some nineteenth-century commentators attributed Flora's virtues to her Edinburgh education, at least two writers have given Pocahontas an Anglo-Christian mother to account for her civility—according to one, Virginia Dare, presumably the first white woman born in North America.[11]

By the middle of the nineteenth century, both Flora and Pocahontas were seen as the acmes of heroism. In much the same vein as Jones's 1838 assessment of Flora is this 1846 view of Pocahontas:

> In all history and in all romance it would be difficult to find a more perfect character than Pocahontas; and taking her as she has come down to us, it appears impossible to say wherein it could have been improved.[12]

Five years earlier another commentator had written that Pocahontas

> is one of those characters rarely appearing on the theatres of life, which no age can claim, no country appropriate. She is the property of mankind, serving as a beacon to light us on our way, instruct us in our duty, and show us what the human mind is capable of performing when abandoned to its own operations.[13]

But perhaps the best of the tributes applicable to both women is this one from 1839, assessing Pocahontas's rescue:

> The universal sympathies of mankind and the best feelings of the human heart have redeemed the scene from the obscurity which, in the progress of time, gathers over all but the most important events. It has pointed a thousand morals and has adorned a thousand tales. Innumerable bosoms have throbbed and have yet to throb with generous admiration for this daughter of a people, whom we have been too ready to underrate.[14]

These mid-century juxtapositions of heroines come at the end of the second major period in the history of Flora's celebrity. The first period, of course, had been the one of almost instantaneous fame as word of her action spread orally through the Highlands and by letter and dispatch to Edinburgh, London, and Paris. Crowds were drawn to Flora in her captivity, and with her demeanor she charmed them. Even if London did confuse her with Jenny Cameron, Flora established herself and her identity with Whig and Jacobite alike. The celebrity of this period was short-lived, perhaps because Flora showed no interest in exploiting it. Instead she lived relatively inconspicuously on Skye and in America for almost forty-four years after her moment in the spotlight, the occasional intruders upon her anonymity being, like Pennant, Johnson, and Boswell, itinerant curiosity seekers with good memories.

Then, in the early nineteenth century as the immediacy of the '45 faded into history, Sir Walter Scott led the Romantics in a reconsideration of the Jacobites and the lost Stuart cause.

The lost Stuart cause had everything a Romantic of the early nineteenth century could want. It invoked the past and tradition; it esteemed pure, country virtues uncorrupted by rationalism and commerce. Even the very fact that it was lost appealed to the Romantics. Simplistic and subject to specific exception as this view has been shown to be, it has prevailed. Its principal spokespeople—Scott, Burns, Hogg, Lady Nairne, and others—celebrated an acceptable, domesticated, and largely sentimental Jacobitism after it had ceased to be a serious threat to the establishment.

British Romanticism, as every boy and girl knows—or used to know, began promptly in 1789, a date usually tied to the start of the French Revolution. That is also the year in which George, Prince of Wales (later George IV),

> donned the garb of old Gaul at a masquerade...and during the evening earned the appellation of the Royal Highland Laddie. The Prince, said one observer, is remarkably fond of Highland reels, which he dances with all the glee and ability of a native of the North.[15]

Scotland came to be seen as the epitome of romance. Wild landscapes, the aesthetic of the picturesque, the love of the past—all are the stuff of romanticism. George IV's visit to Edinburgh, orchestrated in large part by Sir Walter Scott, throws a little more light on Flora and her position at that time. At the time of the King's visit, the *Edinburgh Observer* had this to say:

> We are now all Jacobites, thorough-bred Jacobites, in acknowledging George IV. This seems to be one of the feel-

ings that stimulate people here, at the present time, to make such exertions. Our King is the heir of the Chevalier, in whose service the Scotch suffered so much, shone so much, and he will find many a Flora MacDonald amongst the "Sisters of the Silver Cross", and many a faithful Highlander attending his Throne with a forester bugle and bow.[16]

It was towards the end of King George's celebrated visit to the North that the King promised an annuity of £50 to Flora's granddaughter.[17] "Such was the current Jacobite mood that is seemed only proper that the House of Hanover should honour the memory of the woman who had saved the life of its last active rival."[18]

It seems that by the end of the third decade of the nineteenth century the broadsword is buried, all Scotland is the Highlands, everyone is a Jacobite, George IV is a Stuart, and Flora MacDonald is the embodiment of it all.

The eighteenth and nineteenth centuries are full of anecdotal examples of the establishment's generously tolerating tamed Jacobitism. George III, upon learning that the Laird of Gask, Lady Nairne's father, would not suffer the King's name to be mentioned in his presence, did not send troops to hang the old gentleman as his royal uncle of Cumberland might have done. He sent instead the Member of Parliament from Perthshire with this message:

> Give my compliments—not the compliments of the King of England, but those of the Elector of Hanover—to Mr. Oliphant, and tell him how much I respect him for the steadiness of his principles.[19]

Prince George's (later George IV) wearing of the kilt has already been noted. When, as king, this same George met Flora's son John, he is reported to have said, "This gentleman is the son of a lady to whom my family owe a great obligation."[20] And virtually every monarch since has at one time or another publicly acknowledged either Stuart lineage or the nearness of a Stuart Victory in 1745–46 or both. Victoria spoke of her Stuart blood, noted that she had an attendant named Flora MacDonald, felt the drama at Glenfinnan, drank from a silver quaich the Bonnie Prince once used,[21] loved her Highland home, and in so doing, contributed majestically to the tartanization of Scotland.

George V is said to have told the Duke of Atholl that "Had Charles Edward gone on from Derby I should not have been King of England to-day."[22]

In nineteenth-century Britain, the old order had gone, never to come again. And since it would not come again it was permissible to write and sing praises to it and to recognize the non-partisan virtues in its principal characters. William Aytoun writes of it in "The Old Scottish Cavalier." "It is a song of olden time,/Of days long since gone by," he tells us. The cavalier's father died at Killiecrankie Pass, and the son in his turn rallies to the Prince, follows him, and dies at Culloden. Each of the seven stanzas ends with an adjectival variation on the "old Scottish cavalier(s)/All of the olden time!" The last one:

> Oh! never shall we know again
>   A heart so stout and true—
> The olden times have passed away,
>   And weary are the new:
> The fair White Rose has faded
>   From the garden where it grew,
> And no fond tears, save those of heaven,
>   The glorious bed bedew
> Of the last old Scottish cavalier
>   All of the olden time![23]

The six adjectives leading up to "last" are "brave, steadfast, true, leal [loyal], valiant, and good."

"History is a Romance which is believed; Romance is a History which is not believed." Thus quoting Lord Oxford in their preface to *Tales of the Century*, John Sobieska and Charles Edward Stuart briefly appeared upon the nineteenth-century scene. On their title page they include an invocation from Ossian: "Gairm-sa air-ais gu-luath/Na bli-adhna' gun tuar a bh'ann (We call back, maid of Lutha,/The years which have rolled away)."[24]

Sobieska and Stuart, a couple of pretenders in their own right, go on to deplore the descent of history from "the thirst of glory, the division of power, the love of adventure, the grandeur and the gloom, the rudeness and the magnificence of the Gothic arts, edifices, and manners" to a "dull and simple narration...of contracted and ruptured treaties, [and] of changes of laws and changes of ministries." In this decline, they submit, "truth became allied with poverty of action and juste-milieuism of mind, as the events and the characters of men had become subdued and common-place." But, they are pleased to report,

> between the lives of the common herd and the actions of extraordinary minds, there is the contrast of many ages.... In this combination of veracity and exaggeration, there has appeared from time to time, even to the present day, a solitary shooting star, which gleams and falls upon the dull blank sky of History, with a transient and mysterious light....[25]

Such a star, they conclude, "however little known, and little appreciated," was Bonnie Prince Charlie. And so, let us add, was Flora Mac-Donald.

Flora is ideally suited to personify all that was noble and virtuous in the cause after it was long lost. After all, she bore no arms against the Crown of Britain. Despite the opinion of an extremist few, her relationship with the Prince was above suspicion and beyond reproach. In her few public remarks on the subject she is consistently clear in her position that what she did for Charlie she would have done for anyone in need and that her actions were humanely and not politically motivated. The traditions and responsibilities of hospitality were deeply ingrained in her people, and it is altogether fitting that she merely applied them to the situation at hand. In a slightly different tone, Dr. C. G. Vardell has this to say about the English response to Flora in London:

> The English are good sports, the Prince was gone, the rebellion squelched, and Flora a Scotch maid. She had done a plucky job and saved the country from an embarrassing situation.[26]

All is thus forgiven, and besides, she did England a favor in helping to get Charlie out of the kingdom. We may note again in this regard that in the popular, short-form telling of the Prince's escape Flora is sometimes credited implicitly if not explicitly with Charlie's ultimate removal from the kingdom, and not just from one island to another along the way. The inscription on the back of the Wilson portrait in the Scottish National Portrait Gallery is one such example, and Dr. Vardell's remark another. The typical American or Briton who can identify Flora with Bonnie Prince Charlie probably cannot name another of the Scots who contributed as much as or more than Flora to the Prince's passage to safety. The work and risks of the many are subsumed in the persona of Flora.

In their depictions of the fair conductress, some have presented Flora as a flaming Jacobite devoted to the Stuarts and ready to do anything and sacrifice everything for the Prince and the cause. The earliest Stuart propagandists and later romantics saw her thus, a view which probably leads to the "Liberty-Leading-the-People" image of Flora exhorting boatmen and North Carolina loyalists and naval gunners. The historian Browne, for example, says that Flora

> retained her Jacobite predilections to the last hour of her existence. Though mild in disposition, she was roused to anger when any attempt was made...to deprecate the exiled family; and nothing offended her so much as the absurd appellation of 'Pretender' applied to Prince Charles and his father.[27]

On the other hand, Walter Biggar Blaikie notes that "Kingsburgh who sheltered [the Prince], Lady Margaret MacDonald who cherished him, and Flora MacDonald who saved him were all—in theory at least—on King George's side."[28] And Bruce Lenman says that "Flora MacDonald, herself no Jacobite, felt that it was her duty as a Highland lady to assist the escape of a hunted prince of Scotland's ancient dynasty."[29] Duty or not, Susan Maclean Kybett asserts that Flora resented the Prince's intrusion upon her life. Another piece of evidence by omission comes from W. G. B. Murdoch, who says that "the three Jacobite ladies who exemplify the most intense form of loyalty are Miss Christian Threipland, Lady Balmerino, and Lady Strange."[30] Flora finishes out of the money if indeed Murdoch thinks of her as a Jacobite at all. As noted earlier, Paul Green brought the once-opposing forces together in Flora when he referred to her as "preserver of Bonnie Prince Charlie, loyal daughter of the empire, and ward of his majesty King George the Third." And Alex Paterson could commemorate the American bicentennial and Scottish contributions to the American experience in a play about Flora, who transcends partisanship. Flora herself said much the same thing late in life in that oft-quoted remark about having served two royal houses and having precious little from either one to show for her pains.

In all this it is significant to note that Flora's fame has outlasted that of two Jacobite women more closely identified with the conduct of the rising. Colonel Anne Mackintosh raised a regiment of Mackintoshes, MacGillivrays, and MacBeans to fight with Bonnie Prince Charlie. Her husband was less successful in putting troops into the field in support of the government. As the story goes, in one engagement, Colonel Anne's husband was taken prisoner and brought before his wife. "Your servant, captain," she said; "Your servant, colonel," her husband replied.[31] A wonderful vignette this—the stuff of legend clearly, yet Colonel Anne is far less well known today than is Flora. Jenny Cameron, too, seen early in martial terms and, in London at least, more famous than Flora at the outset, has faded into the footnotes of the '45.

Perhaps General Campbell understood Flora well when he dismissed her as a pretty rebel who had been given some bad advice by those who should have known better. A fair-minded humanitarian, a simple Highland girl moved to action perhaps by the wretched but still charismatic Prince, an intelligent and thoroughly good woman ministering to a man in need: hardly the stuff of treason. Despite the fear for Flora's life that Governor McLean ascribes to General Campbell, as we look back on the events of 1746 it is clear from the outset that no harm was going to befall Flora in captivity. Her character made her a delight to everyone. For six weeks near Edinburgh and for six months in London she was called upon by admirers of both sides. Luke-warm Scottish as well as closet English Jacobites may have embraced Flora to atone in part for their reluctance to "up and rally at the royal prince's word." In yet another of the "Flora's Lament" poems, Henry Scott Riddell picks up this idea when he imagines Flora expressing her own dismay at the indifference of her countrymen to Charlie and his cause. The first stanza:

> More dark is my soul than the scenes of yon islands,
>   Dismantled of all the gay hues that they wore;
> For lost is my hope since the Prince of the Highlands
>   'Mong these, his wild mountains, can meet me no more.
> Ah! Charlie, how wrung was this heart when it found thee
>   Forlorn, and the die of thy destiny cast;
> Thy Flora was firm 'mid the perils around thee,

But where were the brave of the land that had own'd thee,
    That she — only she — should be true to the last?[32]

Though we find no evidence that Flora herself ever commented thus on the allegiance of her countryman, Riddell's bringing of the idea and Flora together is certainly apt.

One recent observer has suggested that "Scotsmen stress the gallantry of the '45 to the degree to which they wish to obscure the shoddy, mercenary self-betrayal of the Union of 1707."[33] In like manner, in the aftermath of the '45 some of the more vehement and virulent Whigs may have celebrated Flora in a kind of unstated apology for their own heavy-handed treatment of their Jacobite countrymen.

Flora's final surge of celebrity came at the end of the nineteenth century: the "canonization" that her descendants mounted as they funded or dedicated monuments and stained glass windows. The celebrations of Flora in literature over the last hundred years derive in the main from this period.

In North Carolina, at least, long after the political implications of the '45 and the American Revolution had faded into history books, Flora lingered on in the local folklore. As a young girl growing up near Laurinburg towards the end of the nineteenth century, Nettie McCormick Henley remembers having heard "hazy stories of Flora McDonald," and even as late as 1915 John R. Black recalled having been told stories of Flora.[34] Such lingering recollections are not always welcome. One preserver of North Carolina's history notes that attention to Flora's sojourn draws attention from the other women who settled in the region at the same time and whose stories are perhaps just as worthy of the telling.[35]

Rassie Wicker speaks of "the dismal failure" of Flora's dream "...to begin the world again, anewe, in another corner of it...." He regrets the losses she and her family suffered in their new homeland, but he regrets even more Carolina's loss of Flora and her extended family.

> The potential worth of this group of educated and cultured people would have been of incalculable value to the infant nation, and there seems little doubt but that given time for reflection, they would have willingly returned and embraced the new Democracy and become the nucleus of an honor-

able and cultured society, and an honour to their adopted country.[36]

But they didn't. In Scotland in 1745, the old order had risen against the established new order, struggled heroically, and failed. The establishment remained in place and eventually could afford to welcome the toothless remnants of the old order into a nostalgic place in the national image. In America, the situation was different. This time the old order was the establishment against which the new order rose, struggled vigorously, and won. Those who celebrated the new American nation had to repudiate the personifications of that old British order; hence Paul Green has Jennie Ban MacNeill turn however reluctantly from Flora's bitterness to the next generation's hope.

Still, it was Flora's, not Jennie's, name that captured the imagination of James MacDonald and prompted his efforts to affix the Highland woman's name to a college in the heart of Scottish North Carolina.

Chapter 17

"Fancy and Tradition"

Thus everywhere to truth Tradition clings,
Or Fancy localises Powers we love.
Were only History licensed to make note
Of things gone by, her meagre monuments
Would ill suffice for persons and events:
There is an ampler page for man to quote,
A readier book of manifold contents,
Studied alike in palace and in cot.

—WILLIAM WORDSWORTH[1]

WHO THEN WAS THIS "FAIR MAIDEN" whose name has so long endured? Flora MacDonald, it has often been observed, is a folk heroine. "Folk" in this sense may have some of the same qualifying effect that it does when preceding "art" or "music": a folksiness that sets Flora and Grace Darling apart from Cleopatra and Boadicea and consigns them to greatness in themselves as opposed to greatness in history; remembered in song and story, the subject of family historians, mentioned perhaps in footnotes but not deemed suitable for serious scholarly investigation.

We are told that Flora didn't understand all the attention being paid to her. Thus unprepared for history, she didn't take or leave many notes. The correspondence that has come down to us is partially revealing but limited; there just isn't enough of it to warrant a collected and annotated edition. Flora had no one following her around recording her every word and movement. By the time she met Boswell, he was already engaged. We can safely surmise that Chambers's *History of the Rebellion* provided nineteenth-century American writers with the background information and that Banks's pamphlet in turn gave Mac-Gregor the basis for his remarks about Flora in America. But it remains clear that much transmission of Flora's story was by word of mouth and is thus lost to us. Here and there we may catch a glimpse of the real Flora—in the recollections of old Mrs. Smith in mid-nineteenth-century Fayetteville or of Mr. Sharpe's mother in Edinburgh a decade or so earlier. We are closest to Flora, perhaps, in Boswell's account of her bantering with Dr. Johnson during their meeting on that September evening on Skye and in some of her own correspondence as she describes herself as "once known to the world"or as she clings to the hope that her sons are alive and well. But we still wish we could hear the original, unpolished, unedited versions of Flora's story which preceded her to Edinburgh, London, and Fayetteville. Folks who did not have personal papers—the stuff of historical research—had a lot to do with sustaining and transmitting Flora's story. And unless some one discovers a cache moldering in some attic, bothy, croft, castle, or (like the portrait Mrs. Wylde mentioned), pawn shop, we must rely on what we have.

Voices have told of Flora as the Highland heroine, and voices have sung hymns of praise to her as "our lady." The epithet is sometimes attributed to the Prince, who seems to use it with to deliberate if ironic Marian overtones. "Beautiful Virgin," reads the English translation of a Gaelic epithet in a poem said to have been written by Neil MacEachain,[2] and Dr. King prays, "Semper amata/Semper honorata, Insignissima Virgo, manebis."*[3] Is it perhaps ironic that to Flora, who "was educated, lived, and died in the Presbyterian faith, the faith of the Church of Scotland, and [who] never sympathized with the religious creed of the Pretender, whose life she saved,"[4] should thus be ascribed these Marian epithets? Not really. Here again Flora transcends sectarian limitations. As Paul Green made her both preserver of Bonnie Prince Charlie and loyal subject of King George III, so she can be both "our lady" and a pillar of the Barbecue Presbyterian Church.

---

* A translation of Dr. King's lines might read, "Ever beloved, ever distinguished, most notable maiden, you will remain with us." I am indebted to Dr. Norman Merrill for his help with the translation and for noting that Dr. King's lines may echo those spoken by Aeneas when he salutes Dido, "Semper honus nomenque tuum laudesque manebunt." "Always will honor and name and your praises remain," (*Aeneid*, I, 609.)

Whether fact or fiction, these Virginal abstractions, like other treatments of Flora, make it difficult to get to know her. By virtue of her symbolic value, she has retained much of her privacy. The abstract heroine masks the specific woman. Inglis Fletcher sensed the vacuum created by Flora's reserve when she told us that "Whatever Flora had in her secret heart, the face she showed the world held the tranquillity and dignity of a great soul."[5] Abhorring a vacuum as much as the next group, biographers have rushed in to fill it with whatever motives and qualities it suits them to place there. Most commentators on Flora have been more interested in her as agent than as woman. The succession of biographers, poets, playwrights, novelists, and philo-gaelic anachronists who have used Flora for their own purposes have not brought us much closer to the real woman. At almost every point in Flora's story one can ask, "Did she or didn't she": receive an Edinburgh education; spend time in the Tower of London; slap Felix O'Neill's face; exhort boatmen, Carolina Highlanders, and naval gunners to do their duties; attend a ball in her honor at Wilmington; commission a portrait to give to Commodore Smith; sit to Joseph Highmore; sell her silver in Charleston; leave two children dead and buried in North Carolina? Answers seem shaped by investigations and predilections.

Historians in this century have worked hard to set the record straight, and it is probably about as straight now as it is going to get until that cache comes to light. But at this distance the on-going efforts to verify how many children Flora brought with her to America or whether she and her family lived four hundred yards farther up or down Cheek's Creek or even a couple of creeks away in one direction or another are but part of what compels in her story. There is also the plethora of facts and artifacts that have accumulated and been taken up into the mythology of Flora, Bonnie Prince Charlie, and the '45.[6]

To look at the Prince and the '45 without the protection of romantic, rose-colored glasses can be quite uncomfortable. The damage that Charles did to Scotland in his ill-considered and futile quest for a throne he could not have is enormous. Better to compose ballads and trot out the old myths, the shortbread, and the Drambuie than to think seriously about Tearlach's chances for success. Better to look at John Pettie's portrait of the confident young man in the flower of his youth than at Hugh Douglas Hamilton's portrait of a sixty-five-year-old man ravaged by excess. Remember how Sir Walter Scott softened the aftermath of the '45 when he wrote of the Jaccobites,

> Their love of past times, their tales of bloody battles fought against romantic odds, were all dear to the imagination, and their little idolatry of locks of hair, pictures, rings, ribbons...might have rendered them dangerous....Yet, as we now recollect them, there could be on earth supposed to exist no persons better qualified to sustain the capacity of innocuous and respectable grandsires.[7]

With or without protective glasses, Flora is safer and more rewarding to contemplate. Her precipitating act was one of disinterested humanity, not partisan politics. Her precipitating act brought her attention in her captivity, and her demeanor in the light of all the attention sustained it. Her fame preceded her to America, where she probably did no more than the other women around her — endure under difficult circumstances. Yet in America, perhaps even more than in Scotland, the precipitating act has retained in Flora special symbolic value. Though Flora played little if any part in the American revolution, Mrs. Ellett included her among the women of that war. Paul Green and Inglis Fletcher found in Flora a perfect figure around whom to tell their stories. And James MacDonald saw in Flora the embodiment of all that was good in a college committed to the Christian education of young women.

Some of the celebrity surrounding this woman was planned and promoted — most visible in the actions of her descendants in the last decade or so of the nineteenth century, and it can be argued that Dr. MacDonald's efforts were promotional. But the enduring power of the images that are Flora have made the promotions possible. Dr. Johnson left us as a description of Flora a simple theme on which two centuries of enthusiastic planners have played endless variations: "She was a woman of middle stature, soft features, gentle manners, and elegant presence."

Notes

Notes for Introduction

1. Bruce P. Lenman, "Some Recent Jacobite Studies," *Scottish Historical Review,* LXX, 1: no. 188: April, 1991, p. 72.

2. H. V. Morton, *In Scotland Again,* London, 1949, pp. 183-84.

3. *Ibid.,* p. 186.

4. The Reverend G. V. R. Grant, "The '45: A Disastrous Mistake," *The 45—to gather an image whole,* ed. Lesley Scott-Moncrieff, Edinburgh, 1988, p. 23.

5. Quoted in Frank McLynn, *The Jacobites,* London, 1985, p. 214.

6. *Ibid.,* p. 214.

7. Conversation with the author, October 29, 1991.

8. Roy M. B. Williamson, *Flower of Scotland,* The Corries (Music) Ltd., 1968.

9. See William Jolly, *Flora MacDonald in Uist,* first published 1886; edition quoted here is that published with the 5th edition of Alexander MacGregor's *The Life of Flora MacDonald,* Stirling, 1932, p. 240. Wordsworth's exact phrase in the third stanza of "She was a phantom of delight" is "A perfect Woman, nobly planned,/To warn, to comfort, and command."

Notes for Chapter 1

1. Bruce Lenman, *The Jacobite Cause,* Glasgow, 1986, p. 10.

2. Flora Maxwell Stuart, *Lady Nithsdale and the Jacobites,* Innerleithen, 1995, p. 51.

3. E.g., 1689, 1708, 1715, and 1719.

4. Susan Maclean Kybett, *Bonnie Prince Charlie,* London, 1988, p. 38.

5. Alasdair Maclean and John Gibson, *Summer Hunting a Prince,* Stornoway, 1992, p. 4.

6. Frank McLynn, *Bonnie Prince Charlie,* Oxford, 1991, p. 127.

7. Kybett, p. 118. See also a note by Barbara Fairweather in *A Jacobite Anthology,* Aberdeen, 1995, p. 4.

8. Charles Sanford Terry, *The Young Pretender,* London, 1903, p. 51.

9. At least Flora said he did. See Chapter 9 and Alasdair Maclean, *A MacDonald for the Prince,* Stornoway, 1982, p. 60.

10. Walter Biggar Blaikie, *Itinerary of Prince Charles Edward Stuart,* Edinburgh, 1975, p. 5.

11. For more on Flora and the Prince in film, see chapter 14.

12. David Duff, ed., *Queen Victoria's Highland Journals,* Exeter, 1980, p. 179.

13. Carolly Erickson, *Bonnie Prince Charlie,* New York, 1989, p. 117.

14. Kybett, p. 123.

15. Frank McLynn, *The Jacobites,* London, 1985, p. 82.

16. Erickson, p. 117.

17. John S. Gibson, *Locheil of the '45,* Edinburgh, 1994, p. 65.

18. *Ibid.,* p. 65.

19. Katherine Tomasson, *The Jacobite General,* Edinburgh, 1958, p. 19. See also Bruce Lenman, *The Jacobite Risings in Britain 1689–1746,* London, 1980, p. 247.

20. *The Sword and the Sorrows,* National Trust for Scotland, 1996, p. 87.

21. Quoted in Kybett, p. 136.

22. W. G. B. Murdoch, *The Spirit of Jacobite Loyalty,* Edinburgh, 1907, p. 146.

23. Walter Biggar Blaikie, *Edinburgh at the Time of the Occupation of Prince Charles,* Edinburgh, 1910, p. 56.

24. "By a lady seeing His Royal Highness the Prince," in *A Full Collection of All Poems upon Charles, Prince of Wales, . . . ,* Edinburgh, 1745.

25. Quoted in J. C. Hadden, *Prince Charles Edward,* London, 1913, p. 266.

26. Margaret Forster, *The Rash Adventurer,* New York, 1973, p. 93.

27. Alexander Charles Ewald, *The Life and Times of Prince Charles Edward Stuart,* London, 1904, p. 282.

28. McLynn, *Bonnie Prince Charlie,* pp. 223–224. For the size of Loudon's force see W. B. Blaikie, *Itinerary . . . ,* p. 39.

29. The Prince's army was by no means wholly Highland. Many men, including officers, came from coastal towns between the Tay and Moray firths. See, for example, Murray G. H. Pittock, "The Myth of the Jacobite Clans: Lowland Recruitment in the '45," a paper presented at the annual conference of the Eighteenth-Century Scottish Studies Society, Aberdeen, July 30, 1995.

30. Andrew Lang, *Pickle the Spy,* London, 1897, p. 23.

Notes for Chapter 2

1. A. R. MacDonald, "A True Account of the Life of Flora Mac-Donald," *Oban Times,* July 8, 1905.

2. Ruairidh H. MacLeod, *Flora MacDonald,* London, 1995, p. 3.

3. In the boat as passengers with the Prince were Col. O'Sullivan (qv), Felix O'Neill (qv), Allan MacDonald, a priest, and Edward Burke, who had guided the Prince from Culloden. In addition to MacLeod there was a seven-man boat crew. Cf. W. B. Blaikie, *Itinerary of Prince Charles Edward Stuart,* Edinburgh, 1975, p. 47.

4. Alasdair Maclean and John S. Gibson, *Summer Hunting a Prince,* Stornoway, 1992, p. 16.

5. Susan M. Kybett, *Bonnie Prince Charlie,* London, 1988, p. 231.

6. For example, Eric Linklater, *The Prince in the Heather*, London, 1987, p. 58.

7. For example, Kybett, p. 227.

8. Margaret Forster, *The Rash Adventurer,* London, 1973, p. 166.

9. John S. Gibson, *Locheil of the '45,* Edinburgh, 1994, p. 154.

10. The fate of one Roderick Mackenzie is instructive. In late summer, 1746, Mackenzie was cornered by Government troops. When asked if he was the Prince, he said that he was. His captors beheaded him on the spot. See, among others, Kybett, p. 246. Had Mackenzie's head been that of the Prince, official Government regret over the impetuous act of overzealous troops would have been preferable to the inevitable trial and execution of a royal captive.

11. Blaikie, p. 53.

12. Kybett, p. 232.

13. The Baron Ernest Porcelli, *The White Cockade,* London, 1949, p. 175.

14. Maclean and Gibson, p. 35.

15. *Ibid.,* p. 31.

16. Frank McLynn, *Bonnie Prince Charlie*, Oxford, 1991, p. 285.

17. Maclean and Gibson, pp. 34, 70.

18. Quoted in McLynn, p. 285.

19. W. W. MacBean, *Miscellanea Jacobitiana,* New York, 1902, vol. 8, p. 157. Mr. MacDonald's obituary adds that on New Year's Day, 1825, at the age of 105, MacDonald danced a reel with four generations of his male issue.

20. Rosalind K. Marshall, *Bonnie Prince Charlie,* Edinburgh, 1988, p. 157.

21. Now, it is said, part of the Royal Hotel.

22. Robert Chambers, ed. *Jacobite Memoirs of the Rebellion,* Edinburgh, 1834, p. 455.

23. Quoted in Forster, p. 177.

24. Anon., *The History of the Rise Progress, and Extinction of the Late Rebellion in Scotland,* Edinburgh, 1759, pp. 159-160.

25. Maclean and Gibson, p. 68.

Notes for Chapter 3

1. Elizabeth Gray Vining, *Flora, A Biography,* New York, 1966, p. 15.

2. Alexander MacGregor, *The Life of Flora MacDonald,* Stirling, 1901, p. 30.

3. Robert A. Logan, "Dates in the Life of Flora MacDonald," *The Scottish Genealogist* XXIX: March 1982, p. 2.

4. Alasdair Maclean and John S. Gibson, *Summer Hunting a Prince,* Stornoway, 1992, p. 59.

5. *The Gentlemen's Magazine,* XVI: August, 1746, p. 429.

6. *Ibid.,* XVI, October, 1746, p. 532.

7. Frederick A Pottle and Charles H. Bennett, eds., *Boswell's Journal of a Tour of the Hebrides with Samuel Johnson, LL.D. Now First Published from the Original Manuscript,* New York, 1936, p. 154n.

8. *Ibid.,* pp. 159–160.

9. Thomas Pennant, *A Tour of Scotland and Voyage to the Hebrides 1772,* London, 1776, vol. I, p. 342.

10. Peter Levi, ed., *A Journey to the Western Islands of Scotland and The Journal of a Tour to the Hebrides,* Penguin, 1984, p. 14.

11. Pennant, vol. I, p. 345.

12. Pottle and Bennett, p. 162.

13. Lord John Drummond was the younger brother of James Drummond, Jacobite Duke of Perth. James shared with Lord George Murray command of the Jacobite army, and John came from France at the head of an Irish brigade. The brothers left Scotland in early May aboard a French privateer.

14. *The Females Rebels, Being some Remarkable Incidents of the Lives, Characters, and Families of the Titular Duke and Duchess of Perth, the Lord and Lady Ogilvie, and Miss Florence McDonald*, Dublin, 1747, p. 55.

15. In February 1715–16, this same Vezzosi, then a servant in the Italian embassy in London, played a bit part in Lady Nithsdale's daring rescue of her husband from the Tower on the eve of his scheduled execution. See Flora Maxwell Stuart, *Lady Nithsdale and the Jacobites*, Innerliethen, 1995, p. 89.

16. *Ascanius: or the Young Adventurer, A True History*, London, n.d., p. 3.

17. Padre Giulio Cesare Cordara, "Commentary on the Expedition to Scotland Made by Charles Edward Stuart, Prince of Wales," Sir Bruce Seton, ed., in *Miscellany of the Scottish Historical Society*, Edinburgh, 1926, pp. 152ff.

18. As described in Voltaire, "Siecle de Louis XV," *Oeuvres*, Paris, 1836, IV.

19. *Ascanius*, pp. 47–48.

20. Voltaire, p. 61.

21. J. C. Hadden, *Prince Charles Edward*, London, 1913, p. 239.

22. C. Day Lewis, trans., *The Aeneid of Virgil*, New York, 1953, VII, 480 ff.

23. *Ascanius*, p. 55.

24. *Alexis* also appeared as *An Interesting and Faithful Narrative of the Wanderings of Prince Charles Stuart and Miss Flora MacDonald*, ed. Peter Buchan, Glasgow, 1839. The 1839 edition does not include the list of characters found in the 1746 edition.

25. Alasdair Maclean, *A MacDonald for the Prince*, Stornoway, 1990, p. 56.

26. Letter reprinted in Henrietta Tayler, *A Jacobite Miscellany*, Oxford, 1949, p. 189.

27. Dorothy Mackay Quynn, "Flora MacDonald in History," *The North Carolina Historical Review*, no. 3: July, 1941, p. 249n.

Notes for Chapter 4

1. Sir Walter Scott, *The Tales of a Grandfather*, London, 1925, p. 1153.

2. *Ibid.*, p. 1169.

3. Robert Chambers, *The History of the Rebellion in Scotland, 1745–1746*, 2 vols., Edinburgh, 1827, II, 153.

4. Forbes was a clergyman of the Episcopal Church of Scotland. In 1762 he was made Bishop of Ross and Caithness.

5. Robert Forbes, *The Lyon in Mourning*, 3 vols., ed. Paton, Edinburgh, 1975, I, 113n. The 1975 edition is a reprint of Paton's 1895 edition. All subsequent references are to the 1975 edition.

6. Robert Chambers, *Traditions of Edinburgh*, Edinburgh, 1931, p. 19n. The notes are those of Robert Chambers and the editor of later editions, C. E. S. Chambers. The latter Chambers says eight volumes, not ten. Later in the book Robert Chambers mentions that he has Forbes's manuscript (177n).

7. A bit of evidence to suggest that those who did know of Forbes's manuscript may have had trouble gaining access to it: Andrew Lang, at work on *Pickle the Spy*, says he had read parts of the MS., but that "difficulties were made when I wished to study it for this book." (*Pickle*, p. 24n) In his Preface to *Pickle*, dated November 5, 1896, Lang notes that *The Lyon . . .* has been printed and repeats, "I was unable to consult the MS. for this book, but it contains, I now find, no addition to the facts here set forth." (xiv)

8. Unsigned article, "Biographical Sketches—Flora MacDonald," *Chambers' Edinburgh Journal*, 1834, pp. 316–317.

9. Joseph Seawell Jones, *Memorials of North Carolina*, New York, 1835, p. 75.

10. John H. Jesse, *Memoirs of the Pretenders and their Adherents*, Boston, 19–?, p. 99ff.

11. The Reverend William Henry Foote, *Sketches of North Carolina*, New York, 1846, p. 157.

12. *Ibid.*, p. 150.

13. *Ibid.*, p. 150.

14. *Ibid.*, p. 152.

15. Elizabeth F. Ellet, *The Women of the American Revolution*, 3 vols., New York, 1848–1850, II, 149.

16. James Banks, Esq., "A Lecture on the Life and Character of Flora MacDonald," *The University Magazine*, np. 1857, pp. 23–24.

17. Banks, p. 4.

18. *Ibid.*, p. 6.

19. *Ibid.*, p. 7.

20. Alexander MacGregor, *The Life of Flora MacDonald*, Stirling, 1932, p. 102.

21. Flora Frances Wylde, *The Life of Flora MacDonald by her grand-daughter*, London, 1875, p. 216.

22. Alasdair Maclean and John Gibson, *Summer Hunting a Prince*, Stornoway, 1992, passim.

23. Wylde, p. 240.

24. MacGregor, p. 28.

25. William Jolly, *Flora MacDonald in Uist*, p. i.

26. *British Biographical Archives*, no. 715, pp. 350–358.

27. A. R. MacDonald, "A True Account of the Life of Flora Mac-Donald," *Oban Times*, July 8, 1905.

28. Scottish Society of America, *Flora MacDonald: A History and a Message from James A. MacDonald, DD, LLD*, Washington, 1916, title page.

29. *Ibid.*, pp. 17–18.

30. *Ibid.*, p. 23.

31. Donald MacKinnon in his introduction to Allan R. MacDonald's *The Truth about Flora MacDonald*, Inverness, 1938, p. xiv.

32. The Baron Ernest Porcelli, *The White Cockade*, London, 1949, p. 209.

33. I am grateful to Eloise Knight, of Pinehurst, NC, Mr. Wicker's daughter, for allowing me to read the MacKinnon manuscript.

34. Elizabeth Gray Vining, *Flora, A Biography*, New York, 1966, quoted on dust jacket.

Notes for Chapter 5

1. Elizabeth Gray Vining, *Flora, A Biography*, Philadelphia, 1966, p. 25.

2. Col. David Stewart, *Sketches of the Character, Manners, and Present State of the Highlanders of Scotland*, 2 vols., Edinburgh, 1822, II, xxxiii.

3. J. Cuthbert Hadden, *Prince Charles Edward*, London, 1913, p. 238.

4. William Jolly, *Flora MacDonald in Uist*, Perth, 1886, p. 21.

5. Alexander MacGregor, *The Life of Flora MacDonald*, Stirling, 1901, p. 55.

6. *Ibid.*, p. 55.

7. Allan R. MacDonald, "A True Account of the Life of Flora MacDonald," Oban *Times*, July 8, 1905.

8. Vining, p. 25.

9. Robert Chambers, *History of the Rebellion in Scotland 1745–1746*, Edinburgh, 1827, p. 153.

10. Walter Biggar Blaikie, *Edinburgh at the Time of the Occupation of Prince Charles*, Edinburgh, 1910, p. 33.

11. *Ibid.*, p. 34.

12. W. G. Blaikie Murdock, *The Spirit of Jacobite Loyalty*, Edinburgh, 1907, p. 23.

13. Samuel Johnson, *Journey to the Western Islands of Scotland*, ed. Peter Levi, London, 1984, p. 55.

14. Murdock, p. 63.

15. W. Drummond Norie, *The Life and Adventures of Prince Charles Edward Stuart*, 4 vols., London, n.d., IV, 47.

16. Winifred Duke, *Prince Charles Stuart and the '45*, London, 1938, p. 266.

17. Alexander Nicholson, *History of Skye*, Glasgow, 1930, p. 233.

18. The Reverend A. MacDonald, DD, *Memorials of the '45*, Inverness, 1930, p. 78.

19. *The Scotsman*, January 6, 1927. Report of W. Forbes Gray, "Romantic Episodes in the History of Edinburgh," broadcast over BBC Edinburgh.

20. Norie, p. 47.

21. *The Female Rebels*, Dublin, 1747, p. 53.

22. Robert Forbes, *The Lyon in Mourning*, 3 vols., Edinburgh, 1975, I, 116.

23. *Ibid.*, p. 117.

24. Allan R. MacDonald, *The Truth about Flora MacDonald*, Inverness, 1938, p. 71n.

25. The Reverend A. MacDonald, p. 78.

26. Stewart, I, 107.

27. William Donaldson, *The Jacobite Song*, Aberdeen, 1988, pp. 40–41.

28. Compton Mackenzie, *Prince Charlie and his Ladies*, London, 1934, p. 75.

Notes for Chapter 6

1. A bit player here, Conway married General John Campbell's daughter, says the plaque on his portrait in Inverary Castle. He continued his military career and served in Parliament, where he made several speeches opposing Britain's American war. When the war ended, he was appointed commander-in-chief. Cf. Christopher Hibbert, *Redcoats and Rebels*, New York, 1990, pp. 254, 336, 340.

2. Horace Walpole, *Correspondence*, ed. W. S. Lewis, et al., London, 1974, vol. 37, letter dated 12 August 1746 (OS).

3. *Ibid.*

4. *Ibid.*

5. Other spellings of the captain's name include "Ferguson" and "Fergussone."

6. Sir James Fergusson, *Argyll in the Forty-Five*, London, 1951, p. 224.

7. Vining, p. 75.

8. Fergusson, p. 231.

9. *Ibid.*, p. 233.

10. Quoted in Angus W. McLean, *Highland Scots in North Carolina*, unpublished ms., 1919, pp. 127–128. The work has been published, but the reference is taken from the manuscript version.

11. *Ibid.*, p. 129.

12. Fergusson, p. 233.

13. Governor McLean's several positions from *Dictionary of American Biography*, vol. XXI, New York, 1935.

14. McLean, p. 108.

15. *Ibid.*, p. 109

16. Fergusson, p. 236.

17. *Ibid.*, p. 246.

18. *The Albemarle Papers*, ed. Charles Sanford Terry, Aberdeen, 1902, letter dated 5 August 1746 from Lord Justice-Clerk Andrew Fletcher to William Anne, 2nd Earl of Albemarle.

19. The Reverend A. MacDonald, DD, *Memorials of the '45*, Inverness, 1930, p. 80.

20. Robert Forbes, *The Lyon in Mourning*, 3 vols., Edinburgh, 1975, I, 112.

21. *Ibid.*, I, 112.

22. *Ibid.*, I, 112.

23. *The Scotsman*, January 6, 1927. Report of W. Forbes Gray, "Romantic Episodes in the History of Edinburgh," broadcast over BBC Edinburgh.

24. *The Lyon in Mourning*, I, 112.

25. Dr. John Burton, *A Genuine and True Journal of the Most Miraculous Escape of the Young Pretender*, ed. E. Goldsmid, Edinburgh, 1891, p. 53n.

26. *The Lyon in Mourning*, I, 116.

27. Alasdair Maclean, *A MacDonald for the Prince*, Stornoway, 1990, p. 53.

28. *The Lyon in Mourning*, I, 113.

29. *Ibid.*, I, 113.

30. *Ibid.*, I, 114.

31. Public Records Office.

Notes for Chapter 7

1. *The Albemarle Papers*, ed. Charles Sanford Terry, Aberdeen, 1901, letter to the Duke of Newcastle, dated 27 October 1746.

2. *Ibid*, p. 39.

3. Fitzroy Maclean, *Bonnie Prince Charlie*, London, 1988, p. 245.

4. Allan R. MacDonald, *The Truth about Flora MacDonald*, Inverness, 1938, p. 61.

5. W. Drummond Norie, *The Life and Character of Prince Charles Edward Stewart*, 4 vols., London, n.d, IV, 82.

6. W. A. Speck, *The Butcher*, Oxford, 1981, p. 186.

7. J. Doran, *London in Jacobite Times*, 2 vols., London, 1877, II, 134.

8. Leonard Burkat, Program notes for performance of *Judas Maccabaeus*, Berkshire Choral Institute, July 30, 1994.

9. W. A. Speck mentions these honors in *The Butcher*, Oxford, 1981, but in "A Great Year for Drambuie," *Times Literary Supplement*,

August 11, 1995, p. 13, acknowledges "retailing uncritically the myth" about the flower.

10. Flora Frances Wylde, *The Life of Flora MacDonald*, London, 1875, p. 240.

11. Henrietta Tayler, "The Lieutenant-Governor of the Tower in 1745–1747," *Scottish Historical Review*, XXV, January, 1928, pp. 73–89.

12. Sir Walter Scott, *Tales of a Grandfather*, London, 1925, p. 1169

13. *Caledonian Mercury*, January 5, 1747.

14. A. Francis Steuart, "Jenny Cameron," *Scottish Arts and Letters*, vol. II, no. 4 (Sept–Nov., 1903), p. 393.

15. W. B. Blaikie, "Jenny Cameron of the Forty-Five," letter dated July 10, from Edinburgh, in *The Scotsman*, July 13, 1907.

16. *Ibid.*

17. *Ibid.*

18. Henrietta Tayler, *A Jacobite Miscellany*, in *Roxburghe Club Papers*, Oxford, 1948, p. 72.

19. Blaikie, *op. cit.*

20. Baron Ernest Porcelli, *The White Cockade*, London, 1949, p. 54.

21. Sir Bruce Gordon Seton and Jean Gordon Arnot, *The Prisoners of the '45*, 3 vols., Edinburgh, 1928, I, 93.

22. *Ibid.*, p. 213.

23. Charles M. Smith, "A Highland Heroine," *Munsey's Magazine*, July, 1897, p. 400.

24. A. R. MacDonald, *Memorials of the '45*, Inverness, 1930, pp. 80–81.

25. Margaret Williamson, "The Real Flora MacDonald," *The Lady's Realm*, September, 1897, p. 674.

26. Alexander Nicholson, *History of Skye*, Glasgow, 1930, pp. 246–247.

27. Smith, p. 400.

28. James Browne, *A History of the Highlands and of the Highland Clans*, 4 vols., Edinburgh, n.d., III, 309.

29. Wylde, p. 240.

30. Sir Walter Scott, *Tales of a Grandfather*, p. 1170n.

31. Doran, p. 254.

32. Norie, p. 83.

33. *Chambers' Edinburgh Journal*, vol. II, nos. 53–104, Edinburgh, pp. 316–317.

34. Jones, *Memorials of North Carolina*, New York, 1838, p. 69.

35. Chambers, pp. 316–317.

36. A. R. MacDonald, "A True Account of the Life of Flora Mac-Donald," Oban *Times*, August 5, 1905.

37. Attributed to W. B. Blaikie; quoted in James A. MacDonald, *Flora MacDonald, A History and a Message*, Washington, 1916, p. 20.

38. Seton and Arnot, I, 215.

39. Robert Chambers, *History of the Rebellion in Scotland, 1745–1746*, Edinburgh, 1827, p. 193.

Notes for Chapter 8

1. Quoted in *The Lyon in Mourning*, III, 67.

2. Dr, John Burton, *A Genuine and True Journal . . .*, p. 59.

3. Flora Frances Wylde, *The Life of Flora MacDonald . . .*, p. 258.

4. Of Mr. Sharpe it is written: "His thin effeminate figure, his voice pitched *in alt*—his attire, as he took his daily walks on Princes Street, a long blue frock coat, black trousers, rather wide below, and sweeping over white stockings and neat shoes—something like a web of cambric around his neck, and a brown wig coming down to his eyebrows—had long established him as what is called a character . . . In jest upon his own peculiarity of voice, he formed an address-card for himself consisting simply of" a single quarter note upon a musical staff depicting C sharp. He lived with his mother at 93 Princes Street. R. Chambers, *Traditions of Edinburgh*, Edinburgh, 1931, p. vi.

5. Quoted in MacBean, *Miscellanea Jacobitiana*, New York, 1902, II, 88.

6. *Ibid.*

7. Dr. Ellen G. Miles, Letter to the author, April 7, 1992.

8. Jacob Simon, notes to *Thomas Hudson 1701–1779, Portrait painter and collector, A bicentenary exhibition*, Greater London Council, 1979.

9. Miles, letter dated April 7, 1992.

10. Elizabeth Gray Vining, *Flora, A Biography*, Philadelphia, 1966, p. 85.

11. Notes in the Scottish National Portrait Gallery, Edinburgh.

12. *Ibid.*

13. Witt Library catalogue, Yale Center for British Art, New Haven, CT.

14. Letter dated August, 1956, in Scottish National Portrait Gallery, Edinburgh.

15. W. G. Constable, *Richard Wilson*, London, 1953, p. 152.

16. *Ibid.*, p. 236.

17. Alison Lewis, *Joseph Highmore: 1692–1780*, Harvard PhD dissertation, 1975, p. 325.

18. Alastair Smart, *The Life and Art of Allan Ramsay*, London, 1952, p. 183.

19. A. E. Haswell-Miller to Mrs. M. McIntyre Wilson, letter dated July 15, 1938, in Scottish National Portrait Gallery, Edinburgh.

20. J. Penderal-Broadhurst, "The Portraits of Flora MacDonald," *Art Journal*, 1899, p. 112.

21. *British Heritage*, December/January, 1992/1993, p. 22.

22. Exhibited at Caledonia Fine Arts Company, Ivoryton, CT, September 21, 1996.

23. See Daphne Foskett, *Miniatures Dictionary and Guide*, Antique Collectors' Club, 1987, p. 625; Mrs. E. F. Ellet, *Women Artists in All Ages and Countries*, London, 1859, p. 166; W. S. Sparrow, *Women Painters of the World*, London, 1905, p. 57.

24. See especially Lady Victoria Manners, "Catherine Read," *Connoisseur*, LXXXVIII & LXXXIX, December, 1931–March, 1932.

25. The portraits, of Mary Gunning, Countess of Coventry, and Elizabeth, Duchess of Argyll, hang in Inverary Castle. The portrait of Flora passed through an auction house in the 1980s and remains at large.

26. M. Fergusson, *Rambles in Skye, with a sketch of a trip to St Kilda*, Irvine, 1895, p. 150.

27. Ellis Waterhouse, *The Dictionary of British 18th Century Painters*, Antique Collectors' Club, 1981.

28. Lewis, p. 455.

29. *Ibid.*, p. 456.

30. *Ibid.*, p. 457.

31. Warren Mild, *Joseph Highmore of Holborn Row*, Ardmore, PA, 1990, chapter 9, p. 1.

32. Lewis, p. 455.

33. Donald B. Chidsey, *Bonnie Prince Charlie*, New York, 1928, facing p. 174.

34. Penderal-Broadhurst, p. 113.

35. John H. Jesse, *Memoirs of the Pretenders and their Adherents*, Boston, 19–?, III, 112–113.

Notes for Chapter 9

1. Alasdair Maclean, *A MacDonald for the Prince*, Stornoway, 1982, pp. 59–60.

2. Hugh Douglas, *Flora MacDonald, The Most Loyal Rebel*, Dover, 1993, p. 97.

3. Allan R. MacDonald, "A True Account of the Life of Flora MacDonald," *Oban Times*, August 19, 1905.

4. See, for example, Douglas, p. 96, and MacDonald, *Oban Times*, August 12, 1905.

5. Donald Mackinnon, *The Life and Adventures of Flora MacDonald*, unpublished ms. shown to the author by Mrs. Eloise Knight of Pinehurst, NC.

6. MacGregor, p. 158n.

7. Maclean, p. 68.

8. John McLeod's Memorial, unpublished ms. in Beinecke Collection, Yale University.

9. See especially, Maclean, *op. cit.*, John Gibson, "The Summer's Hunting," in *The 45—to gather an image whole,*" ed. Scott-Moncrieff, Edinburgh, 1988, and Maclean and Gibson, *Summer Hunting a Prince*, Stornoway, 1992.

10. Maclean and Gibson, p. 65.

11. In November 1840, 52 years after his death in France, Neil MacEachain's narrative of the events of 1745–1746 appeared in *New Monthly Magazine*.

12. Maclean, *A MacDonald for the Prince*, Introduction.

13. *Ibid.*, p. 79.

14. Dorothy Mackay Quynn, "Flora MacDonald in History," *The North Carolina Historical Review*, July, 1941, p. 244.

15. David Greenwood, *William King, Tory and Jacobite*, Oxford, 1969, p. 235.

16. *Ibid.*, p. 236.

17. Douglas, p. 105.

18. A. MacDonald, "A True Account...," *Oban Times*, August 12, 1905.

19. "The Grave of Flora MacDonald," *Gentleman's Magazine*, May, 1868, p. 603.

20. Quoted in Boswell, *A Tour of the Hebrides*, ed. Levi, London, 1975, pp. 243–245.

21. Duane Meyer, *The Highland Scots of North Carolina, 1732–1776*, Chapel Hill, NC, 1961, p. 50n.

22. Samuel Johnson, *A Journey to the Western Islands of Scotland*, ed. Levi, London, 1975, p. 101.

23. Johnson, p. 73.

24. William R. Brock, *Scotus Americanus (A Survey of the sources for the links between Scotland and America in the 18th Century.)* Edinburgh, 1982, p. 82. For the identity of Scotus Americanus, see Ned C. Landsman, "Immigration and Settlement," in *Scotland and the Americas 1600 to 1800*, Providence, RI, 1995, pp. 22–23.

25. Brock, p. 83.

26. Johnson, p. 75

27. Boswell, p. 327.

28. Quoted in Vining, p. 115.

29. Quoted in Angus W. McLean, *Highland Scots in North Carolina*, unpublished ms., p. 111.

30. Boswell, p. 280.

31. Letter from Flora to John Mackenzie quoted in Vining, p. 118.

32. Letter from Flora to the Duke of Atholl, quoted in Allan R. MacDonald, *The Truth about Flora MacDonald*, Inverness, 1938, pp. 110–111.

33. Boswell, p. 261.

Notes for Chapter 10

1. Hugh Douglas, *Flora MacDonald, A Most Loyal Rebel*, Durham, NH, 1993, p. 138.

2. Rassie Wicker, *Miscellaneous Ancient Records of Moore County, NC*, Southern Pines, NC, 1971, p. 441.

3. *Ibid.*, p. 155.

4. J. P. Maclean, "Flora MacDonald in America," *The Celtic Monthly*, vol. 8, 1899, p. 106.

5. J. P. Maclean, *Flora MacDonald in America*, Lumberton, NC, 1909, p. 47.

6. Wicker, p. 441.

7. Bruce Lenman, *The Jacobite Cause*, Glasgow, 1986, p. 120.

8. Joseph Seawell Jones, *Memorials of North Carolina*, New York, 1836, p. 70.

9. James Wolfe, who died while leading British troops to victory at Quebec, wrote to a friend in Nova Scotia in 1751, "I should imagine that two or three independent Highland companies might be of use; they are hardy, intrepid, accustomed to rough country, and no great mischief if they fall. How can you better employ a secret enemy than by making the end conducive to the common good." Quoted in W. Duncan MacMillan (with Patricia Condon Johnston), *MacGhillemhaoil*, 2 vols., Wayzata, MN, I, 16. This same James Wolfe, a major at Culloden, is said to have refused General Hawley's order to execute a wounded Highland officer. Cf. M. Hook and W. Ross, *The 'Forty-Five*, Edinburgh, 1995, p. 117.

10. James Banks, Esq., "A Lecture on the Life and Character of Flora MacDonald," *The University Magazine,* np. 1857, p. 19.

11. *Ibid.*, p. 19.

12. "A Narrative of the Proceedings of a Body of Loyalists in North Carolina," in Wicker, p. 436.

13. Wicker, p. 340.

14. Banks, p. 20.

15. Flora MacDonald's Memorial, in Henrietta Tayler, ed., *A Jacobite Miscellany*, Oxford, 1948, p. 188.

16. *Ibid.*, p. 188.

17. Foote, p. 156.

18. Banks, p. 21.

19. McLean, insert between pages 115 and 116.

20. Wicker, p. 343.

21. McLean, p. 117.

22. *Ibid.*, p. 118.

23. Typescript of an essay written by Dr. Vardell in 1937 in the archives of St. Andrews Presbyterian College, Laurinburg, NC.

24. James E. and Ida C. Huneycutt, *A History of Richmond County*, Rockingham, NC, 1976, p. 121.

25. Paul Green, "Searching for Flora MacDonald's Home in North Carolina," typescript dated 21 October 1953, p. 2.

26. *Ibid.*, p. 3.

27. Eloise Knight, conversation with the author, September 26, 1993.

28. McLean, p. 126

29. Previously quoted from Vining, p. 5.

30. See, for example, J. P. Maclean, *Flora MacDonald in America*, Lumberton, NC, 1909, p. 45.

31. C. G. Vardell, Notes, Scottish Heritage Collection, St. Andrews Presbyterian College, Laurinburg, NC.

Notes for Chapter 11

1. Angus W. McLean, *Highland Scots in North Carolina*, unpublished ms., 1919, p. 121.

2. *Ibid.*, p. 122.

3. Rassie Wicker, *Miscellaneous Ancient Records of Moore County, N.C.*, Southern Pines, NC, 1971, p. 372.

4. This and the preceding quotations from Flora's memorial in H. Tayler, ed., *A Jacobite Miscellany*, Oxford, 1948, p. 189.

5. *Ibid.*, p. 189.

6. McLean, pp. 125–126.

7. "Flora MacDonald," in *Chambers' Edinburgh Journal*, vol II, London, 1834, p. 317.

8. Letter in Donald MacKinnon, *The Life and Adventures of Flora MacDonald*, unpublished ms., 1953, p.154.

9. MacKinnon, p. 155.

10. James Boswell, *The Journal of a Tour to the Hebrides*, P. Levi, ed., London, 1984, p. 265.

11. This is Governor McLean's version of the Memorial (p. 137). Wicker's omits the references to the Duke of Cumberland and Lord Loudon (p. 373).

12. Wicker, p. 373.

13. McLean, insert following p. 136.

14. Alexander MacGregor, *The Life of Flora MacDonald*, Inverness, 1932, p. 173.

15. John Prebble, *The King's Jaunt*, London, 1988, p. 327.

16. Flora Frances Wylde, *The Life of Flora MacDonald*, London, 1870, p. 374.

17. E.E.G., "The Grave of Flora MacDonald," *Gentlemen's Magazine*, May, 1868, p. 608.

18. Chambers, p. 317.

19. Eric Linklater, *The Prince in the Heather*, London, 1987, p. 129.

Notes for Chapter 12

1. Alexander Macgregor, *The Life of Flora Macdonald*, 5th ed., Stirling, 1932, p. 179.

2. Whisky as the traditional drink at Highland funerals is anecdotally documented in David Daiches, *Scotch Whisky*, London, 1969, p. 47. He tells us that in the 19th century a young Highland lass was asked "if her aunt, who was gravely ill, was still alive." Her reply: "Ay. She's no deid yet; but we've gotten in the whusky for the funeral."

3. Alexander Mackenzie, *History of the MacDonalds and Lords of the Isles*, Inverness, 1881, p. 234.

4. Malcolm Fowler, *They Passed this Way*, Harnett County [NC] Centennial Inc., 1955, p. 40.

5. Sir William Musgrave, *Obituary*, ed. Sir William Armytage, London, 1899.

6. *Scots Magazine*, vol. 52 (1790), p. 205.

7. *Gentleman's Magazine*, 1790, p. 398.

8. *European Magazine*, 1790, p. 312.

9. *Gentleman's Magazine*, January, 1831, pp. 85–87.

10. "The Memorial of Flora MacDonald," in Henrietta Tayler, *A Jacobite Miscellany*, Oxford, 1948, pp. 185ff.

11. "The Memorial of John MacLeod," ms. in the Bienecke Rare Book and Manuscript Library, Yale University, 1775.

12. James Boswell, *A Journal of a Tour of the Hebrides*, ed. Peter Levi, London, 1984, p. 269.

13. James Banks, *A Lecture on the Life and Times of Flora MacDonald*, p. 23.

14. *Ibid.*, p. 23.

15. *Ibid.*, p. 23.

16. E. E. G., "The Grave of Flora MacDonald," *Gentleman's Magazine,* May, 1868, p. 600.

17. *Ibid.*, pp. 608–609.

18. The Reverend Alexander MacDonald, Kilmuir, Skye, letter dated April 29, 1926.

19. William M. MacBean, a clipping contained in *Towards a Jacobite Iconography—Miscellanea Jacobitiana*.

20. MacBean, Vol. 5, p. 33.

21. *Scottish Notes and Queries*, Vol. VIII, # 11, April, 1895, p. 163.

22. MacBean, Vol. 12, p. 97.

23. Charles MacDonald Smith, "A Highland Heroine," *Munsey's Magazine*, July, 1887, p. 398.

24. *Scottish Notes and Queries*, October, 1893, p. 68.

25. *Scottish Notes and Queries*, Vol. IX, no. 1 (June, 1895), p. 4.

Notes for Chapter 13

1. Robert Forbes, *The Lyon in Mourning*, ed. Paton, 3 vols., Edinburgh, 1975, II, 82.

2. *Ibid.*, II, 332.

3. *Ibid.*, III, 78. For more on those lines see p. 204.

4. *Ibid.*, III, 67.

5. E. E. G., "The Grave of Flora MacDonald," *The Gentleman"s Magazine*, V (n.s.): May, 1868, p. 608.

6. Ian Jack, *English Literature 1815–1832*, Oxford, 1963, p. 210.

7. *Ibid.*, p. 201.

8. John MacDonald, Letter in *The Gentleman's Magazine*, November, 1828, p. 400.

9. *Ibid.*, p. 400.

10. Alexander Grant, "The Middle Ages: the defense of Independence," *Why Scottish History Matters*, Saltire Society, 1991, p. 24.

11. MacDonald, Letter, p. 400.

12. *Ibid.*, p. 400.

13. *Ibid.*, p. 400.

14. Sir Walter Scott, *The Surgeon's Daughter*, Edinburgh, 1903, p. 256.

15. Edgar Johnson, *Sir Walter Scott, The Great Unknown*, 2 vols., New York, 1970, I, 321.

16. John MacDonald, *Charles Edward Stuart, The Pretender in Scotland, or, The Misfortunes of an Exile,* an Historical Drama in 3 Acts, Paris, 1802.

17. "Obituary—Lieut.-Col. John MacDonald, F.R.S.," *The Gentleman's Magazine*, January, 1832, pp. 86–87.

18. Mrs. Grant of Laggan, *Lines to Colonel John MacDonald, the youngest son of "Flora."*

19. William Donaldson, *The Jacobite Song: Political Myth and National Identity*, Aberdeen, 1988, pp. 3–4.

20. *Ibid.*, p. 107.

21. Cf. James Hogg, *Jacobite Minstrelsy*, Glasgow, 1829; B. H. Humble, *The Songs of Skye*, Stirling, 1934; Andrew Lang, "Jacobite Songs," *Scottish Historical Review*, January, 1911; Dr. K. N. MacDonald, "Poems and Songs in Honour of Flora MacDonald," *Miscellanea Jacobitiana,* New York, 1902.

22. Lang, p. 143.

23. *The Poems of William Aytoun*, Oxford, 1921, pp. 87–92.

24. *Ibid.*, pp. 221–244.

25. Quoted in MacGregor, *Life* . . . ., p. 105.

26. Hogg, *Jacobite Minstrelsy*, p. 105.

27. MacGregor, p. 88.

28. Lang, p. 144.

29. *Ibid.*, p. 144.

30. Hogg, p. 275.

31. Humble, p. 87.

32. Benjamin G. Herre, *Flora MacDonald: A Tale of Freedom and Loyalty*, Lancaster, 1870.

33. *Ibid.*, p. 53.

34. *Ibid.*, p. 56.

35. *Ibid.*, p. 78.

36. *Ibid.*, p. 79.

37. The Reverend George Henderson, *Lady Nairne and Her Songs*, Paisley, 1908.

38. *The Poems of Alexander Macdonald (Alasdair MacMhaighstir Alasdair)*, The Reverends A. Macdonald and A. Macdonald, DD, Inverness, 1924, p. 87.

39. *Ibid.*

40. Sarah Tytler, *The MacDonald Lass*, London, 1895, pp. 150, 240.

Notes for Chapter 14

1. Emmuska, Baroness Orczy, "Flora and the Bonnie Prince," *North China Herald*, Sept. 26, 1934, pp. 477–478. All the quotations which follow are from those pages.

2. Carole May Anima Lenanton, *Over the Water*, London, 1935, *passim*.

3. Paul Green, *The Highland Call,* Chapel Hill, NC, 1941. Quotation from the title page.

4. *Ibid.,* p. 189.

5. *Ibid.,* p. 192. For an introduction to the locally legendary Jennie Ban (or Bahn) MacNeill, see Malcolm Fowler, *They Passed this Way: A Personal Narrative of Harnett County*, Harnett County, NC, 1971, pp. 40-43.

6. 1975 edition, p. 59.

7. *Ibid.,* p. 60.

8. Unsigned article citing the Greenoch *Telegraph* in W. M. MacBean, *Miscellanea Jacobitania*, New York, 1902, vol. 9, p. 110.

9. *Ibid.*; also Glasgow University Library, Drysdale Collection (Cb9 – x.24).

10. Drysdale Collection (Cb9 – x.24).

11. Drysdale Collection (Cb10 – x.17).

12. Inglis Fletcher, *Raleigh's Eden*, Garden City, 1951, p. 416.

13. *Ibid.,* p. 476.

14. *Ibid.,* p. 418.

15. *Ibid.,* p. 481.

16. Inglis Fletcher, *The Scotswoman*, New York, 1954, p. 382.

17. *Ibid.,* p. 382.

18. *Ibid.,* p. 382.

19. *Ibid.,* pp. 36–37.

20. *Ibid.,* pp. 38–39.

21. Elizabeth Coatsworth, *Aunt Flora*, New York, 1953.

22. *The Mammoth Book of Historical Detectives*, ed. Mike Ashley, New York, 1995, p. 372.

23. Lillian De la Torre, *The White Rose of Stuart*, Edinburgh, 1954.

24. David Niven, *The Moon's a Balloon*, New York, 1972, p. 286.

25. Clare Johnson Marley, *Flora MacDonald, Preserver of Prince Charles*, unpublished MA thesis, University of North Carolina, Chapel Hill, NC, 1945, Author's Foreword, pp. iii–iv.

26. *Ibid.,* p. 84.

27. *Ibid.,* pp. 107ff.

28. *Ibid.,* p. 122.

29. Obituary notice, St. Andrews *Citizen*, November 3, 1989, p. 5c.

30. A. B. Paterson, *Flora in Carolina*, unpublished ms., p. 85.

31. A 26-page typescript is in the National Library of Scotland. It appears to be unpublished.

Notes for Chapter 15

1. This chapter title comes from a pamphlet of the same name published in 1900. It is in the archives of St. Andrews Presbyterian College, Laurinburg, NC.

2. James A. MacDonald, *What a Newspaper Man Saw in Britain*, Toronto, 1907, p. 11.

3. Actually there had been a women's college in the area earlier. Floral College, founded in 1841 between Red Springs (then called Dora) and Maxton, had been the first college in North Carolina to grant diplomas to women, but the Civil War and subsequent hard times had led to the college's closing in 1878. One anecdote from Floral's history has it that shortly after the Civil War the Reverend Joseph Wilson came up from Wilmington to preach the Baccalaureate sermon, bringing with him his son Tommie. The lad was apparently a bit too inattentive for the liking of one senior member of the congregation, who chastised the youngster in stern Presbyterian terms. By the time Flora MacDonald College came into being, little Tommie Wilson had grown up to be Woodrow and President of the United States.

4. C.G. Vardell, 1937 typescript in the archives of St. Andrews Presbyterian College, Laurinburg, NC.

5. *Ibid.*

6. Howard A. Banks, "The God-blessed Macs and their college for girls," typescript in the archives of St. Andrews Presbyterian College, Lauringburg, NC, pp. 11-12.

7. Ralph W. Page, *Flora MacDonald College*, reprinted from *The World's Work*, September, 1916, pp. 12-13.

8. "A Message from Doctor MacDonald," a reprint of the May, 1914, speech in Fayetteville, included in *Flora MacDonald: A History and A Message*, Washington, DC, 1916, p. 21.

9. What would have happened if Dr. MacDonald had known of Flora's Canadian sojourn? Would he have named a college in Nova Scotia after her? Would Flora have vied with Laura Secord as Canada's preeminent heroic woman? Mrs. Secord bears further study. She could easily have been the third in a triumvirate of British heroines, alongside Flora and Grace Darling. All the ingredients are present except, so far, the quotation linking her to the other two.

10. Page, p. 13.

11. "A Message from Doctor MacDonald," p. 21.

12. Letter from Dr. Vardell to the Board of Trustees dated Feb. 12, 1915, in the archives of St. Andrews Presbyterian College, Laurinburg, NC.

13. As printed in *The State Journal*, November 24, 1916.

14. What these were and where they are remain unknown at this writing.

15. Commencement program from 1916, archives of St. Andrews Presbyterian College, Laurinburg, NC.

16. Page, p. 16.

17. *Ibid.*, p. 22.

18. Pamphlet advertising Red Springs Seminary, St. Andrews Presbyterian College Archives, Laurinburg, NC, n.d.

19. Page, p. 9.

20. Oft-quoted, this passage is taken from Page, p. 5.

21. Cf. Christina M. Marley, *Expectations for the Daughters of Flora MacDonald College in the 1920s*, Senior Honors Thesis, St. Andrews Presbyterian College, Laurinburg, NC, 1989.

22. The major consistently spells the family surname with the lowercase "d."

23. In his tally Macdonald does not include children of Macdonald women who married into other families, though the women are included. A copy of the speech was kindly given me by the librarian at St. Andrews Presbyterian College.

24. Information on the last years of FMC comes from Herr, Banks, Bracey, Herr, Marley, and documents in the Archives of St. Andrews Presbyterian College, Lauringburg, NC.

25. Typescript of a draft of Dr. MacDonald's message, St. Andrews Presbyterian College, Laurinburg, NC.

Notes for Chapter 16

1. Noel Coward, *Ways and Means,* in *Curtain Calls*, New York, 1940, pp. 205-206.

2. Foote, *Sketches of North Carolina*, New York, 1846, p. 157.

3. See, for example, Jessica Mitford, *Grace Had an English Heart*, New York, 1988.

4. *The Poems of Wordsworth*, ed. T. Hutchinson, Oxford, 1926, p. 540.

5. W. M. MacBean, *Miscellanea Jacobitiana*, New York, 1902, vol. 5, p. 1.

6. Alexander Smith, *A Summer in Skye*, London, 1866, p. 198.

7. Mitford, p. 131.

8. Helen Eliza Finch Parker, *Discoverers and Pioneers of America*, New York, 1856, p. 19. Lady Arabella is the only woman among Mrs. Parker's discoverers and pioneers. It is also interesting to note that Mrs. Parker touches on the "artless tenderness" of Pocahontas in her chapter on John Smith. She does not mention Flora MacDonald in the book.

9. *Ibid.*, p. 19.

10. Quoted in Tilton, *Pocahontas: The Evolution of an American Narrative*, Cambridge, 1994.

11. Tilton identifies Mary Wall as the proponent of this idea.

12. J. C. Pickett, *The Memory of Pocahontas Vindicated . . . by a Kentuckian*, n.p., 1847, p. 86.

13. W. W. Waldron, *Pocahontas, Princess of Virginia and other Poems*, New York, 1841, p. 9. Quoted in Tilton, pp. xv–xvi.

14. Jared Sparks, writing in 1839. Quoted in Tilton, pp. xv–xvi.

15. Michael Fry, *The Dundas Despotism*, Edinburgh, 1992, p. 138.

16. John Prebble, *The King's Jaunt*, London, 1989, p. 206.

17. Not all of Flora's grandchildren fared so well. Around the end of the eighteenth century one of Flora's grandsons, Normal MacLeod, oldest of Anne's children, was shot by Alasdair MacDonnell of Glengarry in a duel over one Miss Forbes of Culloden.

18. Prebble, p. 327.

19. The Rev. George Henderson, *Lady Nairne and Her Songs*, 5th ed., Paisley, Scotland, 1908, p. 34.

20. Compton MacKenzie, *Prince Charlie and his Ladies*, New York, 1955, p. 163.

21. David Duff, ed., *Queen Victoria's Highland Journals*, Exeter, 1983, *passim*.

22. Quoted in Murray Pittock, *The Invention of Scotland*, London, 1991, p. 63.

23. The Rev. Charles Rogers, *The Scottish Minstrel: The Songs of Scotland Subsequent to Burns*, Edniburgh, 1872, pp. 349–350.

24. John Sobieska and Charles Edward Stuart, *Tales of the Century*, Edinburgh, 1847.

25. *Ibid.*, pp. viii–ix.

26. C. G. Vardell, "Flora MacDonald, Scotland's Lady," quoted in J. A. Oates, *The Story of Fayetteville and the Upper Cape Fear*, Charlotte, 1950, p. 55.

27. James Browne, *A History of the Highlands and of the Highland Clans*, 4 vols., Edinburgh, nd., III, 310.

28. Walter Biggar Blaikie, *Edinburgh at the Time of the Occupation of Prince Charles*, Edinburgh, 1910, p. 60.

29. Bruce Lenman, *The Jacobite Cause*, Glasgow, 1986, p. 114.

30. W. G. Blaikie Murdoch, *The Spirit of Jacobite Loyalty*, Edinburgh, 1907, p. 146.

31. Euan Macpherson, "Anne Mackintosh, Colonel Anne of the '45," *Highlander*, xxix: Mar/Apr, 1991, pp. 67ff.

32. Rogers, p. 387.

33. Pittock, p. 101.

34. Nettie McCormick Henley, *The Home Place*, Laurinburg: Scottish Heritage Series, St. Andrews Press, 1989, p. 16. Rassie Wicker, *Miscellaneous Ancient Records of Moore County, NC*, Pinehurst, NC, 1971, p. 342.

35. Kathryn A. Beach, Historian at the Museum of the Cape Fear, Fayetteville, NC, in conversation with the author, September 26, 1992.

36. Wicker, p. 344.

Notes for Chapter 17

1. Lines from the sonnet "Fancy and Tradition," composed 1833, published 1835. From *The Poems of Wordsworth*, ed. T. Hutchinson, Oxford, 1926, p. 393.

2. The poem appears in Gaelic in Alexander MacGregor, *The Life of Flora MacDonald*, Stirling, 1901, pp. 118–119.

3. The Rev. Robert Forbes, *The Lyon in Mourning*, 3 vols., Edinburgh, 1975, III, 78.

4. The Rev. W. H. Foote, *Sketches of North Carolina*, New York, 1846, pp. 156–157.

5. Inglis Fletcher, *Raleigh's Eden*, Garden City, 1951, p. 418.

6. In such repositories as Abbotsford, Dunvegan Castle, Traquair House, the West Highland Museum in Ft. William, and the Museum of the Cape Fear, in Fayetteville.

7. From *Tales of a Grandfather*. Quoted in Ian Jack, *English Literature 1815–1832*, Oxford, 1963, p. 201.

Bibliography

Anonymous, "An Account of the Young Pretender's Escape Written by a Highland Officer in his army," *Lockhart Papers,* London, 1817.

Anonymous, *Ascanius; or The Young Adventurer,* London, n.d.

Anonymous, *A Full Account of all Poems upon Charles, Prince of Wales (published since his arrival in Edinburgh the 17th day of September till the 1st of November 1745),* Edinburgh, 1745.

Anonymous, *The History of the Rise, Progress, and Extinction of the Late Rebellion in Scotland,* Edinburgh, 1759.

Anonymous, *Manlius or, The Brave Adventurer,* Edinburgh, 1749.

Anonymous, *Young Juba, or The History of the Young Chevalier from his Birth to his Escape from Scotland after the Battle of Culloden,* London, 1748.

Armstrong, R., "Grace Darling, The Fate of a Victorian Heroine," in *British History,* 1965.

Ashley, M. (ed.), *The Mammoth Book of Historical Detectives,* New York, 1995.

Aytoun, W. E., *Poems,* Oxford, 1921.

Banks, J. *The Life and Character of Flora MacDonald,* Fayetteville, NC, 1857.

Banks, H. A., "The 'God-blessed Macs' and their college for girls." Typescript, DeTamble Librarry, St. Andrews Presbyterian College, Laurinburg, NC.

Birch, J., "Flora MacDonald," *The Highlander,* vol. 28 no. 6, Nov/Dec, 1990.

Blaikie, W. B., *Edinburgh at the Time of the Occupation of Prince Charles,* Edinburgh, 1910.

—— *Itinerary of Prince Charles Edward Stuart...,* Edinburgh, 1975.

—— "Jenny Cameron and the Forty-Five," *The Scotsman,* July 13,

—— (ed.). *Origins of the Forty-Five.* Edinburgh, 1916.

Boswell, J. *Journal of a Tour of the Hebrides with Samuel Johnson, LL.D.* Edited by P. Levi. London, 1984.

——. Another edition of the same, Pottle and Bennett, eds. New York, 1936.

Bracey, W. R. *A History of Flora MacDonald College.* Unpublished M.A. thesis, Appalachian State Teachers College. Boone, NC, 1962.

British Bibliographical Archive # 715. New York, 1984.

Brock, W. *Scotus Americanus (A survey of the sources for the links between Scotland and America in the 18th Century).* Edinburgh, 1982.

Brown, I. *Summer in Scotland.* London, 1952.

Brown, P. "Flora MacDonald: Beloved Heroine of the Cape Fear." *The Highlander,* vol. 20 no. 4, Sep/Oct, 1982.

Browne, J. *A History of the Highlands and of the Highland Clans,* 4 vols. Edinburgh, n.d.

Brumfitt, J. H. "Voltaire and Bonnie Prince Charlie." *Forum for Modern Language Studies,* 1985.

Buchan, J. "The Company of Marjolaine," in *The Best Short Stories of John Buchan.* London, 1980.

——. *Midwinter.* New York, 1923.

——. *Some Eighteenth Century Byways,* Edinburgh, 1908.

Buchan, P. (ed.). *Alexis — An Interesting and Faithful Narrative of the Wanderings of Prince Charles Stuart and Miss Flora MacDonald.* Glasgow, 1839.

Burkhat, L. Program notes for a performance of *Judas Maccabeus.* Berkshire Choral Institute, Sheffield, MA, July 30, 1994.

Burton, J. *A Genuine and True Journal of the Most Miraculous Escape of the Young Chevalier.* London, 1749.

Campbell, J. L. *Highland Songs of the '45.* Edinburgh, 1984.

Caledonian Mercury. 1746.

Carruth, J. A. *Flora MacDonald, The Highland Heroine.* Norwich, England, 1973.

Caudill, W. S. *North Carolina's Gaidhealtachd.* Unpublished honors thesis. St. Andrews Presbyterian College, Laurinburg, NC, 1989.

Chambers, R. "Flora MacDonald." *Chambers' Edinburgh Journal,* 1834.

——. *History of the Rebellion in Scotland.* Edinburgh, 2 vols., 1827, also 1840.

——. *Jacobite Memoirs of the Rebellion of 1745.* Edinburgh, 1834.

———. *Traditions of Edinburgh*. Edinburgh, 1931.

Chidsey, D. *Bonnie Prince Charlie*. New York, 1928.

Coatsworth, E. *Aunt Flora*. New York, 1953.

Constable, W. G. *Richard Wilson*. London, 1957.

Cordara, G. C. "Commentary on the Expedition to Scotland Made by Charles Edward Stuart, Prince of Wales," in *Miscellany of the Scottish Historical Society*. Edited by Sir Bruce Seton. 1926.

Coward, N. *Curtain Calls*. New York, 1940.

Daiches, D. *Charles Edward Stuart: The Life and Times of Bonnie Prince Charlie*. London, 1973.

———. *Scotch Whisky*. London, 1969.

De La Torre, L. *The White Rose of Stuart*. Edinburgh, 1954.

Donaldson, W. *The Jacobite Song*. Aberdeen, 1988.

Donnachie, I. & C. Watley (eds.). *The Manufacture of Scottish History*. Edinburgh, 1992.

Doran, J. *London in Jacobite Times*. 2 vols. London, 1877.

Douglas, H. *Flora MacDonald, The Most Loyal Rebel*. Dover, NH, 1993.

Drummond, J.(?). *The Female Rebels*. Dublin, 1747.

Drysdale Collection. Glasgow University Library.

Duff, D. (ed.). *Queen Victoria's Highland Journals*. Exeter, 1938.

Duke, W. *Prince Charles Stuart and the '45*. London, 1938.

———. *Scotland's Heir*. London, 1925.

Edinburgh Review. 1790.

"E. E. G." "The Grave of Flora MacDonald." *The Gentleman's Magazine*, May, 1868.

Ellet, E. F. *Women Artists in All Ages and Countries*. London, 1859.

———. *The Women of the American Revolution*. 3 vols. New York, 1848–1850.

Erickson, C. *Bonnie Prince Charlie*. New York, 1989.

European Magazine. 1790.

Ewald, A. C. *The Life and Times of Prince Charles Edward Stuart*. London, 1904.

Fergusson, J. *Argyll in the Forty-Five*. London, 1951.

Fergusson, M. *Rambles in Skye, with a sketch of a trip to St. Kilda*. Irvine, Scotland, 1895.

Fletcher, I. *Raleigh's Eden*. New York, 1951.

———. *The Scotswoman*. New York, 1954.

Foote, W. *Sketches of North Carolina*. New York, 1846.

Foskett, D. *Miniatures Dictionary and Guide*. Antique Collectors Club, Woodbridge, England, 1987.

Forbes, R. *The Lyon in Mourning*. Edited by H. Paton. 3 vols. Edinburgh, 1975.

Forster, M. *The Rash Adventurer*. London, 1972.

Fowler, M. *They Passed this Way*. Harnett County, NC, 1955.

Fraser, A. *The Warrior Queens*. New York, 1989.

Fraser, W. *Memorials of the Montgomeries, Earls of Eglinton*. 2 vols. Edinburgh, 1859.

Fry, M. *The Dundas Despotism*. Edinburgh, 1992.

"G", "Was Flora MacDonald Beautiful?" in W. M. MacBean, *Miscellanea Jacobitiana*. 14 vols. New York, 1902.

The Gentleman's Magazine. 1746, 1747, 1750, 1790, 1828, 1830, 1832.

Gibson, J. S. *Locheil of the '45*. Edinburgh, 1994.

——. *Ships of the '45*. London, 1967.

——. "The Summer's Hunting," in *The 45—to gather an image whole*. Edited by L. Scott-Moncrieff. Edinburgh, 1988.

Gordon, A. W. *Dame Flora*. London, 1974.

Grant, A. "The Middle Ages: the Defence of Independence," in *Why Scottish History Matters*, Saltire Society, 1991.

Grant, G. V. R. "The 45: A Disastrous Mistake," in *The 45—to gather an image whole*. Edited by L. Scott-Moncrieff. Edinburgh, 1988.

Grant of Laggan, Mrs. "Lines to Colonel John MacDonald, the Youngest Son of Flora," in A. MacGregor, *The Life of Flora MacDonald*. 4th ed. Stirling, 1902.

Gray, E. *Meggie MacIntosh*. New York, 1930.

Green, P. *The Highland Call*. Chapel Hill, NC, 1941.

——. *The Highland Call*. Revised edition. Fayetteville, NC, 1975.

——. "Searching for Flora MacDonald's Home." Typsescript, DeTamble Library, St. Andrews Presbyterian College, Laurinburg, NC.

——. *The Sheltering Plaid*. New York, 1965.

Greenwood, D. *William King: Tory and Jacobite*. Oxford, 1963.

Grosart, A. (ed.), *The Townley MSS: English Jacobite Ballads, Songs, and Satires*, privately printed, 1877.

Hadden, J. C. *Prince Charles Edward*. London, 1913.

Hartmann, C. H. *The Quest Forlorn*. London, 1952.

Haswell-Miller, A. E. Letter to Mrs. M. McIntyre Wilson, July 15, 1938. Scottish National Portrait Gallery, Edinburgh.

Henderson, G. *Lady Nairne and Her Songs.* Paisley, Scotland, 1908.

Henderson, T. "Flora MacDonald," in *Dictionary of National Biography.* Oxford, 1906.

Henley, N. M. *The Home Place.* Laurinburg, NC, 1989.

Herr, D. *Red Springs and the Closing of Flora MacDonald College.* Unpublished honors thesis. St. Andrews Presbyterian College, Laurinburg, NC, 1991.

Herre, B. *Flora MacDonald: A Tale of Freedom and Loyalty.* Lancaster, PA, 1870.

Hogg, J. *Jacobite Minstrelsy.* Glasgow, 1829.

Home, J. *The History of the Rebellion in the Year 1745.* London, 1802.

Hope-Moncrieff, A. R. *Highlands and Islands of Scotland.* London, 1925.

Hook, M. & W. Ross. *The 'Forty-Five.* Edinburgh, 1995.

Humble, B. H. *The Songs of Skye.* Stirling, Scotland, 1934.

Huneycutt, J. and I. *A History of Richmond County.* Rockingham, NC, 1976.

Jack, I. *English Literature 1815–1832.* Oxford, 1963.

Jarrett, T. G. "A. P. Paterson—the St. Andrews citizen of the 20th century." *St. Andrews Citizen.* St. Andrews, Scotland, November 3, 1989.

Jesse, J. H. *Memoirs of the Pretenders and their Adherents.* 3 vols. Boston, 19–?

Johnson, E. *Sir Walter Scott, The Great Unknown.* 2 vols. New York, 1970.

Johnson, S. *Journey to the Western Isles of Scotland.* Edited by P. Levi. London, 1984.

Jolly, W. *Flora MacDonald in Uist.* Perth, Scotland, 1886.

Jones, J. *Memorials of North Carolina.* New York, 1838.

Kybett, S. M. *Bonnie Prince Charlie.* New York, 1988.

Landsman, N. C. "Immigration and Settlement," in *Scotland and the Americas 1600 to 1800.* Providence, RI, 1995.

Lang, A. *The Companions of Pickle.* London, 1898.

——. "Jacobite Songs." *Scottish Historical Review,* January, 1911.

——. *Pickle the Spy.* London, 1897.

——. *Prince Charles Edward Stuart.* London, 1903.

Lenanton, C. *Over the Water.* London, 1935.

Lenman, B. *The Jacobite Cause.* Glasgow, 1986.

——. *The Jacobite Clans of the Great Glen 1650–1784.* London, 1984.

——. *The Jacobite Risings in Britain.* London, 1980.

——. "Some Recent Jacobite Studies." *Scottish Historical Review,* 1991.

——. "Union, Jacobitism, and Enlightenment," in *Why Scottish History Matters.* Saltire Society, Edinburgh, 1991.

——. & J. S. Gibson, *The Jacobite Threat.* Edinburgh, 1990.

Lewis, A. *Joseph Highmore: 1692–1780.* Ph.D. dissertation. Harvard University, Cambridge, MA, 1975.

Lewis, C. D. (trans.). *The Aeneid of Virgil.* New York, 1953.

Lewis, W. S., et al. (eds.). *Horace Walpole's Correspondence.* Oxford, 1974.

Linklater, E. *The Prince in the Heather.* London, 1987.

Livingstone, et al. (eds.), *Muster Roll of Prince Charles Edward Stuart's Army.* Aberdeen, 1984.

Logan, R. A. "Dates in the Life of Flora MacDonald." *The Scottish Genealogist,* 1982.

London Magazine. 1746.

Lovat-Fraser, J. A. "Stevenson and the Jacobite Tradition." Paper read before the RLS Club of London, 1927.

Lyne, S. M. *The Rose of Sleat.* London, 1900.

MacBean, W. M. *Miscellanea Jacobitiana.* 14 vols. New York, 1902.

MacDonald, A. *Memorials of the '45.* Inverness, 1930.

MacDonald, A. R. "Flora MacDonald," in *Transactions of The Gaelic Society of Inverness,* xxxvi, 1931-1933.

——. "A True Account of the Life of Flora MacDonald." *Oban Times,* July 8 - August 19, 1905.

——. *The Truth about Flora MacDonald.* Inverness, 1938.

MacDonald, Alex. *The Poems of Alexander MacDonald.* Edited by A. and A. A. MacDonald. Inverness, 1924.

MacDonald, J. "A True and Real State of Prince Charles Stuart's Miraculous Escape after the Battle of Culloden." *Blackwood's Magazine,* October, 1913.

MacDonald, J. A. *Flora MacDonald: A History and a Message.* Washington, DC, 1916.

——. *What a Newspaper Man Saw in Britain.* Toronto, 1907.

MacDonald, J. *Flora MacDonald.* Thurso, Scotland, 1989.

MacDonald, Lt. Col. J. *Charles Edward Stuart, The Pretender in Scotland.* Exeter, England, 1823.

MacDonald, K. N. "Poems and Songs in Honour of Flora MacDonald," in W. M. MacBean, *Miscellanea Jacobitiana*. New York, 1902.

MacGregor, A. *The Life of Flora MacDonald*. 4th ed. Stirling, Scotland, 1902.

Mackenzie, A. *History of the MacDonalds and Lords of the Isles*. Inverness, 1881.

Mackenzie, C. *Prince Charlie and His Ladies*. New York, 1935.

Mackenzie, R. et al. *The Sword and the Sorrows*. Catalogue of "An Exhibition to Commemorate the Jacobite Rising of 1745 and the Battle of Culloden 1746." Culloden, 16 April - 20 September, 1996.

MacKinnon, D. *The Life and Adventures of Flora MacDonald*. Unpublished ms., 1953.

Maclean, A. *A MacDonald for the Prince*. Stornoway, Scotland, 1982.

———. & J. S. Gibson, *Summer Hunting a Prince*. Stornoway, Scotland, 1992.

Maclean, J. P. "Eulogium on the Character of Flora MacDonald." *The Celtic Monthly*, vol. 19, 1911.

———. "Flora MacDonald in America." *The Celtic Monthly*, vol. 8, 1899.

———. *Flora MacDonald in America*. Lumberton, NC, 1909.

Maclean, M. "Flora MacDonald," *The Active Gael*. Glasgow, 1934.

MacLeod, J. Memorial prepared for James Boswell, 1775. Unpublished typescript in Beinecke Rare Book and Manuscript Library, Yale University, New Haven, CT.

MacLeod, K. *The Road to the Isles*. Edinburgh, 1927.

MacLeod, R. *Flora MacDonald, The Jacobite Rebel in Scotland and North America*. London, 1995.

MacMillan, W. D. *MacGhillemhaoil*. 2 vols. Wayzata, MN, 1990.

Macpherson, E. "Anne Mackintosh, Colonel Anne of the '45." *The Highlander*, vol. 29 no. 2, Mar/Apr 1991.

Maitland, W. *History of Edinburgh*. Edinburgh, 1753.

Manners, V. "Catherine Read." *Connoisseur*, Dec., 1931, Jan. & Mar., 1932.

Marchant, J. *The History of the Present Rebellion*. London, 1746.

Marley, C. J. *Flora MacDonald, Preserver of Prince Charles*. Unpublished M. A. thesis. University of North Carolina, Chapel Hill, NC, 1945.

Marley, C. M. *Expectations for the Daughters of Flora MacDonald College in the 1920s.* Senior honors thesis. St. Andrews Presbyterian College, Laurinburg, NC, 1989.

Marshall, R. *Bonnie Prince Charlie.* Edinburgh, 1988.

——. *Virgins and Viragos: A History of Women in Scotland 1080–1980.* Chicago, 1983.

Maxwell of Kirkconnell, J. *Narrative of Charles Prince of Wales' Expedition to Scotland in the Year 1745.* Edinburgh, 1841.

McLean, A. *Highland Scots in North Carolina.* Unpublished ms. De-Tamble Library, St. Andrews Presbyterian College. Laurinburg, NC, 1919.

McLynn, F. *Bonnie Prince Charlie.* Oxford, 1991.

——. *The Jacobites.* London, 1985.

Meyer, D. *The Highland Scots of North Carolina 1732–1776.* Chapel Hill, NC, 1957.

Mild, W. *Joseph Highmore of Holborn Row.* Ardmore, PA, 1990.

Miles, E. *Thomas Hudson Portraitist to the British Establishment.* Ph.D. dissertation. Yale University, New Haven, CT, 1976.

Mitchell, J. H. "Flora MacDonald." *The Celtic Monthly,* vol. v, 1896.

Mitchell, W. *Prince Charles Edward Stuart of Scotland and the Rising of 1745.* Edinburgh, 1930.

Mitford, J. *Grace Had an English Heart.* New York, 1988.

Morison, S. E. *Builders of the Bay Colony.* Boston, 1930.

Mornin, E. "Bonnie Charlie's Now Awa'," in *Forum for Modern Language Studies,* 1988.

Morton, H. V. *In Scotland Again.* London, 1933.

——. *In Search of Scotland.* London, 1949.

Mossiker, F. *Pocahontas, The Life and the Legend.* New York, 1976.

Mundell, F. "Flora MacDonald, the Heroine of the Forty-Five," in *Heroines of History and Legend.* Edited by E. S. Smith. Boston, 1921.

Murdoch, W. G. B. *The Spirit of Jacobite Loyalty.* Edinburgh, 1907.

Musgrove, W. *Obituary.* London, 1899.

Nicholas, D. "Reluctant Heroine: A Brief Life of Flora MacDonald," in *The Stewarts,* vol. xiii, 1968.

Niven, D. *The Moon's a Balloon.* New York, 1972.

Norie, W. D. *The Life and Adventures of Prince Charles Edward Stuart.* 4 vols. London, 1903.

Oates, J. A. *The Story of Fayetteville and the Upper Cape Fear.* Charlotte, NC, 1950.

Orczy, E. "Flora and the Bonnie Prince." *North China Herald*, September 26, 1934.

Ormond, R. & M. Rogers (eds.). *Dictionary of British Portraiture*. London, 1979.

Page, R. "Flora MacDonald College." Reprinted from *The World's Work*, September, 1916, DeTamble Library, St. Andrews Presbyterian College, Laurinburg, NC.

Parker, H. E. F. *Discoverers and Pioneers of America*. New York, 1856.

Paston, G. *Little Memoirs of the Eighteenth Century*. New York, 1901.

Paterson, A. B. *Flora in North Carolina*. Unpublished ms., 1976, DeTamble Library, St. Andrews Presbyterian College, Laurinburg, NC.

Penderal-Broadhurst, J. "The Portraits of Flora MacDonald." *Art Journal*, 1899.

Pennant, T. *A Tour of Scotland and Voyage to the Hebrides, 1772*. London, 1776.

Pittock, M. G. H. *The Invention of Scotland*. London, 1991.

———. "The Making of Jacobite Relics," in *Studies in Hogg and his World*. Stirling, Scotland, 1992.

———. "The Myth of the Jacobite Clans: Lowland Recruitment in the '45." Paper read at annual conference of The Eighteenth-Century Scottish Studies Society, Aberdeen, July 30, 1995.

Porcelli, E. *The White Cockade*. London, 1949.

Power, W. *Prince Charlie*. London, 1912.

Prebble, J. *The King's Jaunt*. London, 1988.

———. *The Lion in the North*. New York, 1986.

Quynn, D. M. "Flora MacDonald in History." *North Carolina Historical Review*, no. 3, July, 1941.

Rogers, C. *The Scottish Minstrel*. Edinburgh, 1872.

Rose, D. "Flora McDonald and the Scottish Highlanders in America." *American Historical Register*, vol. 1, no. 2, April, 1897.

Scholey, A. (ed.). *A Jacobite Anthology*. Aberdeen, 1995.

Scots Magazine, The History of the Rebellion in 1745 and 1746. Aberdeen, 1755.

The Scotsman. Edinburgh, Scotland, January 6, 1927.

Scott, W. *Redgauntlet*. Boston, 1894.

———. *The Surgeon's Daughter*, Edinburgh, 1903.

———. *The Tales of a Grandfather*. London, 1925.

——. *Waverley*. Boston, 1894.

Scottish Historical Review. October, 1917 and January, 1928.

Scottish Notes and Queries. October, 1893; April, 1895; June, 1895; November, 1897; June, 1932.

Seton, B. G. and J. G. Arnot, *The Prisoners of the '45*. 3 vols. Edinburgh, 1928.

Shield, A. *Henry Stuart, Cardinal of York*. London, 1908.

Simon, J. Notes to *Thomas Hudson 1701–1779, Portrait Painter and Collector*. A publication of the Greater London Arts Council, 1979.

Smart, A. *The Life and Art of Allan Ramsay*. London, 1952.

Smith, A. *A Summer in Skye*. Edinburgh, 1912.

Smith, C. M. "A Highland Heroine," *Munsey's Magazine*, July 1887.

Smout, T. C. *A History of the Scottish People 1560–1830*. London, 1972.

Sobieska, J. and C. E. Stuart. *Tales of the Century*. Edinburgh, 1847.

Sparrow, W. S. *Women Painters of the World*. London, 1905.

Speck, W. A. *The Butcher*. Oxford, 1981.

——. "A Great Year for Drambuie." *Times Literary Supplement*, August 11, 1995.

Sprunt, J. *Chronicles of the Cape Fear River 1660–1916*. Raleigh, NC, 1916.

Stevenson, R. B. K. "Bettie Burk's Brogues: The Making of a Relic," in *Review of Scottish Culture*, no. 6, 1990.

Stuart, F. M. *Lady Nithsdale and the Jacobites*. Innerliethen, Scotland, 1995.

Steuart, A. F. "Jenny Cameron." *Scottish Arts and Letters*, vol. 2 no. 4, Sep/Nov 1903.

Stewart, Col. D. *Sketches of the Character, Manners, and Present State of the Highlanders of Scotland*. 2 vols. Edinburgh, 1822.

Swire, O. *Skye, The Island and its Legends*. Oxford, 1952.

Tayler, H. *Jacobite Miscellany*. Edinburgh, 1948.

——. "The Lieutenant Governor of the Tower in 1745–1747." *Scottish Historical Review*, xxv, January, 1928.

Terry, C. S. (ed.). *The Albemarle Papers*. Aberdeen, 1902.

——. *The Forty-Five, A Narrative of the Last Jacobite Rising*. Cambridge, 1922.

Tilton, R. *Pocahontas: The Evolution of an American Narrative*. Cambridge, 1994.

Tomasson, K. *The Jacobite General*. Edinburgh, 1958.

Trevor-Roper, H. "The Invention of Tradition: The Highland Tradition in Scotland," in *The Invention of Tradition*. Edited by E. Hobsbawm and H. Trevor-Roper. Cambridge, 1983.

Tytler, S. *The MacDonald Lass*. London, 1895.

Vardell, C. Typescripts of notes and correspondence. DeTamble Library, St. Andrews Presbyterian College, Laurinburg, NC.

Vining, E. G. *Flora: A Biography*. Philadelphia, 1966.

Voltaire. "Siecle de Louis XV," in *Oeuvres*. Paris 1836.

Waterhouse, E. *The Dictionary of 18th Century British Painters*. Antique Collectors Club, London, 1981.

Whyte, I. & K. *On the Trail of the Jacobites*. London, 1990.

Whitaker, J. *An Almanac for the Year of our Lord 1879*. London, 1879.

Wicker, R. *Miscellaneous Ancient Records of Moore County, NC*. Southern Pines, NC, 1971.

Williamson, M. "The Real Flora MacDonald," in *The Lady's Realm*, September, 1897.

Woosnam-Savage, R. *1745, Charles Edward Stuart and the Jacobites*. Edinburgh, 1995.

Wordsworth, W. *The Poems of William Wordsworth*. Edited by T. Hutchinson. Oxford, 1926.

Wylde, F. F. *The Life of Flora MacDonald*. London, 1870.

Young, I. "To Rescue a Prince." *The Highlander*, vol. 29 no. 4, Jul/Aug, 1991.

Youngson, A. J. *The Prince and the Pretender*. London, 1985.

Index